Lifehouse

Lifehouse

Taking Care of Ourselves
in a World on Fire

Adam Greenfield

VERSO

London • New York

First published by Verso 2024
© Adam Greenfield 2024

The moral rights of the author and translator have been asserted
1 3 5 7 9 10 8 6 4 2

Every effort has been made to contact copyright holders and to obtain
permission for the use of copyright material. The publisher apologizes for any
errors or omissions and would be grateful for notification of corrections that
should be incorporated in future reprints or editions of this book.

Verso
UK: 6 Meard Street, London W1F 0EG
US: 388 Atlantic Avenue, Brooklyn, NY 11217
versobooks.com

Verso is the imprint of New Left Books

ISBN-13: 978-1-78873-835-4
ISBN-13: 978-1-78873-836-1 (UK EBK)
ISBN-13: 978-1-78873-837-8 (US EBK)

British Library Cataloguing in Publication Data
A catalogue record for this book is available from the British Library

Library of Congress Cataloging-in-Publication Data

Names: Greenfield, Adam, author.
Title: Lifehouse : taking care of ourselves in a world on fire / Adam
  Greenfield.
Description: London ; New York : Verso, 2024. | Includes bibliographical
  references and index.
Identifiers: LCCN 2024002434 (print) | LCCN 2024002435 (ebook) | ISBN
  9781788738354 (trade paperback) | ISBN 9781788738378 (US ebook) |
  ISBN
  9781788738361 (UK ebook)
Subjects: LCSH: Community organization. | Social participation. | Disaster
  relief—Citizen participation.
Classification: LCC HM766 .G744 2024 (print) | LCC HM766 (ebook) |
  DDC
  361.8—dc23/eng/20240307
LC record available at https://lccn.loc.gov/2024002434
LC ebook record available at https://lccn.loc.gov/2024002435

Typeset in Sabon by MJ & N Gavan, Truro, Cornwall
Printed and bound by CPI Group (UK) Ltd, Croydon CR0 4YY

For N.

I found a reason to keep living
Oh, and the reason, dear, is you

And Polo said: "The inferno of the living is not something that will be; if there is one, it is what is already here, the inferno where we live every day, that we form by being together. There are two ways to escape suffering it. The first is easy for many: accept the inferno and become such a part of it that you can no longer see it. The second is risky and demands constant vigilance and apprehension: seek and learn to recognize who and what, in the midst of the inferno, are not inferno, then make them endure, give them space."

—Italo Calvino, *Invisible Cities*, 1972

Let's start with the end of the world, why don't we? Get it over with and move on to more interesting things.

—N. K. Jemisin, *The Fifth Season*, 2015

Contents

Introduction   1

1   The Long Emergency   17

2   Mutual Care   57

3   Collective Power   115

4   Beyond Hope   165

Conclusion   207

Acknowledgments   215
Notes   219
Index   253

Introduction

We were out of town when Superstorm Sandy made landfall on New York City, my partner and I, and had trouble catching a flight home. What I recall most vividly about the event itself was the disorientation of seeing a broadcast on CNN of the familiar intersection in front of our building, flooded waist-high. The traffic signals were swinging wildly on their mast arms overhead, in what an excited voiceover described as sustained winds of forty miles an hour or more.

A montage of increasingly surreal footage followed: the tide overtopping a seawall somewhere out in the Rockaways, torrential floodwaters surging into the Brooklyn-Battery Tunnel, then a construction crane snapped in two by the wind, dangling seventy-five stories above Midtown. And finally that unforgettable image of Lower Manhattan, the whole bottom third of the island gone dark after a transformer explosion at the Con Ed electric substation on East Fourteenth Street.

This was plainly no ordinary hurricane. Even before its surge hit New York City, Sandy was already strikingly unusual. The lead winds of a late-season storm, among the largest Atlantic hurricanes on record, had begun to fuse with an existing continental cold front, producing something vastly larger and weirder than either. The combined system would go on to loiter over the northeastern United States for days, stretching ordinary expectations of a weather event to the breaking point, and in doing so defining an entirely new category of "superstorm."

But it was the storm surge, when it came, that literally redrew the maps. Measured at its peak at the Battery at a previously unimaginable 13.88 feet (4.2m)—or some seven feet (2.1m) above flood stage—it was this surge, far more than the rain or the wind, that caused the most severe and lasting damage.[1] As the brackish water streamed inland, it flooded into subway tunnels, utility vaults, basements and hundreds of thousands of other belowground spaces. The Hudson and East Rivers overspilled their banks, as did smaller waterways like the heavily polluted Gowanus Canal. Low-lying areas of New York City, from Manhattan's Financial District to the beach communities of outer Queens, suddenly found themselves submerged beneath a filthy, freezing tide.

It was more than any of the planners, architects or civil engineers responsible for the city's form had ever anticipated, and in the end it was more than the infrastructures they devised could withstand. Failure cascaded through a tight mesh of systems critical to the life of the city that, on any ordinary day, ran quietly in the background. Power, fuel, transportation and communication networks all went down, despite the backups and failovers that had been so carefully designed into them. In the worst-hit neighborhoods, they stayed down for weeks.

In New York City alone, tens of thousands of households found themselves without light, heat or potable water. Elderly people and others with limited mobility were trapped on high floors in their thousands, marooned atop twenty- and thirty-story buildings whose elevator service was not restored for a week or more. Entire housing projects were left to fend for themselves, the maintenance crews responsible for their upkeep and repair stranded offsite by the collapse of the regional transportation network. Attempts to restore service struggled against acute and immediate fuel shortages, amid lengthening lines and spreading mayhem at gas stations. And, in true insult-to-injury style, there was barely time for anyone to internalize any of this before a vicious early cold snap settled onto the area.

By the time my partner and I made our way back to New York, it was already clear that Sandy would turn out to be one of those events that rewrites the way we understand the world we live in. Like the "500-year" floods or wildfires that now seem to strike every few months, the appearance of this storm suggested that the atmosphere had undergone a transition to a volatile new state, in which weather events of a magnitude once thought impossible were plainly now on the table, and those that had been considered exceptional would become routine. It was one of those moments of ruthless clarity: a meteorological disturbance so massive that it defied classification, difficult to attribute with any credibility to anything but human action, had landed on the very capital of Empire. And in a matter of hours, it had laid waste to all the intertwined systems that kept it functioning.

Maybe it's simply that all of this happened to a place as comprehensively mediated (and as endlessly, baroquely self-mythologizing) as New York City. But at least for those of us who found ourselves living through its aftereffects, Superstorm Sandy felt like some kind of rupture or punctuation in history—the advent of a new era, in which the contours of everyday life everywhere on Earth would fundamentally be determined by the consequences of anthropogenic global heating. It will never be possible to point to a given day on the calendar and say, "Yes, that's when everything started to change," and in any event I expect that moment would be different for each one of us. If you were forced to choose a single event, though, a single nodal point at which one set of assumptions about how the future might unfold was replaced wholesale by another, you could do a whole lot worse than this one.

Most of the ways in which Sandy reset our expectations about the world we live in were scary, and hard to accept—but not all of them. If there was one bright light that kept burning amid the devastation, it was that there was in New York an organization able to stand up a logistical network and begin relief and recovery operations almost immediately. This organization had two distribution hubs set up before the last of Sandy's trailing winds had cleared the tristate area. It funneled an enormous volume of donated goods and supplies out to the hardest-hit areas of the city. It furnished crew after crew of volunteers willing to take on the difficult, dirty and occasionally dangerous job of site clearance. And it took on responsibility for

3

providing thousands of displaced, traumatized New Yorkers with shelter, warmth, sustenance and fellowship.

The organization I'm talking about wasn't FEMA—the Federal Emergency Management Agency formally chartered by the United States government to respond to large-scale disasters, whether "natural" or manmade—and it wasn't the National Guard. Nor was it the Red Cross, the superficially benign philanthropy blandly familiar to generations of Americans for its role in distributing blankets and food parcels in the wake of crisis. In fact, it was neither a government agency nor a charitable effort of any kind. It was a spontaneous, self-organized initiative assembled in real time by veterans of the previous year's Occupy Wall Street movement, and consciously guided by the anarchist ideals and values of that movement. It was called "Occupy Sandy."

Occupy Sandy was simply the easiest, fastest and most effective way for an ordinary, unaffiliated New Yorker to get involved with the relief effort in the hours and days following the superstorm's landfall, whatever their political convictions.[2] That I am aware of, it was the only organization that had meaningful and productive things for people without specialized skills to do in the city's moment of maximum need—the only one with the capacity to absorb the massive incoming flows of volunteers, supplies and financial contributions, and the network to direct those materials and energies to the places where they could do the most good.

Some numbers will begin to suggest the magnitude of the things these unpaid amateurs accomplished together, on an improvisational basis, without anything in the way of leadership, institutional infrastructure, existing financial resources or prior planning. Within a week of the peak storm surge, Occupy Sandy had 700 core members working out of two repurposed churches in the Brooklyn neighborhoods of Clinton Hill and Sunset Park, and was serving approximately 20,000 meals a day across a far-flung constellation of thirty or more local "recovery centers" stretching from Red Hook to New Dorp.

4

By the end of November 2012, the initiative could marshal some $700,000 worth of supplies and equipment, and ultimately collected more than $1.3 million in donations intended to support its efforts.[3] All told, some 60,000 volunteers were eventually involved in this bottom-up relief effort in one way or another—roughly four times the number fielded by the American Red Cross—bringing with them insights and perspectives from all walks and strata of New York City life.[4]

I was one of them. And for the first time in my life, I was in a position to *do something* about the consequences of global heating.

It's that *doing something* that I want to spend the rest of this book exploring—both the commitment to local, self-organized action itself, and everything it opens up for us, in a time when so much else about our lives feels like it is shutting down.

Superstorm Sandy, of course, was just one event in the larger pattern of events that we generally think of as "the climate crisis," defined by the heating our long dependency on fossil fuels has visited upon the planet's atmosphere, and all the hurricanes, wildfires, droughts and other catastrophic consequences that now follow from it.

One of the most prominent features of this crisis is that we generally feel helpless to do anything about it. This isn't because we don't know what causes the atmosphere to warm. The causality is straightforward: the upward march of temperature results from three centuries in which our species powered its expansive activities by burning the "fossil" hydrocarbon fuels of oil, gas and coal, slowly saturating the atmosphere with the carbon dioxide that absorbs so much of the sun's heat.

Nor is there any ambiguity about what it would take to slow or reverse the heating—and therefore, eventually, subdue the roiling volatility that now threatens so much of everything we care for. The prospects for that depend vitally on eliminating the combustion of such fuels, which even now account for an overwhelming proportion of everything that powers the global

5

economy—in 2022, an estimated 81 percent of all energy consumed on Earth.[5]

The trouble is that choices concerning energy strategy are made by institutions that are inaccessible to the ordinary person, and which are, in any event, very heavily incentivized to keep on doing just as they have done. Unless you yourself, personally, are a large shareholder of an energy company, or the autocratic ruler of a fossil fuel–producing country, your ability to effect any meaningful change in how the global economy is powered is virtually nonexistent. Until the parties who *do* have the power decide otherwise, then, the mining, the drilling, the pumping and the burning will continue unabated— and with them the unrelenting accumulation of carbon in the atmosphere, the heating and the terrible consequences for all human and nonhuman life.

This is the point at which our sense of helplessness really starts to feel overwhelming, because none of the mechanisms for change that are available to us feel like they're up to the task of addressing these increasingly distressing circumstances.

In liberal democracies, electoral representation is the dominant, and only formal, theory of change on the table. But can we vote someone into office for whom robust action on the climate is an overriding priority? We would have to find someone like that, first of all. They'd have to win election. We'd have to hold them to whatever commitments they made on the campaign trail, against the influence of extractive industries that are boundlessly wealthier and better resourced than we are. And then we would have to trust that a large enough number of voters around the country had managed to do the same in their own constituencies, such that the caucus for change is the dominant force in the legislature.

As improbable as all of this sounds, it's the only game in town. And so many of us still troop off to the voting booth every few years and cast our ballots for those candidates we think will advance our concerns in the halls of power. For the most part, that's where the matter remains: the ambit of public action many people are willing to take is confined to what happens on Election Day, whatever misgivings they or anyone else may harbor about its effectiveness or consequence.

For many of us, of course, registering our concern for what is being done to the climate as an indirect signal every few years feels ludicrously inadequate to the scale and urgency of the crisis. But what's left to us consists largely of our own choices. So we give up the car and take the bus instead, or ride a bike to the market. We cut red meat from our diet, reuse our shopping bags and are diligent about sorting the packaging for recycling. Maybe we go so far as to give up flying, or we forgo having children ourselves. And all the while we do the things we think will give voice to our rising sense of unease. We march and we sign petitions, we make displays of our worthiness and unity and number and commitment in the hope of influencing those who make the laws.

When these things begin to feel irrelevant or pointless, we block highways. If we're feeling particularly brave, we chain ourselves to the doors of the closest oil-company headquarters. But none of that seems to move the needle, either—not on legislation, not on policy, not on any of the decisions made by those whose decisions actually matter. No matter what we do, the figure for atmospheric ppm carbon dioxide ticks ever higher. It often feels like all we can do is look on in horror as the line on the graph continues its relentless upward sawtoothing, bursting through every successive threshold at which we've been told livable conditions might still be preserved on the planet.

We scan the news, and it's full of dust storms and receding glaciers, fracturing ice sheets and catastrophic floods. Or someone's shared video of a runaway wildfire to our neighborhood chat group—we glance at our phone and see trees older than America consumed by flame and the skies a hundred miles away gone an uncanny orange with the smoke of their dying. And then we walk out the door into a world where people are still placidly driving their cars, commuting to work, taking vacations, having kids, buying stuff. What we feel in moments like this is more than disorientation. It's something closer to reality shear.

The findings accumulate, the careful lawyerly precision of interim reports and white papers gives way to more urgent and emotive language. The gentle drizzle we're used to more and more often comes on instead with the suddenness and violence of the monsoon. The bodies of refugees fleeing the devastation continue to wash up on the shore. One day we find the supermarket shelves empty of the things that have been there in such abundance our whole lives. And we wonder why nobody seems to be *doing something* about any of it.

And so we hope. We hope, variously, that carbon offsets, cap-and-trade schemes and all the other market-friendly paraphernalia of soft mitigation work as we have been promised they will. That our elected representatives turn out to be wise enough in the ways of legislature to get a Green New Deal with teeth enacted. That the unaccountable transnational elites who *really* call the shots will eventually insist on decisive, coordinated action to protect the climate, for reasons of raw self-interest if for no other. That a party of the poor and downtrodden will rise in righteous glory, to end the age of oligarchic plunder and impunity and set the world to rights. That there's a garage somewhere, inside of which a genius tinkerer is even now perfecting the technology that will siphon carbon dioxide from the air and sequester it safely somewhere it can't threaten us again. Maybe even that an artificial sentience is gestating, in the anonymous racks of some distant research center, that will somehow be able to seize control of the economy entire, and in that way rescue us from all our errors and mistakes.

What I think we badly need to get our heads around is that *all of these varieties of hope are killing us, and everyone and everything we care about.* Whatever energy we might invest in the conventional mechanisms of change, they are plainly failing to prevent the burning of fossil fuels at scale. But worse, every hour we dedicate to them is an hour we haven't spent in material preparation for the conditions we will live with for the rest of our days on Earth. Our trust in these processes is getting in the way of our dedicating time and energy to the

8

efforts that might actually work to cushion ourselves and our communities from everything coming our way.

If we want to survive the hard times to come together, we need to stop investing our faith and energy in institutions that are demonstrably failing us. We need to admit that we've reached a moment at which we can no longer afford to wait for some external process to save us, whether mechanism, movement or deus ex machina.

What we need, in other words, is to get beyond hope. We've got to stop waiting for someone else to *do something* and start doing for ourselves. And not simply in a way that reproduces all the values and structures that led us into our current predicament, but in a way that places concerns for care, dignity and the achievement of justice at the heart of everything we undertake together.

Guided by everything I learned from watching the way Occupy Sandy worked, as well as the experiences of parallel movements across the past six decades, this book is about how we might accomplish that.

In the end, my involvement with Occupy Sandy was comparably shallow. All told, it amounted to perhaps two weeks of shifts at the 520 Clinton Avenue distribution hub; participation in a few of the general assemblies at which the community reported back to itself what it had learned and decided on courses of future action; and an unforgettable Christmas Eve huddled on a freezing church porch that still smelled of a recent firebombing attempt, singing carols and old Wobbly songs with the other volunteers there that night.[6] What I saw during these few hundred hours, though, did as much to transform my sense of what ordinary, untrained people could achieve together as anything else I've ever experienced.

For my entire adult life, I had been told that the principles of self-organization I believed in were childish, impractical, utopian fantasies that might work tolerably well in small groups of people who already held similar political commitments, but couldn't possibly do so "at scale," among significant numbers of citizens. And yet here was the most concrete proof possible that these same, ostensibly impractical principles could successfully be used to coordinate a highly complex and occasionally life-critical effort, consistently and for a number of months, across the largest and most demographically diverse metropolitan area in North America. If anybody doubted that self-organized, nonhierarchical mutual aid projects could respond to catastrophe every bit as effectively as official disaster-relief agencies—if not, in many cases, markedly more so—their questions ought to have been resolved by Occupy Sandy.

That ordinary New Yorkers could organize themselves to achieve something this complicated and difficult, under immense pressure, put flesh on the bones of my fundamental belief in undirected human capacity. That they could do so with the most limited means, in the face of opposition that ranged from patronizing skepticism to outright arson, said something impressive about their ability to make sound collective decisions, despite the pressure. And for this kind of order to arise spontaneously, in the early aftermath of the most significant natural disaster in the city's living memory, strikes me as nothing short of astounding. I doubt there are 60,000 convinced anarchists in New York City. There may not even be a tenth that number. But there are 60,000 who *did* anarchy, all through the storm and the months that followed, and did so brilliantly. And perhaps this offers us a more general template for ways in which we might organize our communities so that they shelter more of us from more of the hard times ahead.

But what if organizing ourselves in this way also helps to repair other, more chronic insults to our well-being—the overwhelming sense of powerlessness we so often contend with, the dread of the future we barely manage to tamp down, even the damage inflicted upon us by the ordinary disasters of everyday life? What if the experience of coming to the aid of our community affirms us in ways we might not have dared to ask for, or even imagined possible?

In her 2009 book *A Paradise Built in Hell*, the writer Rebecca Solnit discusses just this aspect of efforts that arise in the aftermath of disaster.[7] She writes movingly of the joy one can take, even in the midst of catastrophe, from inhabiting for the first time a civic self, a self rooted in the provision of communal care—one that seems infinitely larger and more capacious than those narrower selves that are invoked by work, family life, consumerism, therapy culture or identity politics. And she goes on to quote the American sociologist Charles Fritz to the effect that the "widespread sharing of danger, loss and deprivation produces ... solidarity among the survivors, which overcomes social isolation, provides a channel for intimate communication and expression, and a major source of physical and emotional support and reassurance."[8]

This isn't some sociological theory of the wouldn't-it-be-lovely-to-think-so variety but a consistent empirical observation. Consider what John P. Clark related about his experience of the Common Ground mutual aid effort that arose in New Orleans following 2005's Hurricane Katrina: "Volunteers and survivors often described the experience of a break with conventional reality, and the emergence of a new time and space of possibility."[9]

The sense of an opening that Clark reports chimes in every detail with what the artist and activist Cassie Thornton found in her visits to the "solidarity clinics" of austerity-stricken Greece in January 2017: "I met a group of middle-aged women who cited 'the crisis' as the birth of their new lives as radicalized people within activist communities, people who had found a purpose, who were now more than just workers and consumers. They felt powerful, connected and interdependent for the first time."[10]

People who participated in these efforts consistently experienced the feeling of interdependence as *healing*, at both the individual and communal levels. "People's differences went by the wayside," said one Occupy volunteer, who spent three months working in the hardest-hit areas of the Rockaways. This same volunteer went on to note the curious fact that the opportunity to contribute to the relief effort was itself part of the relief it furnished: "Helping others became a major coping mechanism for many people. It's much better to have them empowered rather than having these people stand in a line to beg for aid."[11]

Perhaps most poignant of all is the stark contrast between the sense of empowerment Solnit, Clark, Thornton and this unnamed Occupy volunteer all mention and the pursuits that are supposed to produce meaning and value in the rest of our lives. When Clark says that in the provision of mutual aid, "[o]ne could experience one's own activity as intrinsically valuable," the strong implication is that the things we ordinarily do —that we *have* to do, in order to keep a roof over our families' heads, and food on the table—are *not* experienced that way.[12]

The crux of this isn't simply, as Charles Fritz was given to pointing out, that "the everyday, ongoing life of the society" is its own kind of quiet disaster. It's that the way our society is currently organized affords us very few opportunities to step outside the identities we've so carefully shored up, and simply show up for the people who need what we have to offer. It was just such an opportunity that Occupy Sandy extended. If you've ever given blood, maybe you'll recognize these aspects of the way it felt to work at 520 Clinton: that it mattered, that there was no detectable downside to it and that whatever good came of it had not a thing to do with who I thought I was, who the world perceived me to be or how I preferred to present myself.

And in this, there is a clue as to what form our response should take when the excursion from normalcy lasts not just the weeks or months it might take to rebuild after a storm, but forever. You may have noticed that certain words crop up again and again in participants' accounts of mutual aid efforts. They are the exact same things I experienced in the course of my own involvement with Occupy Sandy: *Purpose. Power. Possibility.*

That these are the qualities that stand out in personal narratives of mutual aid work, to the point that people thought they were worth mentioning, suggests just how much we suffer from the pointlessness of the work most of us are ordinarily required to do, as well as the broader passivity and isolation to which our usual roles in life have consigned us. But the same accounts *also* suggest that something profound seems to happen in the moments after some catastrophe has disrupted the ordinary flow of life, in which we stop waiting for rescue and commit ourselves to collective, reparative action. The choices we make in these moments evidently have the power to bind up other, seemingly unrelated wounds. They may even open onto entirely new ways of being in the world.

To me the implications of this extend far beyond either "mutual aid" or "disaster relief," in the very strictest sense of those terms, and invite us to think expansively about what such efforts might mean when unfolded to their fullest extent, in a world where so many of the old certainties no longer apply.

What I'm proposing is that the most productive way of addressing each of the intertwined crises that confront us—the fundamental, planetary one of climate-system collapse, yes, but also the dread and the powerlessness and even the inordinate difficulty we so often seem to have now, in communicating across the genuine differences that cleave us—consists in our application of one and the same strategy.

And happily, this strategy also happens to be the one most immediately accessible to us. It lies in organizing ourselves to take care of one another, without waiting for anybody to issue that care to us as generic subjects, sell it to us as customers or offer it to us as passive recipients of a charity bestowed from above. In other words: finally *doing something* about the straits we're in, directly and in our own neighborhoods, in ways that call upon all the resources and capacities the roles we play in everyday life have no need of and place no value upon. Who knows but that we may finally find selves that we recognize, even here in the most difficult and challenging hours of our lives.

This is what I want us to hold on to, as we move further into the time of storms together. In the rest of this book, we'll learn how to develop this set of ideas and put them to work.

We will confront the complex and cascading conditions of our moment head on, to better understand what they actually ask of us. We will learn to understand how the second- and third-order consequences of global heating give rise to a Long Emergency—a breach in the ordinary that simultaneously challenges the structures of power we're familiar with, endangers most everything we hold dear and furnishes us with a rare opportunity to build something more in line with our deepest values.

By considering the Black Panther "survival programs" of the 1970s, the solidarity clinics of austerity-stricken Greece and Occupy Sandy itself, we'll explore how people under various kinds of extreme pressure organized for their own continued existence, when everything else fell down around them. From them we'll learn how we might tend to our own needs for sustainment, safety and mutual care in the face of the Emergency, especially when the state has failed us (or even, as is so often the case, when it actively moves to thwart us).

We'll turn to the thought of the idiosyncratic American "social ecologist" Murray Bookchin, as well as examples from municipalist Spain and autonomous Rojava, to learn how we might build and apply collective power—a counterpower to the forces of grief and loss at work everywhere around us. We'll glean vital insight into what works and what doesn't work, what tactics we ought to embrace and which ones we might be better off choosing to avoid.

And finally, we will bring together everything we have learned. We'll discover how mutual care and collective power reinforce each other, in the places of refuge that I call Lifehouses. We'll explore how we might set up a whole network of such sites, in which we can nurture the capacities of the communities we belong to, offer respite to all those driven before the storm and get started on the long, difficult work of repair. We will see how building the Lifehouse both gives us a practical means of enduring the Long Emergency and prefigures the methods of decarbonized cooperation and exchange that our lives will necessarily be founded on in the post-Emergency world that follows.

But none of that can fall into place until we finally steel ourselves to take those first few steps beyond whatever hope for the future we still cherish and at long last commit ourselves to *do something* about it.

Whatever you choose to do, though—whatever any of us choose to do, together—we should understand from the outset that it won't be enough. Nobody can prevent all the extinctions and losses, ruptures and severings that are now bound to take place: not any of us as individuals, or even all of us in concert. We've left it too late, the damage is too deep, the destabilizing process too far advanced. We won't be able to forestall any but the least part of the sorrows to come, even if we give everything we have to the effort. But what we *can* still do, perhaps, is join ourselves with the others around us and together make spaces in which more of what we cherish is able to endure. To make life and possibility, where there is otherwise only grief.

Nobody can do that for us. We have to do it for ourselves. This book is about what happens when we let go of hope, stop waiting and start doing.

1

The Long Emergency

Shortly before 5 p.m. on Tuesday, July 19, 2022, the temperature reading at the Royal Air Force base in the Lincolnshire town of Coningsby hit 104°F (40°C), setting an all-time record in a United Kingdom that was then enduring the second successive day of unprecedented heat.

Across Great Britain, train service came to a virtual standstill, as rails buckled, overhead power lines came down and trackside electrical fires compromised the safe operation of those mainline routes that were still running. Highways and airport runways that had been engineered for an era of lower operating temperatures rippled and cracked. Two of the capital's largest hospitals were forced to cancel operations and reroute critically ill patients to other facilities, after the air-conditioning units cooling their data centers failed and their IT systems collapsed. A long arc of wildfires left smoke hanging over much of the country, from North Yorkshire down to Essex; the London Fire Brigade declared a major incident after having attended some 1,146 call-outs on July 19 alone, making it far and away their busiest day since the Luftwaffe bombings of the Second World War.

Once the situation had stabilized over the course of the following week, the true cost became clear. Official sources estimated that a thousand Britons had lost their lives in the swelter, their deaths attributable to no other cause than the heat—a higher number of deaths from this cause, over the two-day period of elevated temperatures, than would ordinarily be expected in an entire year.

For many residents of the British Isles, this was the moment at which everything finally came into focus. The atmospheric heating they had been warned about across forty years of climate research and increasingly urgent rhetoric had become a concrete, uncomfortably physical fact of life. As billions of others around the world had done before them, they were now forced to adapt to circumstances that suddenly seemed unfamiliar and hostile. And all it took to bring this new reality home, and to demonstrate the acute vulnerability of the infrastructural systems their lives depended on, was a forty-eight-hour jolt of extreme temperature.

In the aftermath of that single two-day period, what became clear was that the immediately injurious effects of the heat itself were not the whole story. Bad as they were, those effects were in many cases compounded by shortfalls of planning and investment, maintenance and care. Their impact was ultimately absorbed by public services, infrastructures, a social fabric and individual bodies already weakened by the combined effects of pandemic-driven neglect and longer-term austerity. Officials didn't even bother denying it—one admitted it would take "decades" to proof the country's road and rail infrastructure against the heat, while another chided the British public that it "must learn to live with extreme events."[1]

If 104°F is now inside the bounds of possibility for a July day in Britain, though, you really do begin to wonder what might constitute the next extreme, and just what it is that we "must learn to live with." Because there's worse yet to come—for all of us, everywhere on Earth, no matter what any of us choose to do now as individuals, families, communities or societies.

The issue we face is not simply that legislatures and private interests worldwide continue to make decisions that are inconsistent with a survivable future, or that even the most hesitant, incremental, market-friendly efforts to preserve a livable climate are routinely thwarted. It's that even if all the endlessly ramified operations of the global economy could somehow immediately, instantly and painlessly be rendered carbon-neutral, some further increment of planetary heating is bound to happen, simply as a result of the fossil-fuel consumption that has already taken place. There remains some legitimate question as to just how much heating will occur, over what time frame and with what impact on the delicately equilibrated systems that sustain all Earthly life. But enough oil has already been pumped to the surface, enough coal has already been burned, enough of their carbon has already been liberated to tip the atmosphere into a new and violently hostile state of being.

So bear in mind, as you skim the morning headlines, that everything we have already experienced is just a foretaste. This is what the planetary system looks like, and how it behaves, when the carbon dioxide reading measures 424 parts per million, when the average amount of global warming since the beginning of the industrial era has barely crept past a single degree Celsius.[2]

Once the increase tilts past 1.5°C, we are told that "tree die-offs, drying peatlands, thawing permafrost and other self-reinforcing feedback loops [will] release additional carbon emissions, amplifying the warming further."[3] This is the point at which the transformation of Earth's atmosphere becomes an autocatalytic, self-sustaining process, spiraling "beyond the ability of humanity to influence it."[4] The climate will find a new equilibrium at some point, but no human now alive can say with any confidence where that might be. Whether we or our institutions are prepared for it in any way that matters, we have stepped into a new planetary epoch together.[5]

What is of interest here isn't so much the coming of the heat, in itself. I think most of us accept by now that anthropogenic global heating is a real thing, and that a radically different climate will continue to condition experience across the entire life span of anyone now alive. What we'll primarily be at pains to respond to are the follow-on, second- and third-order effects of the heat and especially the ways in which these cascade, interlock and amplify one another to create a fundamentally new and extremely challenging set of conditions for human life on Earth. In the dryly technocratic language favored by the Intergovernmental Panel on Climate Change (IPCC), these conditions arise out of the interaction of "[m]ultiple climatic and non-climatic risk drivers ... resulting in compounding overall risk and risks cascading across sectors and regions."[6] And we have to imagine all of that intersecting with, and intensifying, the existing patterns of deprivation and injustice we already struggle with. *This* is what constitutes the baseline condition we need to plan for.

Even now, I don't think either the depth or the complexity of the trouble we're in are particularly well understood. The wager here is not that billions of human beings will experience the deleterious effects of heat directly and for themselves. That is overdetermined: as we have seen, it will happen regardless of any action we may take. The wager concerns what happens in the aftermath. The specific assertion I am making is that the combined direct and indirect consequences of the heating *that is already entrained by our past behavior*, no matter what we do now, will in fairly short order exceed the capacity of our social, technical, political and economic systems—in other words, what many of us would think of as planetary civilization—to contain them. And that as a result, the greater part of that civilization's familiar ways of ordering everyday reality, whether enacted through mechanisms of state or market, will not survive.

I'm not expressing any opinion, mind you, as to whether any of that *should* survive—whether it might yet be reformed, repaired or made just, or whether it has earned the benefit of the doubt in any of these respects. I'm simply saying that it *will* not, not in any form that we recognize. And if by "short order" I mean "at some point in the next ten to fifteen years," that's probably optimistic. This is our world now. These are the skies under which we will live out the rest of our days. Welcome to the Long Emergency.

The Long Emergency is my name for the period we've entered together, set off by climatic instability, but ultimately far larger than that alone. It consists of an extended excursion from everything we recognize as normal, of as yet unknown duration and resolution, during which many of the systems and structures that currently shape our lives will be flung to pieces by the force of events. For as long as it lasts, we will be compelled to take on a much greater share of the responsibility of caring for ourselves than most of us are accustomed to, as individuals and communities both.

Even now, in its earlier stages, we can see just how that great undoing will unsettle the world as we know it. Three interlinked circumstances, in particular, spell havoc for any attempt at maintaining the institutional status quo: that a band of the Earth where a billion or more human beings now live may soon be uninhabitable through much of the year; that a considerable percentage of them are likely to flee in desperate search of conditions more hospitable to life; and that no society on the planet is remotely prepared to handle the consequences of that many people being on the move.[7] At the tail end of four decades of disinvestment in public services, especially, the challenges of organizing a safe, dignified and just existence for everyone displaced by the heat and its sequelae will tax our systems to the breaking point. Whatever respite or refuge is to be found we will have to fashion for ourselves, largely using the means we already have at hand.

I imagine that if you're reading this book, you don't particularly need to be convinced of this, any of it. But it's one thing to understand something like this intellectually and quite another to accept it emotionally. This uncompromising set of facts will compel us to adopt new ways of doing things, at every scale. It will transform the most fundamental arrangements of our lives: the structures of power and the institutions that mediate it. The ways in which we organize the fulfillment of our bodily, psychic and social needs. The shape of families and communities. Our methods of organizing the built environment and of moving through the world. Where and how the food we eat and the things we use are produced. Conventions of conduct, comportment, equipment and dress. Even the people we understand ourselves to be, and present to the others around us.

And while our ability to steer any of this will most often be limited, where we *are* able do so, we may find that we have unprecedented scope to reimagine the fundamental terms of our engagement with one another. This is what we'll need to hold fast to, amid all the anguish, loss and grief of a world progressively unweaving itself: the idea that this state of Emergency offers us an opening and a chance to try ways of organizing life in common that are different from everything that has brought us to the place where we stand now.

There are those who consider the prospect of an Emergency world and see, somehow, a near future largely determined by the continuing resilience of late-capitalist normalcy, holding its own against all the converging factors that threaten it, and capable still of bringing new territories and aspects of life under its dominion. Others see the blood-drenched, all-against-all nihility of *The Road*.[8] Personally, I don't think either one of these scenarios furnishes us with an especially helpful guide to the space of possibilities we now inhabit, or the room it affords us for maneuver. But there is a way in which we might approach understanding everything that is at stake and getting at least an initial idea of where big heat is taking us all, and that is to consider our previous collective experience of sustained emergency: the suspension of most all of the norms of everyday conduct that followed the outbreak of COVID-19.

The pandemic tutored us in the intricacies of the planetary supply chain, reintroducing consumers in the global North to experiences of material scarcity we probably thought our societies had transcended permanently. The elaborate logistical systems that underpin the fulfillment of our needs, and that ordinarily work so well that we tend to forget they even exist, had finally failed to deliver what was wanted exactly where and when it was wanted—if not quite for the first time in living memory, then at least since the increasingly distant childhood of those who grew up in the years of wartime rationing. In the worst weeks of lockdown, we found ourselves bartering for bread flour and toilet paper, or buying them by the pallet-load because industrial quantities were the only ones left available, and then sharing out the excess among friends and neighbors.

The globe grew bigger again, as the contrails stopped cross-hatching the sky. Our lifeworlds contracted to the ambit of a square mile or so, and, for a little while, our relationships with the other people in that square mile became the central fact of existence.

All through this time, millions sheltering under strict lockdown relied on neighborhood mutual aid groups for their groceries—in fact, for deliveries of everything necessary to maintain and reproduce our capacity to function as human beings, whether that meant baby formula or methadone, dropped off by masked and gloved volunteers who rang the doorbell and then retreated to a wary distance. We learned to depend more on one another, for everything from check-in calls on vulnerable neighbors to household repairs, and less on systems of state or market.

For the overwhelming majority, this turn to one another was not made out of any prior ideological commitment to anarchism, or localism, or the virtues of self-reliance, but because there simply was no alternative. We took care of one another in all the ways we could, and when some crisis exceeded our ability to manage it using the resources we had at hand, for the most part it simply went untended to.

In many ways, the official response to COVID not merely did not help us look after one another but actively exacerbated our inability to do so. As even the convinced antistatists among us must acknowledge, state action was critical in organizing both the astoundingly rapid development and the widespread distribution of effective vaccines. But throughout the early phase of the pandemic, government on both sides of the Atlantic remained in the hands of almost uniquely incompetent managers, the greatest part of whose incompetence lay in allowing questions of public health to become unduly politicized. Far from summoning us to any sense of common purpose, public policy therefore aggravated the social fault lines that had developed and were allowed to fester all through the years of neoliberal complacency, often badly compromising our ability to care for ourselves and one another.

There was an initial, instinctual flush of high seriousness and spontaneous mutual concern: this was the period of balcony arias in Italy and weekly doorstep applause for the National Health Service in the UK. But as the crisis wore on, to all appearances interminably, the popular mood soured. Dark conspiracy theories swirled, suppressing vaccine uptake just when near-universal adoption was needed most. In time, lockdown came to be marked by an amplification of the ugly qualities and characteristics that so often color the everyday late-capitalist lifeworld: solipsism and self-absorption, mutual wariness and hostility, most of all a preemptive irritation with the demands of others. And this was inevitably reflected in the type and magnitude of risk we assumed whenever we moved in public, with some fraction of those around us loudly refusing to mask up, or even threatening or physically assaulting those who did.

Amid all this, we learned that disruption is not merely an event that lands in one place and at one time, but something that cascades and ricochets, nonlinearly and in unpredictable ways. All through 2021, anyone who wanted to buy a PS5 or an iPad to ease the boredom of long days in lockdown had to contend with the knock-on effects of an achingly drawn-out drought that hobbled Taiwan's water-intensive semiconductor industry, at the very same moment microprocessor factories in Texas were unable to make up the shortfall due to their own, storm-related blackouts.[9] Just about anything with a chip in it was back-ordered for months. And then the container ship *Ever Given* came to grief in a sandstorm, midway through the Suez Canal, blocking for six days the passage of some 16.9 million metric tons of cargo, and complicating matters still further. By the end of the year, weeks' worth of the American consumer supply wound up stacked in holding patterns in the roads off Long Beach.

Sometimes it was the measures undertaken to forestall the virus itself that complicated our efforts at collective self-care. The members of a Buddhist volunteer group trying to source combat tourniquets for the Ukrainian relief effort, in the early weeks of the Russian invasion, found themselves hampered by the fact that almost all production of such tourniquets takes place in China, in cities that were then subject to the strictest COVID lockdowns observed anywhere. They could go on Alibaba and click "buy now" on as many cases of tourniquets as they pleased, but there was simply no way to physically get shipments out of Shenzhen. What might have been straight-forward, even trivial, under ordinary circumstances became impossible under the emergent conditions of the pandemic. In the brittle, interlinked, hyperextended and thoroughly unfor-giving world we have built, each successive crisis prevented a ready response to the next.

Sometimes, in the way of these things, when an official response *did* arrive, it had a certain quality of misempha-sis, overcorrection or overshoot. Faced with economies in post-lockdown freefall, governments around the world took short-term measures to sustain business activity that turned out to be counterproductive in some important way, even demonstrably hostile to the scaled protection of human life. The summer 2020 "Eat Out to Help Out" policy in the United Kingdom is a prime example. The scheme, which offered poten-tial diners a 50 percent subsidy for restaurant meals in the weeks immediately following the relaxation of the first national lockdown, threw the hospitality industry a temporary £850 million lifeline and was at the time regarded (by its architects, at least) as a success. But the resulting surge of indoor dining came some four months before a vaccine became available, at a time when coronavirus was still spreading uncontrolled and uncontained. Eat Out to Help Out is now known to have generated some 70,000 COVID-19 cases in the weeks that followed—or between 8 percent and 17 percent of all newly detected infections, leading to a cascade of onward cases and some unknown but clearly nontrivial number of deaths.[10] What we learned from this, if we were paying attention, is that simpleminded interventions in poorly understood, complex and complexly interacting systems aren't particularly likely to realize whatever benefits were anticipated, and may indeed leave us saddled with worse, to the very point of death.

And, of course, people *did* die, in their millions. Some were world-famous, many were known only to their families, quite a few of them seemed to occupy that space in between—the kind of people who subtly knit a neighborhood together, even if you only knew them from the bus stop, or because they ran the local shoe-repair shop. Whichever category they belonged to, you knew when the virus had taken someone in the area: their passage would be marked by the telltale of an ambulance gliding silently through the side streets, running blue lights but no siren, a faint but unsettling medieval air hanging over the whole thing. It was when this started to happen more than once a day that we truly learned what it meant to live in a time of plague.

This speaks to one final way in which our collective experience of COVID illuminates the stakes of the epoch now underway. It has to do with the toll taken upon those of us who survived by the grief, dread and unrelieved anxiety of the pandemic years. Despite the astounding human capacity for restoration and repair, despite the ways in which some lucky few among us might even have been able to harness the circumstances of lockdown to their advantage, we are each of us less than we were before. Some of us were, no doubt, able to strengthen our local networks and ties with our neighbors, and our confidence in our own capability along with them. But I imagine that most of us will be hard-pressed to say that we are better able to take on significant new challenges than we were in what it is now clear were the last weeks of the dying old order, in the ember days of late 2019. Whatever world it is that we now confront together, we face it harrowed by the emergencies we have already endured.

So: prolonged and cascading disruptions to the systems that undergird the material abundance we are used to. The retreat or outright failure of whatever state provision we might previously have been able to call upon. An array of public policies, postures and measures meant to impose some degree of continuity on a suddenly turbulent world, many of which swiftly come to seem bizarre and misguided, and which in any event fail to work in the way intended. Attempts at repair that do at least as much harm as good; entanglements in which one measure of mitigation or relief forestalls others that are just as urgent and just as necessary. A generalized contraction of the world, and the concomitant foreclosure of possibility. A train of shocks coming over the horizon one after the other, each new one appearing before we have quite managed to deal with the last, and each complicating all the rest. And all of this buffered only by the commitment, compassion, organizational nous and lifegiving selflessness of the ones around us, and whatever capacities for resistance we are able to develop and nurture in ourselves.

If these were the facets of our experience of COVID, they will also be the defining elements of our encounter with the time of heating. The pandemic was, then, two things at once: simultaneously the most vivid preview of how our societies will respond to future catastrophes of similarly global scale, and the first in an inexorable series of such events, each of which subtly erodes our capacity to respond to the next.

Contemplating what we endured during the pandemic and lockdown ought to give us a better understanding of what to expect from the Long Emergency as it unfolds. But our experience of the COVID years can only be, at best, a very approximate guide to some of the other conditions we now face, especially where those specifically arise from the circumstances of heat. What might actually be useful would be to lay out the basic parameters of life on a suddenly and sharply hotter planet, paying particular attention to the ways in which these intersect with the constraints and uneven geographies inscribed on the globe by the way production and consumption have been organized for the past half-century or so. If we are to devise meaningful strategies for collective survival, we will need to come to grips with each one of these separate elements of the interlocking crisis—as well as what they all imply when taken together as a whole.

We start with the sheer unanswerable fact of the heat itself.

Some idea of what sustained exposure to heat does to the human body can be gleaned from David Wallace-Wells, who considers the matter in his 2019 survey of conditions on *The Uninhabitable Earth*.[11] Wallace-Wells's particular contribution to the popular climate literature is a concern for the so-called "wet-bulb temperature," an index combining heat and humidity readings. At wet-bulb temperatures above 95°F (35°C), he tells us, the human body cannot cool itself by sweating, no matter how much water one drinks. Outdoor labor or activity of any sort will be rapidly and reliably fatal to anyone exposed.

He goes on to observe that there is already a broad swath of latitudes in which the wet-bulb temperature exceeds this point throughout much of the year, that most of the places affected are those least likely to have robust municipal cooling facilities or other means of alleviating the heat, and that both the land area and the number of days a year in which these conditions obtain are rapidly expanding.[12] A more recent study, however, suggests that the human body loses its capacity for self-regulation at wet-bulb temperatures much lower than was thought to be the case when Wallace-Wells published.[13] Wet-bulb readings of around 87°F (31°C) are now considered to be the upper limit for survivability—the threshold past which continued exposure reliably entrains organ failure and death, even for the youngest and healthiest. Since far more of Earth's surface can be expected to experience conditions in this range over the summers to come, the clear implication is that the zone that will effectively become uninhabitable is considerably larger than even Wallace-Wells had supposed.

There are legitimate reasons to push back against this narrative, including the idea that increased awareness of the danger among those most vulnerable to conditions of high heat and humidity has itself reduced the risk they contend with.[14] By the same token, though, no amount of awareness can compensate for the facts of our physical embodiment, or the structural factors that limit people's ability to determine when, where and for how long they work, constrain their access to air conditioning and otherwise restrict how much control they have over their exposure to the heat. The latitudes in greatest peril may never be literally uninhabitable in the way that, say, the surface of Mars is. But conditions that approach the upper bounds of survivability unquestionably make the struggle to provide for oneself and one's family that much more difficult, day by day ratcheting up the incentive to seek a better life somewhere else.

Even in regions where humidity, and therefore the wet-bulb temperature, does not present a hazard, heat can threaten life in ways few had imagined before they started showing up in the statistics of morbidity and mortality. For example, the past few summers have seen a steady increase in the number of people across the American Southwest admitted to hospital burn units, having suffered instant second-degree burns from contact with sidewalk or street surfaces superheated to over 170°F (76.7°C).[15] Unsurprisingly, the number of hospital admissions tracks the rise in temperatures associated with hotter summers.[16] A 2019 study found that the risk of pavement burns in areas of direct sunlight begins around the 95°F mark, but "increases exponentially as ambient temperatures rise" into the range that is now routine—a sobering thought, considering that daytime temperatures in Phoenix, Arizona, hit 110°F (43.3°C) or more every day between June 30 and July 30, 2023.[17] In cases where surface contact is sustained for more than a minute or two—as it easily can be for accident victims, elderly people who have fallen to the ground and are unable to immediately right themselves, or opioid users who have nodded out—victims generally suffer full-thickness, third-degree burns over the entire skin area involved. In the hottest places, these burns join more obvious risks to life from sunburn, dehydration, heat exhaustion and heat stroke as factors that already constrain outdoor activity during daylight hours, at least for those who are able to exert control over their working conditions.[18] And this is hardly a marginal concern: Phoenix is the fifth-largest city in America.

Beyond these immediate threats to the functioning of our bodies, none of the hazards presented to us by heating is more fundamental than that it endangers the growth of agricultural crops on which all human well-being ultimately depends. More than 40 percent of the daily calories currently consumed by humanity each day are derived from just three staple crops: rice, wheat and maize. Of these, a single one, rice, is the predominant source of energy in the diets of more than 2 billion people around the world and may constitute 90 percent or more of daily caloric intake among the poor of South and Southeast Asia.[19]

Rice is well adapted to the monsoon conditions of this part of the world, both major subspecies having been domesticated here. But it is vulnerable to heat that strikes at the wrong time in its growth cycle: its ability to grow is limited by the number and intensity of "killing degree days" to which seedlings are exposed, and crop yield falls sharply as temperatures surpass the threshold of cellular damage. Whatever rice does survive to be harvested, further, will be less nourishing, with the grain's levels of protein, iron, zinc and multiple B-complex vitamins all suffering from high atmospheric concentrations of CO_2.[20]

What is true of rice is true of the other staple crops, as well. In any given area under cultivation, some plants will wither and succumb to the heat-driven desiccation of their vital organs, while others will not propagate adequately due to equally heat-driven failures of pollination. All are imperiled by the drought, wildfire and bacterial and fungal blights projected to occur more often, and with greater severity, on a significantly hotter planet. Shortfalls in production may be ameliorated, to some extent, by expanding the territorial range across which staple crops are grown, or by cultivating them at higher altitude; it is even just possible that high ambient levels of atmospheric CO_2 could increase average yields in well-situated biomes. But unless robustly heat-tolerant varieties of the crops much of humanity currently derives the better part of its nourishment from can be developed, the grim prospect of sustained, population-wide hunger, even famine, cannot be eliminated.[21]

And then there are the physical effects of unprecedented heat on the places we live. If we have already seen what a mere two days of extreme temperature do to a polity and a population unprepared for it, consider that by 2050, people living in Beijing, Delhi, Kuala Lumpur, Singapore and dozens of other cities analyzed in one 2019 study will experience "a climatic regime that does not currently exist on the planet."[22] Even this rather hair-raising estimate is based on the IPCC's Representative Concentration Pathway 4.5, an "optimistic" scenario in which carbon emissions are stabilized after mid-century and average global heating is held somewhere between 1.4 and 1.8°C.[23] Whether either is likely to be contained within those bounds is left as an exercise for the reader.

When I argue that many places on Earth that are currently densely settled will become virtually impossible for human beings to dwell in safely, this is the finding I have in mind. As much as the habitability of such places will be constrained via the direct impact of heat, it's not hard to imagine that the closely associated second-order effects will be very nearly as consequential, extending as they will to insurmountable drought, the salinization of aquifers, seawater rise, or such a rise coupled with subsidence of the ground on which the city is built, as in Jakarta.[24]

I'm not suggesting that these conurbations will ever become entirely depopulated. There will always be communities of people who prefer to make a go of it in the wreckage, somehow, because they quite reasonably fail to perceive the makings of a better life anywhere else; because the anonymity and relative lack of oversight they experience in the abandoned city afford them opportunities not otherwise available; or simply because it is their home and they will not desert it. But proofing all of the urban environments most vulnerable against the newly volatile conditions will require an enormous, ongoing financial investment, literally running into trillions of US dollars.[25] Where that investment is no longer considered worthwhile or can no longer be sustained, the electric power, water, gas and sewerage infrastructures that support high-density habitation will swiftly fall into disrepair. And in turn, wherever they do, it will become extremely difficult to sustain communities of any significant size. (At some point, depending particularly on whether or not they can reliably be supplied with sufficient quantities of drinking water, Phoenix, along with Los Angeles, Las Vegas and the other cities of the American desert South-west, may well number among them.)

A further tranche of cities, while not subject to quite the same conditions of existential risk, will be under continual threat from tropical storms: hurricanes in the Atlantic and northeast Pacific, typhoons in the northwest Pacific and cyclones in the south Pacific and Indian Oceans. We know that these storms will both be increasingly frequent and—thanks to the sharper energy differentials of warmer, wetter air—increasingly violent. The Category 4 hurricane Harvey, for example, which made landfall just south of Houston in late August 2017, shed 15 percent more rainfall than comparably sized storms of the pre-warming era.[26] Harvey inflicted $125 billion in damage, making it second only to Katrina as the costliest storm on record—and it was only one of sixteen separate billion-dollar weather events in the United States that year.[27] Houston's experience of Harvey suggests that the magnitude of damage inflicted on the built and social fabric of a place by the wind speeds, rainfall totals and storm surges associated with Category 4 and 5 storms can be shouldered once, possibly twice, though not easily. Asking any human community to do so once or twice *per decade*, however, is unthinkable. That level of insult to the systems and infrastructures that support the maintenance of collective life simply cannot be sustained.

We will be reminded, over and over, that the relevant factors governing the fate of such cities are economic every bit as much as they are geophysical. The tipping point for coastal and low-lying conurbations will be that at which reinsurance firms withdraw their protection, capital investment in the form of real estate effectively becomes uninsurable, and development-loan and mortgage providers abscond from the scene. The calculus in such cases is one of "asset exposure," measured in increments of "capital per inhabitant," and the downside risk they face when they assess the most likely climate scenarios in these terms is already making insurance providers noticeably skittish.[28]

Just how skittish is suggested by the large American insurer State Farm's May 2023 announcement that in response to "rapidly growing catastrophe exposure," it would no longer write homeowner policies in California—not merely in flood or wildfire zones, that is, but everywhere in the entire state.[29] We can be certain that State Farm will not be the last insurer to do so, and that their decision is merely the harbinger of a more thoroughgoing retreat of this sort.

On the far side of the risk curve, the auguries for any further investment in a city are not especially good, and some relatively dramatic dispersal of the population cannot be far off, however improbable it may seem now. The C40 Cities climate initiative speaks frankly of a "managed retreat" from coastal zones, arguing that "[m]ovement away from the coastline will be unavoidable in some places," and that doing so intentionally and proactively "will have significantly lower social and economic impacts than forced, reactive retreat after coastal flooding events."[30] Relocating everyone imperiled by rising oceans is not the project of a few months, or even a few years: in 2018, twenty-one of the world's thirty-three megacities of 10 million or more inhabitants were situated on coasts.[31] Roughly 600 million of us live fewer than ten meters above average sea level.

Whether cities of the threatened latitudes become physically uninhabitable or their future prospects merely judged to be a bad investment risk, the predictable consequence will be a significant intensification of the flight toward the temperate zones of the Earth that has already begun.[32]

Unsurprisingly, the language around this issue is vexed. Experts tell us that the term most commonly used to describe people in flight from ecosystemic collapse, "climate refugee," is misleading on both legal and scientific grounds, so let us simply think of them as being "displaced." What all parties agree on is that their experience of displacement will take multiple forms.

Most of us, when trying to imagine what people go through in the course of such journeys, are likely to picture dust-whipped desert holding camps, perilously overloaded Zodiacs on the Channel, or desperate lunges across the Mediterranean in whatever spavined Libyan fishing boat can be pressed into service.[33] But the reality is that a healthy proportion of such displacements will be internal, such as the waves of outmigration that depopulated panhandle Texas and Oklahoma during the Dust Bowl years of the 1930s. Whether showing up in the form of RVs in Walmart parking lots and FEMA trailers dotted across the American landscape, families doubled or tripled up in inadequate housing, or the millions who wander from city to Chinese city without the all-important *hukou* that confers the right of settlement in any of them, the dislocation will be visible just about everywhere in the inland regions of the habitable zone.[34] As we move deeper into the Long Emergency, both city and countryside will increasingly come to be marked by scenes of mass dispossession, involuntary mobility and the inevitable social frictions that arise in their wake.

What happens at the boundaries between states will be more brutal still. Border crossings on land will increasingly become flashpoints for conflict, with the worst violence most likely to break out at the junctures between polities that appear to offer sharply asymmetrical life chances to the displaced—as, say, along the Rio Grande dividing Ciudad Juárez, Chihuahua, from El Paso, Texas; at the Pazarkule gate on the Turkish-Greek frontier; or at the Spanish North African exclaves of Ceuta and Melilla.[35]

Even where such stark contrasts do not exist, it will become routine and unremarkable for states of the relatively clement latitudes to assert their sovereignty in the way the United States already does, in the form of fortified and heavily militarized frontiers, ludicrously thickened border conditions and rigorously enforced biometric access regimes.[36]

The abject cruelty of exclusions at land borders is, if anything, overmatched by those that take place on the high seas. Here state posture increasingly combines attempts to repel migrant vessels that approach territorial waters with the harassment, interdiction or detention of the humanitarian activists trying to help them survive the crossing.[37] Such operations often result in massive loss of life, as during the June 2023 incident in which the Greek coast guard actively prevented the rescue of hundreds of migrants trapped on the *Adriana*, a Libyan fishing trawler about to capsize in the Ionian Sea.[38]

And for those who do manage to slip through the weave, legally or otherwise, the coldest of welcomes. As the Long Emergency wears on, the tendency will be for states to institute and hunker down behind all the policies and provisions that together make up a "hostile environment" for immigrants of all sorts.[39] Internally, states that perceive themselves to be under pressure from mass migration will do everything they can to make everyday life miserable for the newly arrived.

This will broadly mean an intensification and sharpening of those measures that already exist: routine immigration patrols, grim detention facilities for those scheduled for deportation and mandatory document checks at every point where people avail themselves of everyday services like housing, banking, education and healthcare. With increasing frequency, private employers and landlords will be deputized to make this sort of inspection—directed not merely to refuse service to anyone who cannot furnish the necessary credentials, but to report them to the authorities on the spot.

And more and more often, we'll find ordinary people enlisted to perform "borderwork": the informal and enduring ways communities have of letting newcomers know when they are not welcome, ranging from subtle slights to the most blatant, overt forms of othering.[40]

The picture that is rapidly coming into focus is one of a world without refuge, hospitality or fellow feeling, in which even those who are themselves only a generation or two removed from flight do everything they can to prevent the same welcome being offered to others. What is certain, however, is that all of the people displaced in the waves of collapse and abandonment will need to find homes somewhere. Through its sheer magnitude, the human flow involved will overwhelm any and all measures taken to counteract it. No polity on Earth will be able to completely seal itself off, whatever cruelty it chooses to enact at its borders.

Both transborder and internal migrant flows will continue to be swollen by large numbers of people fleeing armed conflict, which we now know is made more likely by heating.[41] A 2014 study considering thirty-two years of data from sub-Saharan Africa found reasonable grounds to draw a "strong causal" relationship between temperature at the higher end of the expected range and violence against civilians, in particular.[42] The authors of a systematic review published the following year were willing to assert the link between climate and conflict rather more strongly, and with global effect.[43] They were even prepared to put numbers on it: in reviewing fifty-five quantitative studies of interpersonal (i.e., "assault and murder") and intergroup conflict ("riots and war") conducted between 1986 and 2015, their meta-analysis showed that each rise of one standard deviation in a given location's temperature "is associated with an average 2.1 percent net increase in the rate of interpersonal conflict and a 11.3 percent increase in the rate of intergroup conflict." They then dryly noted that, according to an emissions scenario "which is now thought to be conservative," "[a]lmost all inhabited locations are projected to warm by at least [two standard deviations], with the largest increases exceeding [four] in tropical regions." What this suggests above all is just how futile it is to distinguish between those fleeing hostile climatic conditions and other kinds of refugees, as if there's a material difference between fleeing from the prospect of death in a food riot and that of death from heat stroke.

Demands for the restriction of movement will be resisted, of course—most effectively not by displaced people or their advocates, but by a business community that has long depended for its profit margins on the unimpeded flow of underpaid and acutely vulnerable immigrant labor. This is particularly so in sectors like poultry processing or agriculture, where the convenience, variety and plenty we enjoy have largely been achieved on the backs of an immigrant workforce that has long been treated as disposable.

And perhaps the needs of business will mean that some route to relative safety can be preserved, here and there, for at least a small portion of the displaced population, though at the cost of unspeakable working conditions. Otherwise—unless internal migrants become desperate enough to take on the non-unionized, low-pay, high-turnover work on which the everyday bounty depends—the closure of borders will drive acute shortages across every economy that has come to rely on the tacit cruelty of a two-tier labor system.[44] The grotesque irony is that any safe route whatsoever that is made available to displaced migrants may depend on the patronage of forces foundationally committed to their exploitation.

What we must try to comprehend and plan for, somehow, is a world in which hundreds of millions have been set to flight. In the very long term, I think we'll collectively come to understand this titanic, century-spanning process of resettlement as the planet's human population simply adapting en masse, and as best it can, to its violent new conditions of tenure. But in the meantime, the outlook is considerably darker. Consider the repercussions of the Mediterranean migration crisis over the past decade and a half, with knock-on effects extending to the as-yet uncontained right-populist surge across Europe;[45] remind yourself that the number of human beings involved in that migration reached into the millions, at most—and then try to imagine what will greet a population on the move that is not one but two orders of magnitude greater.

The vast upheavals of people during the Second World War and the Partition of India are the only remotely comparable events in recorded human experience, and the ripple effects from those are still driving history the better part of a century later. Everything we know about such wrenching dislocations tells us that abuse, pogrom and attempts at more or less comprehensive "cleansing" are sure to follow, wherever a distinct and identifiable body of people arrives in a place disinclined to welcome them in any particular number. And if history is any guide, some of these will be aimed at populations previously thought to be well integrated, or even fully assimilated.

*

Sharp limits on the movement of people will be accompanied by increasing friction in getting goods from one place to another, in an undoing of the process painstakingly enacted during the era of globalization.

Globalization was, in part, a titanic, decades-long, and largely successful effort to figure the world as a smooth space, where neatly containerized cargoes of all sorts could flow seamlessly between continents through the secured "gateways" and "corridors" of international logistics.[46] During these years, production was increasingly offshored from its traditional sites in the industrial heartlands of the global North to locales offering more relaxed regulatory regimes, fewer taxes and lower wages, in a headlong race to the bottom. Shenzhen was transformed from sleepy Pearl River Delta market town to manufacturing titan and metropolis of 12 million. Impoverished countries like Bangladesh, Vietnam and the Philippines reinvented themselves as powerhouses of global textile production. And warehouses, retail shops and homes beyond number filled up with the low-cost, relatively high-quality things they churned out.

But as you may have noticed, there is a considerable degree of overlap between the tropical locales that benefited most from this offshoring and the places on Earth most imperiled by direct heat, cyclonic storms and sea-level rise. Globalization will be thrown into reverse as tropical cities are subsumed by these threats, a greater share of manufacturing capacity is reserved for desperate local need and the conduits that for so long ducted capital, matter and energy between hemispheres are severed with an almost audible snap.

In this process of involuntary deglobalization, geography will have its revenge. Especially if emissions-intensive air freight falls into increasing disrepute, if not legal jeopardy, on ecological grounds, seaborne cargo will have to shoulder a greater part of the burden of moving things around the world. But ships plying their way between continents are forced to thread certain potentially unreliable bottlenecks—the Panama and Suez Canals, most obviously, but also the Strait of Hormuz, the waters off the Horn of Africa and the treacherous Malacca Strait, rich with gleefully redistributive pirates.[47]

This will increase the difficulty involved in simply getting goods from one place to another, in turn compromising the "just-in-time" logistics on which so much modern production depends. It will become enormously more burdensome, and in some cases may no longer be cost-effective at all, to assemble components drawn from across a hemisphere at a site of final integration before shipping them to a retailer or end user on the other side of the ocean. A greater portion of the complex artifacts people do make and use will therefore, of necessity, be produced closer to the point of actual need, or done without entirely.

Of all sectors of the economy, though, those that are dedicated to the provision of food and other perishable goods are most acutely vulnerable to increased difficulty in getting things from one place to another. If food production is likely to be sharply limited at source—as we've seen, both by the direct effects of heat on crops and by shortages of the necessary agricultural labor—it is equally so that what does get produced may not traverse borders quite as easily as it had in the past.

The July 2023 collapse of the Black Sea Grain Initiative suggests some of the reasons why.[48] Intended to protect shipments of the Ukrainian wheat, corn and sunflower oil much of Africa depends on, the compact was sensitively dependent on Russian assessments of strategic advantage, or even whim. When those assessments shifted, Russia reimposed the blockade on Ukrainian shipping it had maintained since the outbreak of war, and with tens of millions of tons once again piling up in silos, grain elevators and warehouses, Ukraine was compelled to try moving grain overland.[49] But the volume of grain that can be moved via truck or train is inconsequential compared to the capacity of an oceangoing bulk-carrier fleet, and the circuitous routing required of overland journeys means even that small amount moves much more slowly than it had before. The immediate result of the agreement's collapse was price instability on grain markets worldwide and food insecurity for hundreds of millions living half a planet away.

It's true that these are special circumstances, arising amid a conflict that, for once, has not a thing to do with global heating. But as we've seen, the risk of conflict increases sharply in a hotter world, and the same wartime factors that now hobble Ukrainian grain shipments—contested waters, mined sea-lanes, missile strikes on civilian vessels—stand to endanger any shipment moving across the face of an angrier globe, just as they had in world wars past.[50]

None of this makes the already quite considerable challenges of feeding ourselves over the years to come any easier. For the indefinite future the picture is likely to be one of curtailed availability, irregular distribution, range reduction, the increased spoilage of perishables, higher costs and limited stock of what is available, acutely threatening the all-but-inconceivable plenty, variety and on-demand access most of us have experienced for most of our lives.[51]

And what is true of food is also true for medicines and medical devices. You may remember how difficult it was to source N95 masks in the US or the UK during the early phase of the COVID pandemic—again, this was because the facilities capable of manufacturing nonwoven material at the necessary scale had largely been offshored to China. Chastened by this experience, both countries have more recently made noises about redeveloping a robust measure of domestic biopharmaceutical manufacturing capacity, with an eye toward ensuring that all the contents of the standard pharmacopeia can be produced at scale locally.

But while there is certainly a gathering intuition that this might be a wise thing to do, and it even meshes with the kind of protectionism espoused by populist parties everywhere, it has yet to be fully accomplished anywhere. It may never be. As a result, antibiotics, hormones, contact lenses, insulin pumps and a very wide range of other medical and pharmaceutical goods critical to the maintenance of life are still for the most part produced at the far end of a globally ramified supply matrix.[52]

Given the increasing complexity of long-distance transport, we can't bank on uninterrupted access to these vital supplies, either.

There are two further aspects of life in the years ahead we need to consider, without which no picture of an Emergency world is quite complete. The first is that exposure to all of the conditions we've discussed clearly affects some bodies more than others. If the raw conditions of life on a hotter planet fold back against each of us differently, then so, too, do the second-order effects of the heat, from an increased collective propensity for violence to interruptions of the food supply. It is in this sense that the Long Emergency will produce at scale a condition the disability scholar Jasbir Puar thinks of as "debility": a series of psychophysiological maimings and disfigurements of capacity that are unevenly inflicted across the population.[53]

For some of us this will show up as a persistent unavailability of the medicines or prosthetics we depend on; for others it might mean the insults to memory, executive function and cognitive capacity that are broadly entrained by continuous, unameliorated, long-term exposure to stress. For far too many, it will involve the slow depredations of threshold malnutrition. We ourselves will be weakened by our passage through the times ahead, in the most intimate, bodily ways, and the most vulnerable among us most of all.

The second is that our ability to respond to all of the conditions we face is complicated by the fact that we have entrusted so very much of the way we organize the world, as individuals and institutions both, to a finicky, fragile, high-maintenance technology of cloud-based services. Most all the networked services we depend on, for everything from entertainment to wayfinding to payment at the point of sale, are hosted in highly energy-intensive data centers and connected to the user and one another via a perilously vulnerable meshwork of routers, microwave transmitters and fiber-optic cables. None of these have generally been designed to account for operating temperatures that are now considered "extreme" and will soon become far more frequent.[54]

Though important parts of this extended armature have been engineered with redundancy and failover firmly in mind, we have lazily come to regard something as an always-on, always-there utility that is in fact deeply contingent. At any given moment, important components of it are evidently only a few hot hours away from failure.

Here, then, is everything suggested by those two days of a British July in full flower: a hotter world is, eventually, a hungrier world, a sicker world, a more violent world, a smaller and a more crowded world. In all of these dimensions, things may occasionally get better for a little while, here or there. But the frictions will never ease. The sort of disruptions, difficulties and outages that we're just now learning to anticipate and expect: these things do not represent a glitch in the system of the world. They are the best currently available state of that system, functioning as smoothly as it is able to at the moment, given the constraints on it, and likely as smoothly as it ever will again.

There is, of course, an institution in our lives that is supposed to manage risk, protect us from threats to life and provide for the common good. What of the state in the Long Emergency?

In a growing number of places on Earth, the state has already failed, collapsing inward in not so much a managed as an unplanned and headlong retreat from public provision. We see what this process looks like once it has run to completion in countries like Yemen, Somalia, Haiti or, most recently, Venezuela: the state has vanished utterly as a force in people's lives. Its ability to guarantee reliable (or any) access to essential services has evaporated. For most of the population, everyday life has become a desperate scramble to secure the basic necessities of survival.

Those with cash to spare are, of course, always free to purchase whatever safety the market affords them. The *Guardian* columnist Nesrine Malik describes some of the measures resorted to by better-off residents of the Sudanese capital, Khartoum:

There are electric generator providers who will sell you a wide range of devices to keep your lights on when the power goes out. There are sellers of water pumps to tease out the water from the mains, and another set of contractors to build you giant water containers to store that water when even the pumps don't work anymore ... Policing is patchy and unreliable, so you can pay someone to guard your home in the night.[55]

Everyone who can afford to shores up the threadbare remnants of state provision in this way. Everyone who can't is left to fend for themselves.

It's admittedly somewhat surreal to apply the lessons of everyday Sudanese life to, say, the United States, an economy fully 150 times as large. Given the way governments in the global North are already visibly struggling with the basics, though, we can be forgiven for wondering if some more thorough undoing isn't what awaits us in the years to come. Even short of outright collapse, ordinary democratic polities with fully developed economies now often feel as though they are approaching some threshold past which they will no longer have the effective capacity to deliver political goods—and this is true even now, in the early stages of something that will clearly tax that capacity to the maximum.[56]

More of us now know what it is to struggle with unreliable infrastructure, to wait helplessly for degraded public services or to make shift for ourselves when they never do arrive. And while some might see a certain karmic justice in this, in all the slow violence of empire now come boomeranging back onto the imperial core, in any society it is always the powerless who suffer first and most acutely from the retraction of public provision.

The Marxist geographers David Harvey and Ruth Wilson Gilmore both think of the process involved in this retraction as "organized abandonment."[57] Organized abandonment falls unevenly on the land, but if you live in a place that has been deserted in this way, you know it. You can feel it. The long hollowing-out of public investment is a palpable thing, directly accessible to the senses. It's the dogshit, trash and broken glass that accumulate on sidewalks that are no longer swept clean on a regular basis. The long line of ambulances stacked up in front of the emergency department of each hospital. The wait for a bus that used to arrive every few minutes and may now come twice an hour, if it shows up at all. It is the practical inability to access services that are formally yours by right, and the automated "helplines" or long and intentionally dispiriting waits on hold you encounter when you do try to schedule them. It is the shuttering of firehouses and libraries, the intentional discontinuation of street lighting and roadway maintenance—of everything, in fact, that signals a decent common existence. And all of it done intentionally, for the benefit of a vanishingly small (and not infrequently offshore) shareholder class. If this is the condition of neoliberal governance now, I can't imagine how anyone thinks it will suddenly improve once it comes under so much more pressure from so many new directions.

But as Gilmore develops the idea, particularly, organized abandonment is much more than simply a passive process of retreat and disinvestment. There is an active side to it, as well, and it is brought to bear on the bodies of those marked as other. Places that have been stripped of their public goods in this way are at the same time purposively made over into "planned concentrations or sinks ... of hazardous materials and destructive practices," to which marginalized, racialized and criminalized populations are relegated.

Gilmore is specifically speaking to Black experience in the United States, and there remain aspects of her framing that are unique to that experience. But analytically, it's not hard to see resonances and parallels with the ways in which organized abandonment works elsewhere and for other bodies, including all those in flight from newly uninhabitable conditions. Whatever life they knew before, those who have been transformed into "people on the move" by the fact of their displacement will find that they immediately become subject to much the same array of measures that are applied to other despised populations. Their very existence will be defined as extralegal. They will be intimately policed, perpetually surveilled, consigned to sacrifice zones and exposed to all the hazards that live there, with consequences that are more than occasionally lethal.[58]

So while it's tempting to argue that most states of the global North are bound to contract to whatever core military, security, police and judicial functions are required to protect private property, this isn't quite correct. To say that the state will go away is firstly to presume that it was ever there as anything but an actively malign force in people's lives. After some four and a half decades of conscious disinvestment, however, this simply isn't the case, especially for the poor and racialized communities that are invariably exposed to its worst effects.

What Gilmore helps us understand is the curious mixture of passive and active in the state's posture toward those pushed to the margins, and the ways in which it so often simultaneously undermines and overmines their struggle to lead a decent existence. Many, perhaps even most of us, live in communities whose capacity for care has in some way been eroded by the withdrawal of public investment. Some of us, though, live in communities where that capacity has consciously and intentionally been shredded.

Here we're finally in a position to understand the true depths of the trouble we're in. The crisis of our moment consists not of a breakdown of the global climate system, and all the storms and floods and fires and plagues it gives rise to, as terrifying as those things might be. It doesn't even consist of the irreversible proliferation of such events, or their cascading downstream consequences. It consists in the fact that all of that lands not on healthy, robust societies, but on ones whose capacities for care have been thoroughly and intentionally eroded.

These circumstances are multiplicative: what a well-cared-for population might have shrugged off, or taken in course, poses sharply greater risks for bodies that have been debilitated by their passage through a process of organized abandonment.[59] Our ability to take care of ourselves and one another has been undermined, not enhanced, by the structures of state that are nominally there to secure our collective well-being.

Zoom out, and the picture that comes into focus is of a globe quilted with places in which the long process of targeted disinvestment has frayed away the social fabric to the point that it's come undone; places that have been written off by insurers and formally forsaken as sites of human settlement; and places in which a duly-constituted government no longer has the capacity to underwrite public order, even if it wanted to.[60] Though we have come to it by such terribly different routes, those of us who live in any of these places now find ourselves in much the same situation: alone, unsure what to do and unable to look to the state for meaningful assistance with the conditions that threaten our well-being. We simply cannot count on it to be there for us in the moment that it matters most.

If nothing else, this ought to be radically clarifying. To me, the relevant question we face isn't whether the state *can* or *should* furnish everyone with at least the rudimentary makings of a decent and dignified life, but something far more concrete: whether it is *likely to* in this time and place. Here Harvey states what should be obvious: "[I]f the state withdraws from [the provision of public goods] then there is only one possible response, which is for populations to self-organize to provide their own commons."[61]

This is the insight on which everything turns. As the circumstances of the Long Emergency pick up pace and blend into one permanent condition of omnicrisis, it's time for us to think about building something else.

Are things really that dramatic, though—that far gone? Is it really our lot to stand by and watch as big heat wreaks chaos on the institutional architecture of the world? Aren't there *any* policy directions or technological developments at hand that might yet prove consequential in the struggle to maintain a survivable climate, and therefore the social arrangements we're accustomed to?

For reasons I'll explain, I do not believe that there are. There will of course be attempts to prevent further heating, most of them diligent, clever and sincere—but they will very likely fail, as will attempts to mitigate the heating that does take place. I'm making three separate assumptions here: that a so-called "green energy transition" will not take place in time to prevent the most consequential drivers of change from happening; that reparative "geoengineering" will not be attempted at the necessary scale or, if attempted, will not work as intended; and that in the time available to us, we will not invent some other technology capable of siphoning carbon from the atmosphere at the necessary scale, and rescuing ourselves that way.[62]

Let's start with the notion that a green energy transition will not happen in time to shelter us from the impacts of big heat. In the near term, it's a safe bet that incumbent actors will continue to prioritize the lowering of energy prices, accumulation of domestic political capital or strategic energy access considerations over what is necessary to stabilize the atmosphere. For evidence of this, we need look no further than the Democratic Republic of Congo's May 2022 announcement that it would auction off its peatlands and old-growth rainforests for oil drilling, Germany's return the following month to coal-fired energy generation, Prime Minister Rishi Sunak's declaration that it would be "economically illiterate" to wean the UK off of oil and gas, or the fact that China and India continue to approve new coal-fired power plants, even amid a season of record-shattering heat that shed tremendous suffering on both countries.[63] The price of solar power keeps dropping, yes, and the fact that it and other renewable sources are responsible for an ever-greater percentage of the annual planetary energy budget may well be excellent news for the long term. But decisions like those recently made by India, China, Germany, the UK and the DRC are clearly inconsistent with the pressing need to halt emissions. So while it's certainly *possible* that humanity may successfully complete a transition to renewable sources of energy over the next several decades—and therefore, eventually, the decarbonization of the atmosphere, and a slow subsidence of the heating—it's not currently in the cards. And in any event, no such thing can take place swiftly enough to prevent global average temperatures from proceeding past the point of safety because, again, *they have already done so.*

If we can't act quickly enough to prevent dangerous concentrations of heat-absorbing carbon dioxide (and the still-more-problematic but less-attended-to methane) from building up in the atmosphere, the next line of defense would be to prevent the sun from warming the atmosphere in the first place. This is, in fact, the goal of the various geoengineering techniques gathered under the rubric of "solar radiation management," the most developed of which conceptually is something called stratospheric aerosol injection.[64] This is based on a natural phenomenon that has been noted at least since the "year without a summer" that followed the 1815 eruption of Mount Tambora in present-day Indonesia, the largest volcanic event observed in recorded history: sulfur dioxide lofted into the stratosphere by the blast aerosolized and circulated worldwide, continuing to filter sunlight for months, and cooling average global temperatures by around half a degree Celsius.[65] As a strategy for countering global heating, stratospheric aerosol injection turns on the notion that what happened accidentally at Tambora can be achieved intentionally, programmatically and for as long as proves necessary.

Enthusiasts generally wave a hand at the complexities involved in stratospheric aerosol injection, but they are profound. In her book on geoengineering, the science journalist Elizabeth Kolbert tells us that achieving anything like the necessary coverage would require fleets of aerosol bombers continuously strafing the upper atmosphere with particulates.[66] Not merely does the necessary fleet not yet exist, neither does an aircraft that can carry the required twenty-ton payload to an operating altitude of 60,000 feet—nor, for that matter, does the technology to power such an aircraft's engines and keep it continuously aloft without dumping yet more carbon into the atmosphere. All of that would need to be funded, designed, developed and deployed before heating was reduced by so

48

much as a hundredth of a degree. And even then, unless some other process was drawing carbon down in the meantime, the cooling effect would only last as long as the injection sorties were maintained.

But even this isn't the best argument against geoengineering attempts of this sort. The real trouble is that, despite all the computational power we throw into building models of heat exchange between the planet's atmosphere and its oceans, we still don't understand the complexities of this interaction very well. It's all too easy to see how some well-intentioned but ham-fisted intervention in this entangled system might disrupt climatological patterns that condition literally billions of human lives—the ocean current known as the Atlantic Meridional Overturning Circulation, for example, which both regulates the climate across much of the Northern Hemisphere and circulates nutrients that sustain sea life, or the equally life-giving monsoon rains of South Asia.[67] The Tambora eruption, after all, did just this, resulting in an estimated 105,000 deaths from the direct consequences alone.[68] But advocates appear remarkably cavalier about such prospects: according to a project director for something called the Solar Radiation Management Governance Initiative, "We live in a world where deliberately dimming the fucking sun might be less risky than not doing it."[69] (If you are anything like me, you quail at the thought of how much work the word "might" is doing in that sentence.)

Assuming, then, that geoengineering based on solar radiation management does *not* turn out to work safely or well, a remaining possibility for lowering the heat resides in the technology of direct air capture, or DAC.[70] Here the picture is somewhat more encouraging. To begin with, we know DAC actually works. Each the size of a shipping container, DAC units can be deployed anywhere, and the amount of carbon that a given installation extracts from the atmosphere can in principle be more or less finely tuned, allowing for small-scale tests that don't run the risk of short-circuiting the monsoon or turning the entire sky white as a side effect. But here again, there are limitations: whatever carbon dioxide is absorbed from the air will still need to be sequestered in some way, the DAC process is itself hugely energy-intensive, and the technology has so far only been deployed in pilot programs of limited extent and ambition. While DAC shows significantly more promise—and beyond that, feels in every way wiser and more measured— than stratospheric aerosol injection, spinning it up to any scale at which it might make a difference will take years. Even in the best-case scenario of DAC deployment, we would still be in for many years of historically anomalous temperatures and all the extreme weather events and third-order effects that follow on from them.

And that really is the bottom line in any of these discussions. We are already committed to decades of severe storms, wildfires, droughts and floods, no matter what technology is developed, no matter what policies are enacted, and no matter what any state, transnational or corporate governance body decides to do now. At this point, no force on Earth can prevent the breakdown from progressing. The process that has already begun will run its course, conditioning the shape of possibility on this planet until long after we are gone from the scene. It will be the central determining factor in virtually all human endeavors for centuries to come and will only finally resolve itself many, many years from now, when the climate system has achieved its new stable state, and whatever human population remains has either learned to live within that balance or is unable to disturb it to any salient degree.[71]

The idea I've tried to flesh out here—that the society we live in is on the edge of a catastrophic transition to a new order of being, catalyzed by widespread ecosystemic breakdown—is not an especially novel one. The basic contours of this scenario have been explored, with lesser or greater sophistication, in literally hundreds of essays and books, dating back as far as the 1960s—and, indeed, society's manifest failure to fail over all this time has lent most of these titles an undeniable Chicken Little quality.[72] What this entire body of literature has proven unable to explain is something most people no doubt find utterly unremarkable: that high-complexity societies organized around the conventional Westphalian state and the globalized market continue to thrive, a quarter of the way through the twenty-first century, despite the mounting pressures on them.

The writer and climate activist Andreas Malm has taken would-be catastrophists to task for their failure to connect the dots in this regard. What is lacking in their just-so stories of societal collapse, he argues, is an account of "*how environmental stress factors [are] translated into hardship*" for a society's "dominant classes."[73] That is: How are disruptive climatic conditions—which may well be debilitating or even fatal for individual bodies—mediated to the dominating structures and institutions of society, such that their ability to continue arranging the world for their own benefit becomes and remains degraded? By extension, how will the heat somehow prove incommensurate with the continuity of all the political, territorial, technical and economic arrangements that together make up our familiar world? How, above all, is an institution as enduring and well defended as the state supposed to recede from our lives so thoroughly, when confronted by heavy weather, that we are forced to shift for ourselves?

These are excellent questions, and I've tried to suggest some of the mechanisms that are likely to be involved in our case. But a richer and perhaps more satisfying answer lies in a brief essay called "How Complex Systems Fail," self-published in 1998 by an anesthesiologist named Richard Cook.[74]

By "complex systems," Cook means the intricate, multilayered processes of technical orchestration that are everywhere in modern life, from operating theaters to air-traffic control centers to nuclear power plants, but the same principles can be extended to an economy or a society without doing them too much conceptual damage. Cook tells us a few things about the working of such systems: that they are inherently hazardous and involve multiple points of risk. But they are also well defended against the risk of failure, furnished with abundant safety features and multiple layers of redundancy.

Cook observes that, whatever safety mechanisms they may have been equipped with, what all such systems have in common is that they are kept within safe operating margins via the continuous adjustments of human operators. This seems commonsensical enough. But what he argues next is somewhat startling: these adjustments are invariably in the nature of a "gamble." Whatever decision is at hand, it will always be a bet made about the future in the presence of imperfect information.

Most of the time—in fact, virtually *all* of the time, by definition—the gamble pays off. The system reacts in the way its operators expect it to: the nuclear reactor continues to run smoothly, the satellite reaches a stable orbit, the tumor is excised and the patient successfully revived. Paradoxically, though, trouble arises when operators have insufficient experience of failure. Lulled by their unbroken record of success in keeping it going, they can't sense when the system they've been entrusted with is close to the edge of its performance envelope, and miss or don't recognize the signs that it is closing in on failure. They make a gamble that the system will continue to operate normally, as all their previous experience has counseled them to expect that it will, and they allocate their resources accordingly. And then change comes arcing in from some unforeseen quarter: the gamble is lost, and everything comes undone all at once.

In his essay, Cook says one other interesting thing about complex systems, which is that it is quite possible for them to "run in degraded mode" for extended periods. That is, they are so well defended by their many layers of backups that they can accumulate damage for many years before hitting the point of absolute breakdown. They simply go on working, without either their operators or anyone else necessarily realizing the extent to which everything under the hood has corroded away to nothing.

The most obvious example of this in societal terms is the Soviet Union, which continued to maintain a certain façade of robustness even after the fall of the Berlin Wall in November 1989, and indeed right up to the point of its dissolution on

Christmas 1991. Not merely did the USSR manage to hide its advanced state of decrepitude from all but the canniest external observers, whether sympathetic or hostile; it even managed to prevent its *own* decision-makers from perceiving the truth of their situation.[75] The lesson for us seems obvious: even those arrangements of the world that seem imperturbable may simply be tottering along "in degraded mode," way out past their margins of safety, and vulnerable at any time to the final insult that will bring them all crashing down.

I don't want to discount capitalism's astonishing tenacity, or dismiss that darkly impressive ability it seems to have of reframing disaster as growth opportunity and discovering new markets even amid the rubble. There are plenty of bright people who believe, or have anyway managed to convince themselves, that the systems undergirding everyday life in the late-capitalist period are more than resilient enough to carry the day, even given the new constellation of climatological threats they face.[76] Nor would it necessarily be wise to bet against them, however desperate, self-deluded or willfully unseeing their arguments might seem.

For well over a century now, its critics have continuously underestimated capitalism's sheer vitality: its genius for adaptation, its propensity to generate entirely new lifeways requiring entirely new material supports, its capacity to develop intensively when extension was no longer a viable option. The engine, somehow, keeps turning, despite the analytical predictions (and frequently enough the heartfelt desires and lifelong efforts) of those who have prophesied its failure. It may well somehow continue to do so, even amid the most disruptive scenarios considered here.

I also don't want to suggest that the process of destabilization I describe will necessarily unfold in quite the same way in every place on Earth. Given the present reality of uneven development, it will likely be possible to maintain some pastiche of the late-capitalist lifeworld we recognize in many places—at least with great effort, and exclusively for the most highly favored—and it is even possible that these won't simply amount to a series of buffered enclaves, fortified redoubts and the secured corridors between them. For those lucky few able to avail themselves of these sheltered environments, and blithe enough not to care about the fate suffered by anyone else, not a single topic I raise for consideration in the rest of this book is likely to be in any way germane.

But for the rest of us, the normality to which we've become so accustomed over the past forty years is already dwindling in the rear-view mirror. Nor will there be, as the cliché has it, a "new normal" we might clamber up onto and cling to for dear life. If an emergency, an emergent situation, is a sudden and unexpected excursion from the accepted bounds of the normal—an exceptional case in which the ordinary rules and procedures are temporarily suspended—what we now confront is an excursion that has become permanent.

And so we find ourselves contemplating the end of the systems that have defined the ordinary through all our lives, that have framed and given grounding context to everything we've ever experienced. There's a line of thought that putting things this starkly is bound to be counterproductive, if not actively reactionary in consequence.[77] On this theory, predictions of any particularly widespread social breakdown in the wake of ecosystemic collapse are slipshod analysis: sloppy thought that unduly universalizes and naturalizes something that was done by specific, identifiable historic actors, and for which they should be held accountable. Worse still, from this point of view, is that discussions of breakdown are supposed to subtly commend rugged-individualist responses, and therefore erode the bases for solidarity and the mass collective action that are seen as necessary to a just survival.

One of the strongest criticisms levied against framing our situation in such uncompromising terms, though, isn't directed toward any putative weakness of analysis, or of the political choices that result. It's that doing so can easily be psychologically overwhelming. The argument is that being hammered by the unrelenting facts produces a kind of lassitude in people, a blackened quietism that couples fundamental acceptance of the facts with an overcoming and total sense of one's own powerlessness. Or worse yet—since things are already *so* bad that nothing we do could possibly matter—a careless, profligate abandon.

And here I'm considerably more sympathetic. But as I see things, there are two strong counters to this argument, one of which is ethical and the other pragmatic. The ethical aspect is straightforward: it's a matter of basic respect, as well as a bedrock principle of informed consent, that each of us be furnished with an account of our situation and the options available to us that is as complete and accurate as possible. As importantly, though, we need to grasp what our circumstances consist of, what they imply and how they amplify one another, if we're ever to figure out how to navigate this harsh new world together.

There will be shock and rage and overpowering grief in this—as there should be. I doubt many of us will be able to contemplate the true contours of the world we now inherit without being undone, at least for a little while, by the things we feel in response. If we sit with these feelings for long enough to let them subside, though, we may find ourselves ready to face up to what they are really asking of us. Not only that: we may come to realize that there are others who've been on the same journey and are every bit as ready for that encounter as we are. What lies before each of us now is to find those others. It's only by confronting the new terms of our tenure on the planet, however stark or bleak or frankly unnerving they may be, that together we can begin to *do something* about them.

2

Mutual Care

It is one of the worst bodily sensations you will ever experience: that clammy, cold-sweat certainty of knowing you're alone, at a moment in which you desperately need the help of others. When the support structures you expect to rely upon have fallen away, or were never there in the first place, you arrive with terrible clarity at the understanding that this is it. There's no one you can call. Or there's no one on the other end of the line to answer. Maybe the line itself is dead. In any of these cases, though, the result is the same: no help is forthcoming.

The awful isolation of these moments is something you experience at the somatic level as much as the intellectual or emotional. Every fiber of your being rebels: surely, *surely* it's not supposed to be this way—not here, not in the twenty-first century.

There is a way of refusing to let that isolation stand as the unquestioned law of life, or to acquiesce to the privatization of the terror and grief that accompany it. We call that refusal "mutual aid." The activists Kelly Hayes and Mariame Kaba cite a definition of mutual aid offered by Seattle's Big Door Brigade, and I can't improve on it: "When people get together to meet each other's basic survival needs with a shared understanding that the systems we live under are not going to meet our needs and we can do it together *right now*!"[1]

The commitment to mutual aid doesn't emerge from any kind of prior theory, in other words, simply from the recognition that when the institutions to which we've entrusted our care fail us, the only thing standing between us and the darkness is our own capacity for collective, self-organized action. Mutual aid is simply how people without resources have always arranged the means of their own survival: cooperatively, outside the structures of market or state, using whatever tools they had ready to hand. This is the sense in which the anarchist philosopher Peter Kropotkin first used the term, in his enduringly lively 1902 classic *Mutual Aid: A Factor of Evolution*.[2] Holding that the capacity for cooperation is a trait far older than humanity itself, which has been conserved across deep time for the enhanced likelihood of survival it confers on populations, Kropotkin insists that it is a possibility that remains available to us, even now, and that it might continue to sustain human communities through their darkest hours.

But mutual aid isn't quite as simple as cooperation toward the shared goal of survival in a time of emergency. Nor is it quite coextensive with the set of practices political scientists rather clunkily describe as the "non-state provision of social welfare," though it is that in schematic.[3] In its modern sense, the term primarily refers to those citizen-driven emergency relief efforts that both stem from and reproduce a distinct set of values, most central among which is horizontality.

In this context, horizontality is much more than an organizational structure. It is the refusal to impose, observe or respect any sort of power relation between the person who is extending help and the person who requires it. This is the fundamental quality that distinguishes mutual aid from other models of voluntary, nonstate service provision, like charity. Where charity insists on a show of gratitude from the recipient—or at least tacitly expects them to nurture a sense of obligation that must someday be discharged—mutual aid rejects the savior/saved dynamic entirely.[4]

This is not the only thing that sets the practice of mutual aid apart from charity. Mutual aid starts from the recognition that exposure to risk falls unequally across the population, and aims at nothing less than transforming the circumstances that produced that inequality in the first place.[5] It aims, in other words, at liberation.

*

If Kropotkin had seen collective, cooperative practices under-girding the everyday life of communities just about everywhere, for most of us those habits have long since been overwritten by systems of state and market. In modern times the instinct toward cooperation only seems to reappear in times of the most acute peril, when all of that falls away. The terrible gift we're offered in these moments is a chance to practice all those capacities for self-organization that are so badly under-developed in our ordinary late-capitalist lives. This was the story of the Common Ground Collective, a mutual aid group established in the Algiers district of New Orleans following the August 2005 landfall of Hurricane Katrina.[6]

New Orleans is a particularly low-lying city, protected from the higher surrounding waters of Lake Pontchartrain and the Mississippi River only by an elaborate system of levees. These levees failed at six points during Katrina, inundating 80 percent of the city and damaging a full 70 percent of its occupied housing units.[7] Just about the entire population of Orleans Parish was displaced.[8]

The hurricane's direct and indirect effects were particularly lethal for the city's poor and majority-Black neighborhoods, where they were compounded further by the lack of any mean-ingful official response to speak of.[9] As the days dragged on without any effective relief effort being mounted, the stories that filtered out of the region took on a frankly apocalyptic tenor: bodies lying unrecovered in the street being devoured by rats, or patients stranded in a flooded hospital being euthanized (at least seventeen reported) when it became clear that they could or would not be evacuated.[10]

Galvanized by the anguished recognition that "help was not coming," Common Ground was founded by "three friends sitting around a kitchen table, with only a cell phone, $50, and their own energy, imagination, and compassion to work with."[11] The effort eventually grew to some 28,000 volunteers, an especially impressive level of commitment when you con-sider that in 2005, the population of New Orleans proper was only about sixteen times that number.

Common Ground's founders Malik Rahim, scott crow and Sharon Johnson were clear about what their initiative would offer: "Solidarity not Charity." The effort was "the first movement to visibly mobilise grassroots disaster relief with radical social and ecological principles in the US," and it was explicitly organized "to provide relief, aid and support to underserved [and] marginalized communities" on a Kropotkinian, horizontalist model.[12]

Rahim, crow and Johnson knew what it meant for people to be marginalized and underserved: Algiers, where they founded Common Ground, has a median household income lower than 99.5 percent of American census tracts.[13] But where people living in places like this were all too often treated as Katrina's "faceless or helpless victims," when they were even seen at all, Common Ground insisted that they be acknowledged "as active participants in the struggle to make their lives better."[14]

Taking their inspiration from the Spanish anarchism of the Civil War years, the Black Panthers and the Zapatistas—Rahim himself had actually been a Panther—the three founders wrote down a set of values that would guide their effort, among which were autonomy, anticapitalism, cooperation, solidarity and the commitment to direct action. Common Ground would maintain a properly wary distance from the state, which had done so little for the people of New Orleans, and organize itself from among the people of the communities hit hardest. It would ask no payment for its services and at the same time reject the patronizing model of charity that, subtly or otherwise, conditioned the aid work of conventional organizations. Above all it would *do something* about the catastrophe that had befallen residents of the city's poorest neighborhoods, rather than wait passively for the help from above that was never destined to come.

Starting from a single "distribution center"—a makeshift tent set up in Rahim's driveway, lashed together from PVC pipes and nylon tarps—Common Ground volunteers started sharing out food parcels they'd trucked in from Texas themselves. They set up a rudimentary clinic, whose volunteer medics rode through the streets on bicycles, asking locals if they needed anything in the way of help and offering first aid to those who had been injured in the storm or its aftermath.

The network expanded, over the next several months growing to include multiple distribution hubs and medical clinics, a women's center and a community kitchen. Common Ground crews fanned out through the neighborhoods, pulling down houses that had been rendered uninhabitable by the rains and toxic floodwaters, gutting, tarping and doing mold abatement on the ones they could save, and training volunteers to handle these specialized tasks safely. Yet other initiatives spoke to the wider needs of a community under pressure, from a local newspaper and radio station to "a biodiesel [fuel] program, computer classes, childcare co-ops, legal assistance, eviction defense, prisoner support, after-school and summer programs, anti-racism training, and wetlands restoration work."[15]

None of this went unopposed. Some of the backlash came from the very people you might imagine might contest an autonomous effort at self-determination organized by the residents of poor and Black neighborhoods: Common Ground's volunteers faced down physical threats not merely from the armed white vigilantes roaming Algiers Point, Central City and the French Quarter in their pickup trucks, but also from the National Guard that had ostensibly been deployed to the region to help. But other challenges came from less predictable quarters. The French ultraleftists known as the Invisible Committee remark, in apparent sympathy with the charge, that "Common Ground has been criticized ... for the fact that its activities were geared towards a return to normality—that is, to the normal functioning of things."[16]

But I don't think this is at all fair. Just as the Black Panthers and the Zapatistas had left traces for the founders of Common Ground to pick up, interpret and make their own, Common Ground laid down tracks for the ones who followed, building not so much a network across space as one across time. In navigating by the cues left by the ones who had gone before them, they inscribed the trail more deeply and signposted it for all those who would follow in the years to come. And among those who did pick up the traces was a group of Occupy Wall Street veterans who organized themselves to counter the effects of Superstorm Sandy. They called themselves Occupy Sandy.

If the full circumstances of Sandy's apocalyptic descent onto New York City were difficult for anyone on the ground to grasp in real time, they will be virtually impossible for me to convey to you now, even given the benefit of time and distance. Like all such events, the storm and its aftermath appeared in our lives as a hyperobject, too large and ill defined at its edges for anyone to see clearly.

What did become evident, as the storm surge receded, was that in many places the devastation was little less than total. Whole communities had been reduced to sodden splinters all along the city's coastal frontage, from Edgemere and Arverne in the Rockaways to Midland Beach on Staten Island. In Breezy Point, Queens, at the far western end of the Rockaway Peninsula, an entire neighborhood burned down to nothing when rising seawater first sparked electrical wiring into flame, then prevented firefighters from reaching the scene of the blaze.[17]

In one part of town after another, what had been the stuff of people's lives mere days before now clogged the gutters in abject heaps of undifferentiable material, wedged in tangles of rusted rebar. Many of the buildings that did survive the storm's immediate onslaught were too dangerous for people to venture into unprotected—with 17 percent of the city's land area flooded, tens of thousands of structures had been soaked to chest height in sea salt and sewage, or the toxic waters of the flooded Gowanus Canal, and were now being subsumed by rapidly spreading colonies of mold.[18]

All told, Sandy caused an estimated $19 billion in immediate damage and lost economic activity.[19] Roughly 69,000 housing units were damaged in the five boroughs of New York City alone, and at least 300 destroyed entirely, rendering as many as 40,000 people temporarily homeless.[20] Forty-four New Yorkers lost their lives to the storm's direct effects.

Even neighborhoods that weren't hit directly by flooding or fire absorbed a body blow. With power out through much of the city, with water mains, emergency services and regular food deliveries in broad swaths of Brooklyn and Queens disrupted for weeks, life for millions teetered on the cusp between challenging and perilous. And amid all the chaos, what became obvious was that New York City had never been designed to absorb this kind of impact, at any level: not in terms of its architecture, not in terms of its physical or institutional infrastructure.

On any ordinary day, these infrastructural systems sustained the life of the city so quietly and with such unremarkable efficiency that they receded from collective awareness. In their failure, everyone who relied on them was reminded that "ordinary" is an achievement. The consequences of infrastructural collapse were plainly visible everywhere you went in the days and weeks after Sandy, made manifest in the form of raw human need.

There were and are agencies that are chartered specifically to assist in the wake of such disasters, primarily by organizing emergency shelter, sustainment and financial assistance for all those who find themselves displaced. In New York City, the public-sector response to Sandy was chiefly coordinated by Region 2 of the Federal Emergency Management Agency, or FEMA, and that of the charitable or philanthropic sector by the American Red Cross. But these are lumbering, dinosaurian entities, whose very nature and organizational structure makes them incapable of reacting to events at the speed of calamity itself.

"What we're hearing, even from FEMA and the Red Cross themselves, is that because they're such large operations, it takes them weeks just to get set up," said Rev. Michael Sniffen, rector of an Episcopal church in Brooklyn, a few days after the storm had receded. "You know: FEMA comes and knocks on someone's door and says, 'OK, we've done an assessment, you'll hear from us in ten days.' But for folks who are living without power, without water, without food, ten days is too long to wait."[21]

This was an infrastructural failure of a different sort, and it was particularly terrifying given the plummeting temperatures that settled onto the region in the first days of November. With no heat, no light, no food, no water that was safe to drink and no help in the offing, millions living across the tristate area now found themselves up against the unthinkable. There is a very real sense in which they owe their survival to the efforts of the thousands of their neighbors who organized themselves under the banner of Occupy Sandy.

It is overwhelmingly likely that we would not have anything like an Occupy Sandy to discuss now, whether by that name or any other, had it not been for the original Occupy Wall Street encampment in Zuccotti Park the previous fall.

The legacy of OWS was evident in the incredible speed at which the relief effort took shape: it was because of the social connections, and the trust for one another, that activists had forged in the course of those ecstatic and difficult weeks in the park that they were able to stand up the sprawling network of sites and activities so very quickly.[22] It was evident in the immediate sophistication of the logistical systems they organized at each of those sites, which owed something to the pop-up infrastructure of the makeshift society formed over the fifty-nine days and nights in Zuccotti.[23] And it was most evident of all in the set of values that guided the relief effort—which should surprise no one, given that they were the selfsame values, held by a group that included many of the same people.[24]

These ideas, techniques, connections and beliefs—much of what made Occupy Wall Street what it was, in other words—had lain dormant for the better part of a year, slumbering beneath the surface of everyday New York City life. They remained available as a set of latent and unrealized potentials, there to be picked up, dusted off and brought to life again when the conditions were right.[25] This is what accounts for the circumstance that so mystified official observers at the time: how a non-organization that to all appearances had come from nowhere was able to field hundreds of motivated volunteers within the first days after landfall and sustain high-intensity recovery operations from their sudden network of warehouses and distribution hubs.

One of these hubs was set up in the Episcopal church where Sniffen was rector: the Church of St. Luke and St. Matthew at 520 Clinton Avenue, on the border between Clinton Hill and Prospect Heights. My partner and I showed up there on the afternoon of the fourth day following the storm. At that point, neither of us had any particular experience, skill or competence in disaster relief and recovery work; if that came at all, it came later. All we knew was that we wanted to help and had been summarily rebuffed by the first two organizations we'd initially tried to volunteer with.[26]

We could have followed the crisply designed yellow directional signs that someone had hung up, pointing the way to 520 from the Clinton-Washington C train stop at the corner. But there was no need to: there was a long column of delivery trucks backed up in front of the church, the best signpost anybody could ask for. We found the church halfway down the block, set back from the sidewalk behind a low chain-link fence.

Someone had zip-tied a homemade banner onto the fence that read "OCCUPY SANDY: Mutual Aid Not Charity," in conscious or unconscious echo of the slogan that had rallied Common Ground during Katrina. The banner told us, from these very first moments, that here was something very different from the Red Cross that had turned us away so curtly. (Lest anyone miss the point, the first letter in "aid" was replaced with the universal circle-A symbol of anarchy.)

Two or three volunteers sat at a folding table set up alongside the fence, walking a nearly continuous stream of arrivals through the process of registering themselves. They were extraordinarily efficient: we didn't have a chance to open our mouths before someone responsible for intake had greeted us, thanked us for coming, handed us materials to make name badges with and showed us what to do to get signed up. We filled out a brief questionnaire—contact information, useful skills, languages spoken—and then waited for a group of ten or so to accumulate, at which point we were given a short lecture explaining the values we would be expected to uphold as volunteers. And that was it. We were part of Occupy Sandy.

Let's return for a moment to that banner, and what it implied.

In her book on the aftermath of disaster, Rebecca Solnit suggests that we can best understand what happened in New York that October as a hybridization of two preexisting currents in the city's public life.[27] What emerged fused the spontaneous, largely apolitical self-help efforts that sprung up in the wake of the September 11 attacks to Occupy Wall Street, which was of course intensely politicized. And there's a strong argument to be made that it was the anarchist sensibility suffusing the latter that accounted for Occupy Sandy's remarkable effectiveness.

In other words, what made Occupy Sandy work was precisely the fact that it was *Occupy* Sandy. The effort was explicitly founded in a particular set of commitments, which were articulated in its every space and evident at its every stage.[28] Though they had unquestionably been distilled through the experience, the perspectives and the language of the Zuccotti Park occupation, at core they were much the same set of values that scott crow had described as driving Common Ground's work in New Orleans six years previously: autonomy from the state, solidarity with the marginalized, horizontality in organization and decision-making, and directness of action.

As we'll see, these were all qualities that helped the relief effort achieve what it did, concretely and materially, but they weren't pursued for the sake of that alone. They were deployed toward a larger end. As 520 site coordinator Samantha Corbin told the documentary filmmaker Josh Fox, "Aside from simply being antiracist, antisexist, antihomophobic, anticlassist ... we believe that in the work that we do, we have to be actively undermining those structures that separate us, and keep some people down and elevate others."[29] That belief determined not merely *what* was done by Occupy Sandy (OS) but *how* it was done. The best way to really grasp what I mean by this is to see what it looked like in action.

Once our little group had moved inside the church, we found that its nave had been converted into an impromptu warehouse, complete with areas to receive incoming relief supplies, store them until needed and then stage them for delivery. A human chain ten or fifteen people long was handing boxes in from the street, steadily moving them off the trucks and into a holding area distinctly smelling of damp cardboard, where each one was opened and checked. Donated supplies filled the pews all the way down to the sanctuary, carefully sorted by row: winter coats and hand warmers here, soap and tampons there.

A member of the intake team explained the various sections OS was organized into, listing all of the many things that needed doing—we could prepare hot meals in the church kitchen if we wanted, or help with coordinating transportation, or even get trained to do direct relief or demolition work out at the field sites, if we felt up to it. All of this sounded equally necessary, interesting and urgent, but I could see for myself that the two volunteers handling incoming packages were struggling to sort them into the pews fast enough to keep them from piling up at the entrance. So that's what I got stuck into, and for the most part that's what I wound up spending the balance of my time at 520 doing.

I quickly learned that, however rustic this logistics hub might have seemed to casual inspection, it was a sophisticated operation. Once I got used to the system, it rarely took me any more than a few minutes to put together a care package custom-tailored to the needs of someone out in one of the ravaged coastal communities. This wasn't simply a matter of some shrewd sorting protocol, either. In a particularly clever hack, activists hijacked Amazon's wedding-registry functionality as a way to funnel donations; by visiting the gift registry notionally set up for "the wedding of Sandy and Sandy," supporters from around the world were able to purchase whatever was needed most urgently, from cleaning supplies to bottled water to blister-packs of batteries. (This, of course, was the ultimate source of the long tailback of trucks we'd encountered when we first arrived at 520, which would continue to clog narrow Clinton Avenue for weeks thereafter.) When people who'd been displaced, or were holding out in whatever remained of their family home, told volunteers in the field what they needed, that information was fed directly into the wedding registry. It often enough meant that they were able to get just what they'd asked for.

That they were asked about their needs at all, though, speaks to the contrast between the way OS did disaster relief and how a hierarchical, command-and-control organization like the National Guard set about doing things. When the National Guard set up their distribution sites for blankets or food or fuel, they would generally broadcast over the radio the times and places these supplies would be available. The supplies themselves were free, but anyone who needed them would have to make their way across town to claim them—and this was highly challenging, to say the least, on a sprawling terrain of flooded streets where public transit was effectively nonexistent and fuel shortages were beginning to bite. And what if your radio had shorted out in the flood, or its batteries were dead, or you didn't have one in the first place? How were you even supposed to know these facilities were available to you?

The Red Cross wasn't much better, judging from a "scene of clumsily administered relief" a journalist witnessed in Midland Beach, two weeks after Sandy: "At the nearest intersection, a Red Cross van announced, via megaphone, 'hot soup!' to no one in particular … The truck left not long after arriving. It fed no one."[30]

This is entirely consistent with scenes others witnessed, as well as things I saw for myself when I came across Red Cross teams on my way to or from 520.[31] The distinct impression I was left with was one of salaried staff listlessly executing a plan that had been thought up in some windowless operations center dozens of miles away, with neither input from nor any real consideration for the communities who were supposed to benefit from this largesse. Fairly or not, it was also commonly understood among OS volunteers that Red Cross workers in particular were unwilling to venture up the dark stairwells of the high-rise public housing projects where so many of our fellow New Yorkers were stranded.

By contrast, Occupy Sandy's volunteers actively fanned out across the worst-hit neighborhoods. Like Common Ground's bike-mounted medics, they went door-to-door and household-to-household in Red Hook and the Rockaways, checking in with everyone they encountered. They went into the housing projects and up to the darkened floors, keeping faith with the places, and the people, other relief workers evidently found so daunting. And rather than presuming that those they came across were victims in need of rescue—and offering them generic aid packages in response, as a Red Cross outreach worker might—the members of OS field teams treated them as peers and equals, the ones who knew better than anyone else what their actual needs consisted of.[32] Each interaction between a volunteer and someone affected by the storm therefore started not with an assumption, an assessment or a judgment, but with a question: "How are you doing?"

No attempt was ever made by Occupy Sandy to sort bodies into those that were deserving of care and those that were not, the way other relief organizations did. Nobody involved with the effort would ever ask for proof of address, a Social Security number or any of the other documentation required by government agencies like FEMA before they'd furnish aid. Nobody made you fill out paperwork just to prove that you were who you said you were. OS volunteers offered assistance to anyone who asked, whatever their immigration status, whichever side of the law they were compelled to operate on.

There was a fundamental respect for people's autonomy in all of this, not to mention their dignity. It was one of the qualities that most sharply differentiated Occupy Sandy from the Red Cross or the National Guard, and it emerged directly from the principled distinction between mutual aid and charity. But the way OS went about doing things was also hugely time- and labor-intensive. In pragmatic terms, it wouldn't have been possible had the effort not had enormous numbers of volunteers to draw on. The fact that it *did* had something to do with a quality I think of as "invitationality."

My partner and I had experienced this quality from our very first moments on the sidewalk in front of 520 Clinton. Where the other efforts we had tried to volunteer with in those first days after the storm were indifferent, or even faintly hostile, Occupy Sandy literally and actively welcomed us, and I've never forgotten it. I don't think the power of a greeting like that can be overstated, as a way of piercing the routine isolation of late-capitalist lives and kindling the first flickers of something that might in time become a sense of belonging.

But this wasn't the only way the invitational quality was expressed. It was there in the informal way we were encouraged to identify ourselves as new volunteers and would remain known to one another throughout the entire period of our involvement: as first names only, scrawled in Sharpie across a piece of masking tape slapped to our chests. And it was there in the orientation briefing we were given, where it was made clear that while bigotry of any sort would never be tolerated, anyone who could agree to treat the people around them with dignity and respect would always be welcome and appreciated in the effort.

Other ways in which the sense of invitationality manifested itself were less explicit than that, and more a matter of the shared ethos that saturated and sustained the whole effort. Part of this was simply that anyone could make a meaningful contribution just by showing up, whatever their ability or level of commitment. Nobody who volunteered for Occupy Sandy was ever assigned to a role or task—who, after all, had the authority to assign anyone anything? Newcomers were encouraged, instead, to find a role organically, to "plug themselves in" to whatever seemed like it needed doing most, just as I'd found my way to organizing donations in the pews.[33] With so much going on, people never seemed to have much of a problem finding something to do that was a good fit for their capabilities and predilections.

This wasn't necessarily a matter of any ideological commitment—it was surely down to OS being an informal, ad hoc initiative, with neither the inclination nor the capacity to inflict bureaucratic procedure on anyone. But it meant that the relief effort was to a very great degree genuinely self-organized, and it kept the barriers to entry low. As a result, the operation made places for all sorts of people—some of whom had clearly never before interacted so closely, over so long a stretch of time, with people as different from them as the ones they met in Occupy. Its invitationality helped OS field the numbers necessary to pull off labor-intensive strategies like door-to-door canvassing.

These were all ways in which the values animating the effort were expressed concretely. There was one final way in which those values were expressed, which is that everyone who showed up for Occupy Sandy had a voice in the way it was run. Just as Occupy Wall Street had before it, OS made its decisions collectively, democratically and by consensus. Concerns were aired and courses of action hashed out in regular general assemblies that lasted anywhere up to several hours, and anyone who participated was welcome to speak, to raise items to the agenda and to block the adoption of measures they felt they could not support.

I saw real efforts made to convene as much of the community as possible in these gatherings, and they continued to be held through the entire time I was involved in Occupy Sandy. But while I believe that the commitment to purely horizontal, consensus-based decision-making was something sincerely held by most OS volunteers, as the effort expanded it became functionally difficult to honor in full.

By late November, despite an agenda that made space for reports from a wide range of local activities and working groups, my feeling is that the people participating in the general assemblies had mostly abandoned any pretense that they gave voice to everyone who was involved in the effort in any way. By that point, "Occupy Sandy" was tens of thousands of bodies working at dozens of sites strewn across three states. It was simply too large and diffuse to fit in a single room, and possibly too diverse to allow everyone who did gather there to reach full consensus on all the matters before them.

Was this anarchy in action, then? Well, as the proudly libertarian writer Colin Ward always maintained, ordinary people are doing anarchy all the time, without ever identifying as anarchists, or even necessarily approving of "anarchism."[34] And as we've seen, this was true of Occupy Sandy as well.

But that it worked, and was broadly seen to work, gave the lie to the snide critique so often levied at anarchist ideas, in Ward's time and our own. Nobody could credibly accuse Occupy Sandy of being childish, or impractical, or utopian. If anything, just the opposite was true. The imperative of treating those who suffered from the storm as peers fundamentally deserving of dignity may have been founded in a political stance, but it led directly to a practical result, a far tighter coupling between what they needed and what the relief effort was able to offer them. The commitment to horizontal, leaderless organization meant that relief teams in the field could respond to emergent situations as they saw fit and deploy their resources in whatever way seemed most appropriate. Autonomy meant that the effort was able to reach the most vulnerable New Yorkers, those who had a great deal to fear from becoming visible to agents of the state, or simply lacked the formal tokens of twenty-first-century citizenship. In each of these cases, the principles that guided Occupy Sandy were tested against some of the most trying and stressful conditions experienced in the living memory of New York City, and in each they proved their worth many times over. Occupy Sandy delivered the goods, and it did so in ways no hierarchical body could match.

And it does bear repeating that a relief effort founded in the ethos of mutual aid simply worked better than any of the conventional alternatives. In the wake of the storm, a broad institutional consensus emerged that Occupy Sandy had outperformed official disaster-response organizations like FEMA and the Red Cross, even on their own terms. In mainstream-media coverage, in government circles, there was astonishment at the claim that OS achieved what it did on a total budget amounting to "a mere $1.34 million—roughly 1 percent of the entire Red Cross payroll and less than the sum of three Red Cross executives' salaries in 2012."[35] Figures like these led to the curious specter of New York City's Special Initiative for Rebuilding and Recovery and the US Department of Homeland Security studying this horizontally organized, avowedly anti-statist effort to see how it might be co-opted.[36]

But in the end, such direct comparisons miss the point. They are to reduce OS to a study in operational efficiency. Its real value was that it did what it did in a way that upheld people, affirmed their ability to provide for one another under the most difficult circumstances and maybe even shifted their understanding of the world they lived in. In other words, it was *liberatory*.

The activist Dean Spade proposes four criteria for evaluating the success of a mutual aid effort on this question:

> Does it provide material relief? Does it leave out an especially marginalized part of the affected group (e.g., people with criminal records, people without immigration status)? Does it legitimize or expand a system [resistant left movements] are trying to dismantle? Does it mobilize people, especially those most directly impacted, for ongoing struggle?[37]

Occupy Sandy unambiguously succeeded on at least three of these four counts.

There is no question whatsoever that it furnished communities and individuals both with significant material assistance. It turned nobody away, as either volunteer or recipient of aid, who was willing to treat the others around them with a threshold minimum of respect, and made places for people irrespective of their citizenship credentials. It profoundly, and lastingly, undermined many of the claims to competence that are routinely made on the part of actors like FEMA and the Red Cross, at least so far as the New York region is concerned.

The only remaining question is whether OS encouraged the people who encountered it, whether as participant, recipient or onlooker, to undertake further acts of liberatory self-provision. On this question, the evidence can only be described as "mixed." While concerted mutual aid efforts did arise in neighborhoods throughout New York City during the time of COVID, and some of them did indeed involve veterans of Occupy Sandy, no broader or more sustained infrastructure of self-organized care has appeared there in the years since the storm.

I think it's nevertheless fair to understand OS as a stepping stone toward liberation, as much for the way it transformed subjectivity and the sense of the possible as anything else.

This wasn't anybody's job. Nobody was paid for the grueling hours they put in. Occupy Sandy offered tens of thousands of New Yorkers a rare opportunity to exercise their skills and talents in the service of their community—to *do something* about the terrible thing which had befallen them and their neighbors—and this was its own considerable reward. There were other rewards, too. Without anyone telling them what to do or how to do it, everyone involved in Occupy Sandy had a chance to grow into their autonomy, and their power, in a way that little if anything about their previous lives might have prepared them for.

For me, the chance to for once do something of actual utility—even if it was no more than shifting boxes—stood in the starkest contrast with my working life in the weeks and months before the storm, amid the empty play of symbols that characterizes so much of twenty-first-century existence. The chance to break out of the siloed identities and stilted routines that kept us from ever getting to know one another as anything other than strangers on the street corner was extraordinary. To do all that in service of a larger vision of a community where people cared for one another was unforgettable. The great secret of Occupy Sandy is that being part of it *felt wonderful*.

It registered in the psychic life of the city, as well. Even in a metropolis of 8.5 million, a headcount of 62,000 was enough for the effort to establish a tangible presence on the streets. For a little while, the yellow OCCUPY SANDY MUTUAL AID patch safety-pinned to someone's sleeve or backpack was a common sight around town, and on one level it worked just like any other brand encountered on the sidewalks and subway stairs of New York City: as a declaration of affinity, affiliation, belonging. But part of what that patch meant, too, was that none of us would ever again have to wait in hope for someone to come rescue us, even in the face of events so terrible they challenged the ability of the city itself to function. If there was rescue to be had at all, it would be because we'd organized it ourselves.

For all my enthusiastic embrace of the practice, mutual aid is not a panacea. Whatever context it arises in, this way of doing things is not without its limitations and drawbacks.

As we've seen, in mutual aid efforts the boundaries between caregiver and recipient are, by definition and intent, less sharply drawn than they are in other forms of provision. It derives much of its value from this refusal to make cleavages between the helper and the helped, and for that matter, it may not always be clear just who is acting in which role. To participate in mutual aid projects is necessarily to accept the interdependence of intertwined lives. But especially in smaller communities, this can open the way to a multiplicity of worries—intrusiveness, violations of privacy, judgment, even the withholding of care, which can in turn be used as a cudgel and a means of control. People who are denied care in this way, whether because they are controversial within the community or merely unpopular, often have no real way of doing anything about it.

Unlike the services furnished by a state, as well, nobody has any statutory right to mutual aid. There is no such thing as a minimum level of service, no guarantee of the completeness or competency or even basic adequacy of what you might be offered.[38] And again, barring the rare circumstance in which one has been agreed upon beforehand and explicitly articulated, there is no formal accountability process or means of redress when things do go wrong. You might conceivably go after the Red Cross or the Coast Guard in court, should they somehow fail you in the course of a rescue attempt, and you might even recover something. It's hard to imagine any such thing coming to pass where a self-trained, horizontally organized, entirely voluntary effort is concerned.

And finally, there is the line of critique often levied against mutual aid efforts by those who think of themselves as occupying the revolutionary left: that mutual aid is little different than any of the other institutions of bourgeois voluntarism. That it drains away or mutes the flashpoints of popular rage that might become insurgent. That it shores up a capitalist order that is in its death throes and should be allowed to fail.

I think it's fair to say that mutual aid efforts sometimes generate (or preserve) value that is thereafter folded right back into circuits of capital accumulation, or that their presence in a community can prepare it for later capture by market actors. But, again: the argument is not that mutual aid is perfect, or even that it is the best among all possible ways of doing things. The argument is that it is *what we have* when things go sideways—and a set of practices we can build on, as the crisis in our lives turns from acute to permanent.

We know mutual aid works, at scale and under pressure. But as we lean into the long years of permacrisis, it might pay to think a little bit about just what it is that mutual aid efforts are set up to furnish—what they're good at, and where they necessarily fall short.

What is actually at risk in catastrophic events has to do with the basic Maslovian facts of our embodiment, and the needs imposed upon us by the nature of metabolism. These needs are simple, consisting first of all of hydration, nourishment, shelter and clothing. We need to be clean and able to rest, in an environment sustained within a fairly narrow range of temperatures and conditions. And we need some measure of protection from physical hazards like fire, electrocution or carbon-monoxide inhalation, as well as the bacterial, viral or fungal vectors of disease. Absent any of these, no human body will survive for much longer than a few days.

On any ordinary day, the fulfillment of our bodily needs is sustained by the most elaborate infrastructures—so elaborate, indeed, that a good portion of the institutions of state ever developed have been consecrated to their management. But when some catastrophic event takes place, some or all of the infrastructures we count upon fail. That's what catastrophe *is*: the power goes down, and with it the lights and the refrigeration (and the air-conditioning, if you're lucky enough to have any). The water from the taps smells wrong and doesn't feel safe to drink. The groceries you were counting on to make the week's meals with, the formula for the baby, the medicine you need for your diabetes—none of that ever made it out of the warehouse, it all sits rotting by the pallet-load on a rainswept loading dock, miles out of reach.

This is the central set of issues that mutual aid efforts take it upon themselves to address, at least once the most acute threats to life have been dealt with. Whether Common Ground, Occupy Sandy, the Centros de Apoyo Mutuo set up in Puerto Rico after Hurricane María or the nameless groups without number that popped up all over during the pandemic, what these groups all constituted was a parallel, ad hoc delivery infrastructure, conceived of, managed and experienced in very different ways than those which undergird our lives "on any ordinary day."[39]

But as ingenious as these efforts may have been, as products of the event, they were never designed to be sustained. We can talk about "aid" when need is acute, but when need becomes intractable over the long haul, we have to think in terms of something else. If self-organized processes were effective in distributing aid under these circumstances, in the aftermath of crisis events, might we also productively use these same techniques to reorganize broader swaths of our lives? And especially, might they help us fend for ourselves, collectively, over the longer term, in situations where the state is indifferent, hostile or simply absent? The concept we need to mobilize, if we want to bridge these situations, is *care*.

In English, "care" is one of those words that folds in a great many shades of overlapping meaning. It is, among other things, the mobilization of attention—the dedication of some

77

portion of our cognitive resources to noticing another. But more than that, what we care about *matters* to us. We become personally invested in its fate and thereafter commit our own energy and effort to ensuring its continuance, as best we can. I think of care, then, as acts of nurturance, maintenance and repair, undertaken in the presence of an affective commitment.[40]

These acts of care are required continuously. Whenever and wherever we have endured as some recognizable "we," it was because some among us—the overwhelming majority of whom were women whose names are lost to history—did the draining, thankless, utterly necessary work of making sure we would still be there the next day. This work is feminized and therefore implicitly devalued. It's all but never celebrated in any of the stories we tell ourselves, and only very rarely compensated in any proportion to its actual importance to our lives. But carework is the labor that knits the world together.

To say that carework has been systematically undervalued, even in the progressive tradition, is not merely an understatement but even something of a category error. If you accept the Marxian distinction between "productive" and "unproductive" labor, care is by definition literally unproductive activity. Similarly, where Hannah Arendt opposes the "work" that produces durable objects of use to the "labor" that gives rise to intangibles or consumables, care falls decisively in the latter category.[41] Anyone who has ever spent much of their day washing or cooking or cleaning—and does all of it in the full awareness that it will have to be done all over again the next day, and the one after that, in unending series—might be inclined to agree.

But none of the work that either Arendt or Marx reckons as productive becomes possible without the daily replenishment and restoration of the laboring body.[42] And as Silvia Federici has it, these "day-to-day activities by means of which we produce our existence" are simultaneously sites at which "we can develop our capacity to cooperate and not only resist our dehumanization but learn to reconstruct the world."[43]

Here Federici seems to be getting at the very quality that 520 Clinton site coordinator Samantha Corbin had seen in Occupy

Sandy's ability to "actively undermine those structures that separate us." If carework is, or can be, a way of remaking the world, though, it is prevented from doing so when the people undertaking it are individualized, shattered, severed from one another and alone. Its politically transformational qualities only begin to appear when care is consciously thought of as a matter of collective self-provision, outside the obligations of the family, the impersonal structures of state and market or the vertical relations implied by charity. This is the sense in which we now grasp care.

It is no longer merely the means of individual bodily survival. It is the means by which we sustain ourselves, as communities of people working together toward our common liberation. As a tactic for those intent on resisting oppression in the near term, Hayes and Kaba call this "care-driven organizing."[44] As a way of tending to our needs over the longer term, especially when other modes of provision have fallen away, it is, as I see it, a practice of *mutual care*. And it points toward the habits of collective self-provision we will need to learn (or relearn) if we propose to survive the rigors of the Long Emergency together.

The point of framing things in this way is to address two qualities that existing mutual aid efforts only begin to gesture at: the multiple dimensions of bodily and psychic need, and the extension of those needs over time. Taken together, these demands suggest that mutual care will work best when organized as an integrated *solidarity network* of interlocking efforts—each one targeted toward one discrete facet of carework, like nutrition, education or medicine, each supporting all the others. This is the sort of structure we'll need to call upon when the emergency in our lives becomes permanent and the institutions and services we ordinarily rely upon to sustain us fall away.

Who better to learn from, then, than a group of people for whom life was always an emergency, who responded to their conditions by organizing just such a network of collective self-provision? The first steps on the way toward mutual care were taken by the Black Panther Party for Self-Defense (BPP) in the Bay Area of the late 1960s.

Such ideas have never been more fully developed than they were in the panoply of "survival programs" organized by the Black Panthers between their launch of the Breakfast for Children program in early 1969 and the shuttering of the last such initiative, the Oakland Community Learning Center, in 1982.[45]

What the Panthers organized to defend themselves against was, in a word, racism, though the word scarcely seems adequate until we consult Ruth Wilson Gilmore's definition: "the state-sanctioned or extralegal production and exploitation of group-differentiated vulnerability to premature death."[46] Some of the ways in which this vulnerability appears are independent of class or income, notably a risk of harassment and assault at the hands of the police so acute that Black parents have always had to have "the talk" with their children as soon as they were of an age to leave the house on their own. But all of its manifestations have invariably fallen most heavily on those who are both Black and poor, and this was so even in the Bay Area of the 1960s, in the midst of a society then approaching the historical peak of its power and affluence.

For poor Black people in the Oakland of 1966, "vulnerability to premature death" took a fearsome number of forms; the foreclosure of educational, training and employment opportunities. The institutional denial of credit. Woefully substandard housing. In the medical professions, a general indifference to conditions that disproportionately or predominantly afflicted those of African descent, like hypertension or sickle-cell anemia, a painful and potentially fatal blood disorder. Malnutrition or outright hunger. And, of course, the likelihood of beatdowns, jailing or worse, any time someone was unlucky enough to cross paths with the police.

The spectacle of entire communities bearing up under this kind of malign neglect ultimately proved so incompatible with American self-regard that it led to action, and that action took the form of an expansive program of state provision. The

America into which the Panthers emerged in 1966 was not one undergoing state failure or a process of managed retreat. Quite the opposite, in fact: during the Lyndon B. Johnson administration, between 1964 and 1968, the United States formally committed itself to nothing less than an all-out War on Poverty. In concrete terms, this consisted of a range of targeted activities administered by an independent federal agency called the Office of Economic Opportunity, including the Job Corps vocational training initiative; an early-childhood education, health and nutrition program called Head Start; the college-preparation scheme Upward Bound; Volunteers in Service to America, or VISTA; and the ambitious, controversial Community Action Programs.

Technocratic though it surely was in conception, the War on Poverty represented a massive expansion of the care services available to the many millions left behind by the postwar economic surge. Many of its initiatives were specifically intended to address the needs and problems of what was then called "the ghetto." And by the standards of the day, it was relatively well funded, more than tripling government expenditure on issues of poverty and amounting to some 15 percent of the entire federal budget by the time it was rolled back under the Nixon administration.[47]

There were glimmers of something far more radical in the War on Poverty, as well. In their original conception, the Community Action Programs were the closest any official policy of state ever came to involving the American people in their own self-determination—by comparison with anything devised in the years since, especially, they can seem like something drawn up in Cuba, or Chavista Venezuela.[48] The authors of the Economic Opportunity Act of 1964 famously envisioned that these local initiatives were to be "developed, conducted, and administered with the maximum feasible participation of residents of the areas and members of the groups served."[49]

Perhaps inevitably, though, this was a commitment destined to be honored more in the breach than in any observance.[50] Practically in the same breath that he affirmed "the necessity

81

of including the poor in all our activities," Office of Economic Opportunity director Sargent Shriver clarified what this really meant: "We have no intention, of course, of letting any one group, even the poor themselves, 'run the jobs' or 'run the programs.'"[51]

And just as bad as the seeping paternalism was the sense that the scheme as a whole amounted to a titanic misdirection. As a contemporary observer, the activist urban planner Robert Goodman, described it, "maximum feasible participation" amounted to little more than "allowing the poor to administer their own state of dependency": they "could direct their own welfare programs, have their own lawyers, their own planners and architects, so long as the economic structure remained intact—so long as the basic distribution of wealth, and hence real power, remained constant."[52] This left most Americans who were both poor and Black more or less right where they'd started: unseen, underserved, under-resourced and perpetually at risk.

The gulf between the War on Poverty's promise and its reality was something keenly felt by two young Oakland residents named Bobby Seale and Huey P. Newton, who developed their critique at close range, during their work at a Community Action Program called the North Oakland Neighborhood Anti-Poverty Center in the summer of 1966. Over the course of their involvement with the Center, Seale and Newton had seen how government action consistently failed the very people it was supposed to uphold, how state agencies used the pretext of "community outreach" to intensify their surveillance of Black lives.

Now they laid out the contours of something very different. Setting out from a blank sheet of paper, Newton distilled the principles of Black self-determination he and Seale had absorbed from their readings of Malcolm X and Frantz Fanon into a concise list of positions and demands. This was the Ten-Point Platform and Program, the founding charter of the Black Panther Party for Self-Defense.

Newton designed the party's platform to appeal to Black

Americans by restating the raw facts of their situation "in some basic instructive thing that [ordinary people] can understand, instead of a bunch of esoteric bullshit."[53] The Ten-Point Program was, accordingly, divided into two sections called "What We Want" and "What We Believe," with a point-for-point correlation between each specific policy demanded in the former and one of the articles of belief outlined in the latter.

There was an insurmountable contradiction in the program from the jump, in that it simultaneously demanded that the United States government furnish Black people with decent housing, healthcare and employment (points 2, 4 and 6) and called for the overthrow of that same government (point 10). But it nevertheless gave voice to a conclusion that was becoming increasingly hard to avoid: that if no real relief from their troubles was forthcoming, despite all the Head Starts and VISTAs a wealthy society could dream up, Black people would just have to set about organizing that relief for themselves.

The earliest Panther activities were dedicated to patrolling the police. Taking advantage of what were then generous provisions in the California state legal code for the open carrying of firearms, armed Panthers shadowed the Oakland PD on their sorties through the ghetto, observing their interactions with residents at close hand and ensuring that any arrests they made remained strictly within the letter of the law.[54]

This phase of activity culminated in a May 1967 protest on the steps of the California state capitol building in Sacramento, during which Seale read a statement decrying the proposed Mulford Act, "legislation aimed at keeping the Black people disarmed and powerless at the very same time that racist police agencies throughout the country are intensifying the terror, brutality, murder and repression of Black people."[55] (In a front page story, the *Sacramento Bee* duly reported this scrupulously legal demonstration as the "invasion" of the capitol by an "armed Negro band."[56])

Despite Seale's efforts, the California Legislature swiftly passed the Mulford Act—ironically enough, on an "urgency" provision driven by the protest itself—and it was signed into law by Governor Ronald Reagan two days later, putting a permanent end to the Panthers' armed patrols in California.

By now, however, the Panthers' inability to prevent the passage of the Mulford Act almost seemed beside the point. The audacity of their tactics, and the media attention they garnered, electrified Black radicals across America. Wildcat groups calling themselves "Black Panthers" began to spring up all over the country, just about anywhere there was a significant Black population. Unwilling to countenance the reputational hazard this presented—or perhaps more to the point, the dilution of their authority—in spring 1968 the party leadership began officially chartering these chapters. Local groups were required to swear allegiance to the central committee in Oakland, formally adhere to the Ten-Point Program and send anyone who wished to become a branch officer to headquarters for a six-week course of political education.

The list of official chapters eventually grew to thirteen, with affiliated organizations operating in at least sixty-one cities in twenty-six states and the District of Columbia, vastly multiplying the party's reach, influence and ability to inspire.[57]

But the Panthers' increasingly high profile also shed the most unwelcome kind of attention on Huey Newton personally. In the early hours of October 28, 1967, while looking for a parking space on Seventh Street in West Oakland, Newton was ordered to the curb by OPD officer John Frey. Realizing immediately that the driver he had pulled over was none other than "the great, *great* Huey P. Newton," Frey ordered Newton out of the car and proceeded to frisk him in a manner that Newton found "degrading," "disgusting" and humiliating.[58]

The details of the altercation that followed remain murky still, despite multiple trials, but what has never been in any doubt is that shots were fired, wounding both Frey and Newton as well as a second OPD officer at the scene; Frey, hit four times, died of his injuries.[59] In September of the next year, Newton was convicted of voluntary manslaughter for the killing of Frey and was sentenced to two to fifteen years in the California Men's Colony at San Luis Obispo. He remained imprisoned until the overturning of his conviction in May 1970, removing him from direct influence over the party's activities, but furnishing it with a "living martyr"—and, in "Free Huey," giving the new left of the period one of its most potent rallying cries.[60]

Contesting the police violence Black people were exposed to on a daily basis may have put the Panthers on the map, but it was far from the only aspect of their challenge to white supremacy, and arguably not the most effective or consequential.[61] That accolade belongs instead to a wide-ranging set of community-based care efforts the Panthers devised from the middle of 1969 on, designed to forestall "vulnerability to premature death" in all its many forms. These were the famous "survival programs": a dizzying array of twenty or more distinct initiatives offered to the Black and poor communities of the Bay Area free of charge and, at least in part, eventually rolled out across BPP branches nationwide.

The turn toward the survival programs originally stemmed from a sharp internal dispute between the revolutionary strategies advocated by different factions among the Panther leadership. On one side was Minister of Information Eldridge Cleaver, famously a fiery proponent of the armed struggle. This was undoubtedly in sync with the temper of the times, with hard-left factions worldwide—the Weather Underground, the nascent Baader-Meinhof, Italy's Red Brigades, the Irish Republican Army and the Japanese Red Army—committing themselves to insurrectionary violence. But Newton took up the opposite position: against the overwhelming reality of US power, he considered any embrace of the armed struggle a recipe for revolutionary suicide.

There was a very great deal of justice to Newton's perspective. The Panthers operated under the heaviest sort of government surveillance and repression throughout their entire existence, at first involving local police departments in the Bay Area but, as their notoriety grew, swiftly expanding to include the entire federal law-enforcement apparatus. Their early successes made them a central concern of the nationwide, covert and thoroughly illegal effort the Federal Bureau of Investigation embarked upon in August 1967, at the personal instruction of Director J. Edgar Hoover: the "Black Nationalist Hate Groups" strand of the bureau's longstanding domestic Counter-intelligence Program, better known as COINTELPRO.[62]

This was intended "to disrupt, discredit and destroy" not merely upwellings of emergent Black consciousness in America but Black activists themselves, reputationally and bodily.[63] It was brutally effective. COINTELPRO's direct effects extended to the outright murders of Panthers Fred Hampton and Mark Clark by Chicago police in December 1969, but almost as destructive was the bureau's relentless whisper campaign of poison-pen letters and ginned-up *kompromat*, and the internal fissures and suspicions it gave rise to.[64] Knowing what we now do about COINTELPRO, and the lengths Hoover was willing to go to in order to destroy even the mildest advocacy for Black self-determination, there can be little doubt that any party committing itself to the strategy advocated by Cleaver would in one way or another have been extinguished to its last member.

Newton was no less a revolutionary than Cleaver, but he did recognize something that Cleaver evidently could not: that, in the Marxist-Leninist terms the party leadership was always fond of using, the historical conditions of Black America at the end of the 1960s were not yet ripe for the seizure of power from the oppressor. "[A]s revolutionaries we must recognize the difference between what the people can do and what they will do," he explained. "They can do anything they desire to do, but they will only take those actions which are consistent with their level of consciousness and their understanding of the situation."[65]

And what prevented poor Black Americans from develop-ing a revolutionary perspective, in Newton's analysis, was the abjection and violence of the conditions they contended with in daily life. Anyone interested in seeing them claim their due role as the subjects of history would therefore have to sustain them in body and mind, until they had achieved a level of consciousness at which revolution would appear organically and of its own accord. This was the genesis of Free Breakfast for Children, the People's Free Food Program and all the many other ways in which the Panthers proposed to care for the people. "All these programs satisfy the deep needs of the community but they are not solutions to our problems. That is why we call them survival programs, meaning survival pending revolution."[66]

Cleaver, for his part, had dismissed the notion of working toward the revolution by caring for the people as "sissy."[67] However pungently expressed his feelings may have been, though, they became moot in the fall of 1968, when he chose exile in Algeria over the prospect of returning to prison. With Cleaver out of the frame and Newton still behind bars, Seale, "a staunch advocate of community programs," assumed responsibility for setting the party's agenda.[68] Under his leadership, emphasis shifted decisively toward the survival programs, where it would remain for the balance of the party's time as an effective political organization.[69]

After several months of planning and recruitment, the first Free Breakfast for School Children program opened in January 1969 at St. Augustine's Episcopal Church in West Oakland.[70] It was an immediate success and swiftly led to the formulation of other care initiatives along still more ambitious lines. By 1972, the party was offering an extensive list of survival programs, including

the People's Free Food Program, the Intercommunal Youth Institute, the Legal Aid Educational Program, the Free Busing to Prisons Program, the Free Commissary for Prisoners Program, the People's Free Shoe Program, the People's Free Clothing Program, the People's Free Medical Research Health Clinic, the People's Sickle Cell Anemia Research Foundation, the People's Free Ambulance Service, the People's Free Dental Program, the People's Free Optometry Program, the People's Free Plumbing and Maintenance Program, and the Community Cooperative Housing Program.[71]

Some of these were clearly "programs" in name only, consisting in a service that was only ever offered on a very limited basis, but others were maintained for years and ultimately went on to impact the lives of millions.[72] In the light of Gilmore's definition, especially, we can see these programs more clearly for what they were: lifesystems in a world designed to produce death.

At the level of daily sustenance, the People's Free Food Program furnished recipients with "an ongoing supply of food to meet their daily needs."[73] Each participant in the program was furnished with standardized bags of staple items such as "eggs, canned fruits and vegetables, chickens, milk, potatoes, rice, bread [and] cereal," with a "minimum of a week's supply of food" included in every bag. Whenever conditions permitted, this was extended to "[p]eriodic mass distributions of food to reach a larger segment of the community than can be serviced from the ongoing supply." What people got through the Free Food Program was both more generous and more closely tailored to their expressed desires than any package of support any government program of the time was able to offer.

The People's Free Medical Clinics were dedicated to longer-term maintenance of the body, addressing the demand for "completely free healthcare for all Black and oppressed people" made in Point 6 of the Ten-Point Program.[74] Eventually extending to thirteen cities, these were often rudimentary affairs, set up in trailers or abandoned storefronts; in Boston, the clinic ran on electricity tapped illegally from a nearby lamppost.[75] But most were nevertheless able to offer a respectable range of primary-care services, from basic wound care and blood-pressure testing to nutrition advice, childhood vaccinations and prenatal screenings.[76] Equally important, the care offered at the clinics upheld the dignity of the people they served, in ways that contrasted sharply with the alternatingly neglectful, dismissive, patronizing or authoritarian treatment poor Black patients especially were used to receiving from public hospitals.

The clinics placed a strong emphasis on preventative health-care, doing everything they could to address the totality of the circumstances that produced sickness. This attention to the underlying social and structural causes of disease required an intimate (and labor-intensive) degree of involvement in patients' lives, in a way that would be unthinkable for mainstream medicine, then or now. "We'd go in, and there would be an elderly person in some apartment who needed, really needed, to see a doctor but they were afraid to go to the doctor," recalls Harlem Panther Cleo Silvers.[77] "[In] almost every apartment, there was somebody who had some kind of illness that needed to be treated right away. But the only way to find that out was to go and do the door-to-door work and find out what's really going on in the community." This unusually direct access also gave clinic workers the opportunity to offer their patients advice about housing issues or legal services that were available to them.[78]

Where the People's Free Medical Clinics corresponded with Point 6 of the Ten-Point Program, the Intercommunal Youth Institute spoke to the demand for free education expressed in Point 5. Later renamed the Oakland Community Learning Center, this was the longest-lasting of all the Panther survival programs, and it served as the model for the "liberation schools" the party established elsewhere.[79] Set up to offer education for the children of BPP members, the Learning Center indicted the broader failures of a public school system "which has systematically produced individuals totally incapable of thinking in an analytical way."[80]

The Panthers therefore worked with national education experts to develop a curriculum for the Learning Center that was based on the acquisition and application of critical-thinking skills, and developing these skills among its students was always its primary mission. But the center also served as something of a nexus between the various survival programs. Director Ericka Huggins explained how families benefited from these synergies:

> A number of new programs have developed just from having the school here. We find out, for instance, that a mother

needs certain things, otherwise she won't be able to get her
child to school. So, we have a welfare rights referral system.
There's a senior citizens program functioning here. Quite
often, the grandparents and older guardians of the children
are involved.[81]

Again, as with the clinics, there is a holism to this approach,
founded in the recognition that no child who is hungry, sick
or compelled to take on the burden of caring for the others
in their household will ever be likely to reach their full intellectual potential.

Though never developed anywhere as extensively as they
were in Oakland, for a time the party attempted to roll out
the survival programs across Panther chapters nationwide.
Soon after chartering them in 1968, the party's central committee ordered the regional chapters to commit themselves to
the policy, "including, minimally, a Free Breakfast for Children program"; in April 1970, each chapter was additionally
required to launch a People's Free Medical Clinic of its own.[82]
Some went further still: the Winston-Salem branch operated a
highly successful ambulance service, while the Dallas chapter
offered "pest control programs, citizen police patrols, a liberation school, and a tenant information center."[83]

Whatever the hopes and energies invested in these local
initiatives, however, they were not destined to be sustained for
very long. In 1971, Panther leadership made the decision to
consolidate around their base. The Panther chapters in major
cities like Boston, Detroit, Houston, Philadelphia and Seattle
were shut down, alongside all of the smaller ones.[84] The most
dedicated volunteers at each branch were relocated to headquarters in Oakland. The party's days as a national organizing
force were over.

With the shuttering of the Oakland Community Learning
Center in 1982, one of the most extensive experiments with
care-driven organizing ever attempted came to its formal
conclusion. The Black Panther survival programs were

administered fitfully, over a brief existence. They covered a mere handful of cities and directly involved, at most, hundreds of thousands of people in a nation of 200 million. And even so, the Panthers had to draw on much of the Black revolutionary population of North America to do it. But for all that, they were so audacious in their conception that we are still reading, thinking and talking about them half a century later.

The performance of these programs can't really be evaluated independently of COINTELPRO, because there never *was* any "independently of COINTELPRO." The survival programs, like every other initiative undertaken by the Black Panther Party throughout its existence, suffered tremendously from the FBI's decades-long campaign of harassment, rumor-mongering, subversion, defamation and sabotage, which has to be regarded as the central factor conditioning their success or failure. But let's see if we can nevertheless draw out some insights about what did and did not work about the Panther effort to "serve the people, body and soul."

The survival programs were undermined by a degree of ambition that, while no doubt justified by need, nevertheless amounted to a perilous overreach. There was, if not quite a one-to-one correlation, then certainly a broad correspondence between the Johnson-era War on Poverty programs and their BPP equivalents. But without anything like the resources of the state to draw upon, it's hard to see how the latter ever could have done anything but fall short of the scale, comprehensiveness and universality required by any real program of community care.

This was clear at the time, as well. No less a sage than Bob Avakian, not yet chairman of the Revolutionary Communist Party, USA, could observe in 1972 that Breakfast for Children was "a rather ridiculous attempt to apply literally the standard Maoist 'serve the people' strategy ... the notion that the Panthers could compete with the Welfare Department or the Baptist Church in feeding the ghetto poor is simply ludicrous."[85]

Avakian certainly had his own, self-serving reasons for talking the Panthers down, but he wasn't wrong to question how, or whether, the programs could be sustained. Over the party's history, the net monthly income of $40,000 generated by sales of its newspaper *The Black Panther* represented by far its largest single source of revenue.[86] But the survival programs were also substantially funded by the local Black business community, with contributions coming in the form of both cash payments and donations in kind, and this was not always purely out of the goodness of anyone's heart.

Panther leadership had announced early on their intention to "support the businesses that supported their survival programs and … criticize and mobilize against the businesses that did not," and there was little ambiguity in anyone's mind about what this "mobilization" might entail:[87] Panthers had firebombed a North Oakland store that had donated only one dozen eggs for the Breakfast Program rather than the requested six dozen.[88] Newton's spin on such tactics was that "Black capitalism will be transformed from a relationship of exploitation of the community to a relationship of service to the community, which will contribute to the survival of everyone."[89] But he had earlier spoken, provocatively, of "opening clothing and shoe factories to provide for more of the needs of the community."[90] We are left to wonder what might have happened had the Panthers developed their own organic production capability—setting up affiliated cooperatives to furnish jobs and training, as well as inputs for the survival programs, rather than depending upon a wary business community for unreliable infusions of resource.

And, of course, not one of the programs would have been possible absent massive drafts of unpaid administrative, organizational and care labor—labor, as the testimony of Huggins, Elaine Brown and others who were there at the time makes painfully clear, that was almost exclusively undertaken by the women of the party.[91] Even in the ranks of an organization nominally dedicated to the total liberation of Black Americans, Panther women were second-class citizens and struggled to be acknowledged for their contributions to the cause. As Brown memorably put it, they had "to fight for the right to fight for freedom."[92] This, too, was obvious at the time, for anyone with the eyes to see it, but it's only with the passing years that most accounts have reckoned with just how badly the party's efforts were stunted by its own sexism.

That the personal prejudices, failings and limitations of all-too-human leaders could so deform the party's potential can be directly traced to its top-down organization. In both their centralization of authority and their reliance on charismatic leadership, the Panthers left themselves vulnerable to a decapitation attack, which is of course exactly what happened. Even beyond this, though, it's startling to realize just how antiquated the party's whole architecture now seems to those of us more accustomed to leaderless, self-organized movements. It's unfair to ask that the survival programs anticipate organizational strategies that wouldn't arise for a good twenty years after their eclipse, but any such thing would have put real flesh on the bones of the Panther slogan "All Power to the People."

Perhaps the biggest question hovering over the survival programs, though, concerns what they were ever really intended to achieve. One common line of thought suggests that the Panthers never meant for them to bear the full weight of need, either in West Oakland or anywhere else, but rather intended them primarily as a way to show up the state and shame it into reparative action. This interpretation was bolstered by Bobby Seale himself, who, in enumerating the benefits of the Breakfast for Children program, argued that it "could highlight the government's failure to provide such a crucial social service, as well as add another dimension to [the Panthers'] public image and potentially broaden their base of support."[93] And indeed, the programs were hugely successful in attracting support from elements of the Black community that had previously been indifferent or hostile.[94]

But what Seale neglects to mention here is that Breakfast for Children also fed hungry kids. The People's Free Medical Clinics screened patients at risk for hypertension and sickle-cell disease. The Free Busing to Prisons Program made visits with incarcerated relatives possible. And if these programs and the others directly sustained people against a hostile world, their downstream consequences unfolded with all sorts of time signatures, and in ways that could not easily have been foreseen.

The free clinics in particular resonated widely with other communities under pressure. Their insistence that medicine serve the people directly inspired a succession of actions undertaken in New York City by the revolutionary Puerto Rican advocacy group the Young Lords, notably their hijacking of a city X-ray van so they could offer tuberculosis screenings on the block, and later the audacious 1970 seizure of Lincoln Hospital in the South Bronx.[95] (The demands made as a condition of ending the occupation—for "door-to-door preventative medicine programs, [the right] to choose the doctor you want to have, to have free daycare centers in all hospital facilities, [and] to receive free healthcare"—were eventually written into the New York State Patients' Bill of Rights.[96])

The ripples set up by BPP education programs were felt at a still further remove in space and time: Common Ground cofounder scott crow notes, for example, that he was first exposed to notions of egalitarianism and cross-racial solidarity in the Panther-organized East Dallas preschool he attended as a small child.[97] So while most accounts of the period conclude bluntly that the Panthers' arc across history ended in failure, I wonder if anyone who owes the sustenance of body and soul through those years to one or another of their survival programs would be inclined to judge them quite so harshly.

The Black Panthers are today fondly remembered for their impossible, insurgent glamor, as it has come down to us through a series of iconic images. These come readily to mind: the armed Black Panther Party for Self-Defense of its earliest days, gathered in righteous defiance on the Sacramento capitol steps. A long rank of Panthers in formation at a 1968 Free Huey rally in West Oakland's De Fremery Park, immaculately turned out in their uniform of black beret, black leather jacket, black turtleneck. Or the freed Huey himself, restored to his peacock throne, spear in one hand and bolt-action shotgun in the other. There is a truth depicted in these images, and it certainly comported with the party's idea of itself: Black people as agents of history, dazzlingly unbowed in the face of a state power that aimed to sever and destroy them using all the means at its disposal.

But if America itself has always constituted the permanent emergency in Black lives, the enduring need is for a force that is able to counter *all* of the ways in which bodies are made vulnerable to premature death, and ultimately that has to do with the extension of care. Of all the facets it presented to the world, then, the party that aimed to "serve the people, body and soul" through the survival programs strikes me as the most truly revolutionary. It proposed that the most radical strategy anyone can adopt is the provision of loving care to people their own society would prefer to see erased—and still more so, enlisting them in the effort of extending that care for one another over the long haul.

This is why my favorite picture of the Black Panthers is one in which there are no leather jackets and no berets, no sunglasses and no rifles, in fact no uniformed party members at all—just two Black women in floral-print dresses, one middle-aged, the other heavier-set and a few years older, sitting on a bench before a drab cinder-block wall.[98] At their feet are two kraft-paper grocery bags stuffed to overflowing with bread loaves and packaged food, boldly screened with the words PEOPLE'S FREE FOOD PROGRAM and the party's pouncing-cat emblem. The older woman clutches a copy of *The Black Panther* for Saturday, August 12, 1972, the headline of which reads: "Survival Pending Liberation."

It looks like a hot day in the picture. It looks like a time and place in which people understood that their struggles were linked with the struggles of others. (I wonder how many people, on seeing this image, notice the United Farm Workers button one of the women is wearing.) Most of all, though, what you see in this picture is what it looks like when people refuse to be defeated—when they endure because they organized themselves to endure, despite everything that was arrayed against them.

*

In their respective ways, Common Ground, Occupy Sandy and the Black Panther survival programs all managed to address shortfalls of care, and there is no question that in doing so each of them saved lives. But as we've seen, there were nevertheless real limits to what each was able to achieve. If we're interested in imagining a structure that is able to redress lapses in care that afflict an entire society, and that can manage to subsist outside the state for years on end, we'll have to look further afield for inspiration.

Ideally, what we're looking for is a way of organizing the self-provision of care that combines the ambition and scope of the Panther survival programs with the bottom-up, self-organizing qualities of latter-day mutual aid efforts. It would consciously be organized as a network, able to facilitate the sharing of tactics and practices between nodes, without over-riding their ability to respond to local conditions (or their respect for local knowledge). By operating outside conventional institutional structures, further, this care effort would be free to innovate with respect to approach, method and process—to do things in ways that no profit-driven enterprise or entity of state would ever be likely to attempt, let alone adopt.

As it happens, there is a real-world example of a system of mutual care with just such qualities. It never faced anything like the same pitch of opposition that did so much to under-mine the success of the Panther programs. But it did manage to see millions through a virtually complete collapse of social provision in their society, and to do so in a way that enhanced their capacity, their autonomy and their dignity. I am speaking of the "solidarity networks" of post-2011 Greece.

On paper, there's a clean distinction to be made between organized abandonment and outright state failure. But the conditions experienced by the Greek people in the years since the global financial shock of 2008 suggest that there may not always be a great deal of practical difference between the two.

In Greece, the economic downturn was both more severe and more protracted than elsewhere, eventually so total in its effects and consequences that Greeks refer to it simply as *I Krísi*, "The Crisis." In some sense, the roots of the Crisis can be traced to Greece's original adoption of the euro in 2001, which geared the national economy directly to a far larger European one that worked in a different way and responded to a different set of imperatives—one that was, furthermore, overseen in the main by French and German administrators not particularly well disposed toward their neighbor to the southeast.[99]

A balance of trade deficit opened up between Greece and the higher-productivity economies elsewhere in the Eurozone, as Greece spent more heavily on imported goods than it took in through overseas sales of its own; debt began to accumulate. (Every perceived sign of Greek fiscal liberality in this period, however minor, was accompanied by dark mutterings that "Germany had not signed up to the euro 'in order that it could pay for Greece's debts.'"[100]) It was this imbalance that brought about disaster when global recession overtook the Eurozone: the Greek government found itself pinned beneath a mountain of obligation it had no ready way of servicing, given the scale of the domestic economy and the tax revenue it was able to raise.

To finance repayment of its sovereign debt, Greece was between 2010 and 2012 forced to borrow 240 billion euros from the International Monetary Fund, the European Commission and the European Central Bank, collectively known as the "Troika." But inevitably, there were strings attached: in return for their largesse, the Troika compelled the Greek government to adopt successive "economic adjustment programs" imposing a punitive regime of austerity, in which public spending was pared back to a minimum. Together, the measures constituted "the most extreme package of spending cuts, tax rises and privatizations ever faced by any developed country"—nothing less than a "liquidation of the public welfare system."[101]

This was a storm entirely of human making. The cuts were felt in every sphere of Greek life, resulting in unprecedented levels of unemployment, poverty and social deprivation.[102] But they landed with particular force on the health sector. The two memoranda of understanding that the Greek government signed with the Troika contained provisions explicitly intended to reduce healthcare capacity, via the "rationalization" of state provision.[103] These measures included drastic cuts in hospital budgets, a drawdown of the national healthcare workforce and a reduction in salaries and benefits paid to the healthcare workers who remained in employment.[104] As a direct result, at least 2.5 million people, almost a third of the population, found themselves excluded from access to public healthcare.[105]

The consequences of this unprecedented withdrawal from public provision were as swift and awful as they were unsurprising: plummeting measures across just about every way we have of assessing health.[106] The ramifications included unchecked outbreaks of West Nile virus, H1N1 influenza and malaria; sharply higher rates of HIV infection among injecting drug users; and a spike in the bleakest of all indicators: the number of suicides recorded in Greece rose by more than 60 percent between the pre-Crisis year of 2007 and 2013.[107] The effects of austerity were stark enough to be manifested in the figures for all-cause mortality, with a study in the gold-standard *Lancet* medical journal finding that in 2011–12, some 2,200 excess deaths were most likely attributable to the impact of "economic adjustment" measures.[108]

Greeks were by no means inclined to remain passive in the teeth of the Crisis or to bear its insults in silence. Those who had been compelled to watch helplessly as the Troika and its partners in the Greek government laid waste to their dreams called themselves *Aganaktisménoi*—in Greece as in Spain, the Indignant.

On May 25, 2011, in response to the passage of yet another tranche of austerity legislation, their indignation boiled over. In Athens, tens of thousands of them occupied the central Syntagma Square, just opposite the Greek parliament building, while parallel demonstrations took place in Thessaloniki, Patras, Larissa and the country's other major population centers.[109] Though immediately (and at various times thereafter) subject to vicious repression on the part of the police, the occupation of Syntagma went on for weeks, until the tents were finally cleared from the square on July 30; occupations in Thessaloniki and Heraklion lasted into early August.[110]

At some point during these weeks, a profound transformation of affect and perception took place among a fraction of the Aganaktisménoi gathered in Syntagma; they moved from protesting the circumstances of their collective immiseration to *doing something* about them.[111] The first rhizomatic tendrils of what would become a nationwide solidarity network grew outward from facilities organized by the Syntagma Square assembly to support the immediate needs of those participating in the occupation.[112] As at Zuccotti Park just a few months later, this infrastructure encompassed a collective kitchen, a first-aid clinic/"informal hospital," and a "neighborhood organization center" set up to coordinate actions taking place elsewhere in the city.

The self-organized, grassroots institutions that would play such a pivotal role in sustaining Greek life over the decade to come were already present in embryo in each of these impromptu provisions. But among them, it was the clinic that held the most radical implications for the future. Conceived as a "solidarity project" from the start, according to the architect and activist Elisavet Hasa, it pursued "an alternative mode of care" founded in a new relationship between the providers and seekers of medical services. What originated as a matter of immediate practical necessity, amid the chaos and tear gas of the protest camp, developed into an expansive vision of "autonomous self-organized care practices" and eventually a far-flung constellation of sites at which that vision was realized.

For all its humble beginnings, this was by no means a marginal effort, in either scale or ambition: by 2020, there were more than thirty social clinics operating across Greece, providing "primary and specialized care for roughly 10 percent of the population and a rising number of migrants."[113] With so many denied access to the national health system, this network played a critical role in maintaining the physical and psychological health of millions living through one of the most sustained contractions in peacetime living standards ever experienced by a population of the global North.

What requires some explanation is how the solidarity network came to spread beyond Syntagma and the parallel occupations of public space in the other cities of Greece, and become woven into the rhythms and habits of everyday life. There were two facets to this, one social and the other physical.

The social aspect is easy enough to account for. Some 29 percent of the Greek population reported themselves to have participated in anti-austerity protests in one way or another.[114] Having met their own neighbors in the course of the protests—some of them, seemingly, for the very first time—people tended to maintain these connections as the squares were emptied and they returned to the life of their communities.[115] What they brought back with them wasn't merely a new way of doing politics, complete with its own characteristic modes of organizing and collective decision-making. It was also the sense that everyone in the streets around them was struggling with the same punitive conditions they were.

From the latter half of 2011 onward, a panoply of popular initiatives expressing this newfound sense of solidarity appeared in Greece, each of them organized and managed by assembly, in the way the protest camps had been. Running alongside them were the *Den Pliróno* ("I Do Not Pay") movement, whose guerrilla electricians reconnected power for thousands whose accounts had been shut down for nonpayment (and, from time to time, disabled the electronic payment gates in the Athens Metro), and several hundred "without middlemen" markets, where produce that had been sourced directly from growers was sold at cost.[116]

For the most part, these were simple, practical measures, directly oriented toward the basic Maslovian needs of everyday life. But other initiatives emerged to address the terrible shortfall in healthcare capacity that had opened up—and here, especially, the expression of solidarity took a distinct spatial form. The concentration and "rationalization" of state services stipulated by the Troika had an immediate, tangible effect on Greek cities: "Portions of the building stock that housed welfare services were abandoned ... hospitals and health clinics were merged, medical centers, schools, and daycare centers were closed."[117]

Then the wave of abandonment settled onto private spaces. Neighborhoods came to be pocked with vacancies and sudden voids—each a place where some commercial storefront or residential premises had been forsaken by its owners, in a curious echo of the nation's own throes, when whatever debt had been taken on in its acquisition could no longer be serviced.

This evacuation clearly presented communities with a challenge, but it also offered them the means of addressing it. In neighborhoods across Greece, activists set about occupying abandoned public, commercial or domestic premises and reworking them into clinics and pharmacies. (Other properties weren't so much occupied as freely offered to local solidarity initiatives by their owners, on "the understanding that the initiatives would cover property taxes and utility bills" or undertake needed repairs.[118])

Even in the years before the Crisis, this kind of adaptability had been a hallmark of activist spatial practice in Greece, as when empty apartments in Athens's Alexandras Prosfygika housing complex were converted into a free guesthouse for the visiting families of cancer patients being treated at the adjacent Agios Savvas hospital.[119] Now just about anywhere that *could* conceivably be used as a site for the delivery of care actually *was* pressed into service in this way—private residences, the ground-floor storefront spaces of the low *polykatoikía* apartment blocks ubiquitous to Greek cities, even the grounds of a tile factory that had been taken over by its own workers after being abandoned by the owners.[120] All were reworked room by room, in a politicized process of adaptive reuse that didn't merely transform the use of space, but also its meaning: "living rooms [were] converted into administrative areas or waiting rooms, and bedrooms repurposed as medical examination rooms or storage spaces for pharmaceuticals."[121]

In neighborhoods especially hard-hit by the Crisis, where little that could pass the test of commercial viability survived, a mesh of mutually reinforcing solidarity efforts emerged alongside the clinics. The effect was to create an archipelago of spaces in which refuge was possible, burrowed termite-like through the fabric of the uncaring city. A different set of values held sway in these spaces, articulated in terms virtually identical to those espoused by Common Ground and Occupy Sandy: in crossing the threshold of any among them, you entered a zone in which "charity" was a dirty word, and the fact of someone's need was more important than their ability to pay or the credentials of citizenship they might hold.

In all cases, these were "small local operations, closely intertwined with the life of the neighborhoods in which they were situated."[122] Perhaps unsurprisingly, given everything we know about the gender dynamics of care, women were disproportionately represented in them, comprising more than 60 percent of volunteers.[123] But they reinforced one another, multiplying the capacity of the solidarity network as a whole: clinic and pharmacy workers were able to draw upon free "social kitchens," while the ability to access comparably free healthcare supported a wide range of autonomous collectives in other domains, from legal-support clinics to small-scale urban farms.[124]

There was a circularity or wholeness to these interactions; in particular, the value to other institutions of a place where anyone who needed to might eat, drink, shower and restore themselves at no cost clearly cannot be overstated. (The economics of such projects were further bolstered when members of parliament representing the radical-left party SYRIZA agreed to tithe 20 percent of their salaries to the support of solidarity initiatives.[125])

In order to share resources, extend their capacities and generally amplify their presence in Greek life, the solidarity clinics forged a nationwide network. At an assembly in Athens in November 2013, they adopted a shared "10-Point Charter of Constitution of Solidarity Clinics and Pharmacies"—those ten points, of course, unavoidably reminiscent of the Black Panthers'. What this charter committed the clinics to wasn't simply an attempt to replace the healthcare services that had evaporated in the course of the Crisis on a like-for-like basis, though that might have been welcome enough given the circumstances. It was a reframing of the entire relationship between the person seeking medical care, the provider of that care and the society that contained both. And this in turn required a wholesale deinstitutionalization of the practice of medicine.

No one could accuse the solidarity clinics of lacking ambition. What they aimed to do was nothing less than supplant "the biomedical, hierarchical, and profit-centered model of modern medicine with horizontal and noncommodified modes of care."[126] As anything so complex would have to, this project proceeded on multiple fronts.

The fundamental and in many ways defining quality of solidarity care was, of course, that it was offered for free. The question of one's ability to pay ceased to be a gating mechanism, or a way of allocating medical or pharmaceutical resources. No one using the clinics received a higher standard of care because they could afford to pay more for it.

Deinstitutionalization also meant that the sites of care had to be purged of any visible aura of authority. This turned out to be not so very difficult, when the examining room of your local clinic might have been a sales office or a preteen's bedroom six months previously. To be sure, this was making a virtue of a necessity, but it was a virtue nonetheless: it meant that clinical appointments took place in human-scale settings that had been divested of any power to overawe or intimidate.

This egalitarian sensibility extended to the way that people were greeted when some malady or upset first drove them to seek medical attention. In the solidarity clinics, the person our healthcare systems would ordinarily call a "patient" was instead referred to as an "incomer," the Greek word for *patient* conveying unavoidable "connotations of feebleness."[127] A new reception protocol was developed, to "greet incomers in empowering ways," and it sounds an awful lot like intake for Occupy Sandy, right down to the attempt to help incomers "internalize the values of the clinic."

At the Workers' Medical Center in Thessaloniki, for example, care seekers were seen by a three-person team, in a conversation no more hurried than it had to be. Their approach stands in the sharpest contrast with the procession of rushed, mechanical fifteen-minute slots that so often constitutes general practice elsewhere.

> Every new incomer meets with three health practitioners at the same time on their first ninety-minute visit: a general physician, a psychotherapist, and a social worker … There is a health card that the social worker or third member fills out, asking questions to which the patient can answer or not … The health card covers the mental, emotional, and physical health, but also is used to note the conditions of the family, home, work, food, sleep patterns, and family relations.[128]

All of these were considered salient to the question of overall health.

The American activist Cassie Thornton, who spent time at the Social Solidarity Health Center in Thessaloniki in 2017, later incorporated its methods into her own strikingly innovative proposal for guerrilla healthcare.[129] She explains that the point of this inquiry is "to make a hologram of every person: a three-dimensional image of health as clear as possible" to both the clinical team and the care seeker themselves. This mirrors Occupy Sandy practice, as well as what I was taught at the Berkeley Free Clinic, when I trained and worked as a primary-care medic at the beginning of the 1990s. Reframing this first encounter as a collective inquiry, conducted among peers and invoking the gifts of everyone present, goes a very long way toward subverting the "savior/saved" dynamic endemic to modern Western medicine—and can also bring to the surface information critical to a successful resolution of the health crisis, which a more typical examination might have missed entirely.[130]

The clinics differed from traditional medical institutions in *whom* they extended care to, as well. The solidarity network served everyone denied institutional care in Crisis Greece—not merely those excluded by virtue of their inability to pay but also, in a time of desperate human flow, the undocumented newcomers that made up a growing part of the population. The Greek national health system had always required a social security number of those wishing to book appointments or fill prescriptions, limiting anyone who lacked one to whatever care they could manage to cobble together from repeated visits to the local hospital emergency room.[131] With undocumented immigrants and refugees in Greece numbering somewhere between 600,000 and 1 million, though, this failure of inclusion was staggering, as irresponsible as it was unconscionable.[132] The solidarity clinics stepped into this breach, asking neither proof of citizenship nor any other form of credential from care seekers before offering them treatment.[133]

The final aspect of deinstitutionalization was possibly the deepest of all. It was that care seekers were invited to participate directly in the management of the clinics themselves. Each of the clinics in the solidarity network was managed by an assembly that coordinated all aspects of its operation, from fundraising and the procurement of necessary supplies to counseling of the clinic staff itself.[134] Anyone who came to a clinic to be treated for their ailments was encouraged to join the assembly and actively participate in its deliberations. Beyond a general commitment to directly democratic forms of governance, this turned on the profound and enduring insight that "the incomer's active participation in their own health and community is *itself* a central form of their health treatment."[135] Here scott crow's description of Common Ground's understanding of the people they worked with as "active participants in the struggle to make their lives better" was echoed virtually word for word, inscribed in a practice that defines mutual care about as well as anything could.

This, then, was deinstitutionalized care, responsive to the needs of a population laboring under all the physical and psychic assaults of Crisis. All of the practical knowledge involved in setting up a clinic that worked this way, and running it on an ongoing basis, was shared through the solidarity network: how they went about securing the resources they needed, what kind of maintenance was required by their more delicate equipment, when and under what conditions they pursued alliances with other local actors, even how they physically laid out their spaces.[136]

Each clinic maintained an archive that went into an impressive amount of detail regarding its day-to-day operations, consisting of "bills and cost templates, shift schedules and medicine catalogs, inventories of equipment and sketches of spatial layouts, architectural drawings of the property and photographs," and these, too, were distributed widely. Such protocols were surely more complicated than, say, instructions for the assembly of flatpack furniture, but they required nothing a motivated community couldn't scrape together from the resources at hand. It was as if the source code underlying the whole solidarity-clinic project had been uploaded for sharing and could, therefore, be reproduced locally by every community in Greece that felt the need of one.

Formerly middle-class people seeking care in such settings were most likely reassured to learn that in some ways these clinics worked exactly like the state or private medical practices they'd relied upon previously. Anyone issued a prescription by a solidarity pharmacy, for example, could have it filled locally, or by any other pharmacy within the network.[137] But such markers of familiarity were largely cosmetic and served to camouflage the far deeper transformation that had taken place. In the midst of the worst contraction of possibility any of them had ever known, the solidarity network offered Greeks an entirely new model of care. In Federici's terms, solidarity clinics weren't merely places where people resisted their dehumanization. They were also classrooms, or better yet laboratories, in which together they might learn how to reconstruct the world.

*

An objection that is very often raised by skeptics of deinstitutionalization is that there are shortfalls in what any facility set up along these lines can do. And to a degree, there is some justice to this: by and large, the solidarity clinics did not actually have the capacity to offer cancer care, or advanced trauma medicine, or diagnostics of any sort involving the latest scanners. Anyone requiring that kind of intervention, whether they'd been in a car crash or needed an MRI, would still need to visit a conventional hospital. In such cases, providers in the solidarity network were often able to lean on connections with sympathetic public and private hospitals and arrange referrals for free treatment.[138]

But none of this should be taken to imply that the clinics were incapable of delivering *healthcare*. Because, just as the Black Panthers found (and I can confirm, out of my own few years at the Berkeley clinic), the great majority of people walking through the door of such a facility don't require anything so elaborate as acute trauma care. They may well be suffering from a relatively minor injury or infection of one sort or another, but mostly they are worried. It may even be the case that what nominally brings them to the clinic is not the situation in their life they really want and need to talk about. In most such cases the patient—the incomer, the seeker of care—is very well served by the things an autonomous clinic actually does best: listening to them, demonstrating that someone cares and giving them advice about over-the-counter medications or simple, low-cost treatments they might reasonably undertake at home. None of these measures requires elaborate or expensive infrastructure, but they bear disproportionately on "patient outcomes."

And this extends past the time of the visit. Our health is very greatly determined by factors that are only ever, at best, under our partial control, including where we live, what we can afford to eat, how we earn a living and who we spend most of our time with. What distinguishes radical healthcare providers from their mainstream peers is their understanding that these aspects of our existence cannot be grasped, let alone treated, in isolation from one another. The ailments of the body are connected to those of the society that body moves through.

A suggestion to "eat more leafy greens," for example, is easy enough to accommodate for someone used to doing their grocery shopping at a high-end market. But it's all-but-worthless advice to anyone who lives in what nutritionists call a "food desert," where the only affordable options they might have access to are fast-food chains, convenience stores or ultraprocessed vending-machine snacks. And, of course, it's a stinging slap in the face to anyone compelled to make their home in a refugee camp and feed themselves on whatever is served to them. This is something the Greek solidarity clinics dealt with by maintaining close links with a range of small-scale, democratically managed urban farms, "without middleman" farmers' markets and fishing cooperatives. The care they offered was *integrated*, in other words, and it responded to the structural constraints on health in a way our own institutionalized systems evidently remain unable to, even in conditions as yet unbound by crisis. Why, then, has their model of care not spread everywhere?

CareNotes, the collective editors of an insightful book on the Greek experience called *For Health Autonomy*, note a widespread perception that the solidarity clinics were merely "temporary materializations [organized] by and for activists," destined to fade away once the state had recovered its senses and returned to the universal provision of care.[139] This would certainly seem to dovetail with what one regional solidarity-clinic coordination group had in 2015 described as its "single aim": "to cease to exist, to be no longer needed, to have the state provide each and every one with the access to the fully operational national healthcare system."[140] And it was what actually seemed to be in the offing when the SYRIZA-funded Solidarity for All network announced that it was creating a register of clinics and allied efforts in preparation for folding them into a coordinated national effort once the party had assumed power.

But from the perspective of other activists, this was a blatant land grab: an attempt to co-opt the energy of their movement, drain it of its revolutionary content and reassert the normalcy of business as usual under a shallow mask of left authenticity. Their hostility was implacable—not merely to the Solidarity for All registration effort, but all other forms of normalization, including several cases where an originally self-organized clinic was taken under the auspices of a sympathetic local government. (Indeed, initiatives that had voted in assembly to accept municipalization in this way were compelled to leave the solidarity network.)

These tensions came to a head when a euphoric SYRIZA prevailed in the national elections of January 2015, and what had been internecine squabbles among tendencies of the activist left were overnight transformed into questions of official government policy. The boundaries between SYRIZA and the solidarity movement had always been somewhat blurred, particularly given SYRIZA's establishment of Solidarity for All—the umbrella support group to which the party's MPs had donated 20 percent of their salaries—in autumn 2012.[141] There was even a statute in the party's charter requiring its members to invest their time and energy in solidarity initiatives.[142] Many Greeks therefore expected that, in power, its strategy to defeat the Crisis might involve a mixed ecology of care services, in which those who preferred to do so (or continued to have no other option, like undocumented migrants) would be free to secure their care from the solidarity clinics, while everyone else returned to a newly revivified national health system. Why would a party that had invested so much in supporting grassroots efforts not incorporate them into its grander vision for a better tomorrow?

Others had so much faith in SYRIZA, especially after a 2015 reform granting the uninsured access to the public health system, that they saw no place at all for a national network of solidarity clinics. And it was evidently this view that prevailed. According to the psychologist Ilektra Bethymouti, one of its earliest participants, the solidarity network effectively came to an end at the Fifth Panhellenic Meeting of Solidarity Clinics, in Thessaloniki in April 2016.[143] From that moment forward, each of the clinics that survived was obliged to navigate whatever hazards it faced alone.

In voluntarily dissolving the network they'd worked so hard to build, healthcare activists placed a tremendous wager on SYRIZA's ability to restore the national health system to its full capacity. As the CareNotes collective observed, though, the confidence they placed in SYRIZA relied on "a nostalgic misperception of the permanence of a stable and benevolent social welfare state." In other words: there was nothing worth returning to. Even at its most complete, the care that people accessed through the state was always contingent, conditional on a government remaining in power that was willing to undertake robust and continued investment in the national health. Any faith that such conditions might persist into the indefinite future was a faith misplaced.

Just how badly misplaced was made brutally plain when the new SYRIZA government, under Prime Minister Alex Tsipras, immediately executed what has to be regarded as a world-historical "backflip" and "surrendered abjectly and totally to the Troika institutions."[144] In July 2015, the Tsipras government agreed to a third tranche of "economic adjustment," imposing some of the harshest austerity measures yet seen in Greece, and though they had to rely on the votes of opposition parties to get it across the line, the package was approved by the parliament in August. The scars of this betrayal lingered for years. At the next opportunity, in the national elections of 2019, Greek voters handed a landslide victory to the center-right New Democracy party, under whom refugees were once again excluded from the national health system. Everyone who had staked so much on the idea that another care was possible now had to watch as that possibility slipped through their fingers once more.

There's a powerful lesson in the Greek experience for those of us afflicted by the deliberate hollowing-out of the UK's once-mighty National Health Service, the slow cratering of profit-driven healthcare provision in the United States, or the more thorough abandonments that are surely yet to come. The only way for any of us to secure even the rudiments of care, when the systems we're used to relying upon become unreliable, is to develop the capacity to care for ourselves.

And this is a possibility that remains open to us. Other than a squeamishness about operating outside the law, perhaps, there is not a thing that stops any of us from organizing our own solidarity clinics, pharmacies and networks right now. In fact, given the often-enough lethal shortfalls of care that increasingly manifest themselves in our communities, I wonder more and more frequently why this hasn't already happened.

But if we *do* nevertheless manage to establish self-organized systems of mutual care, at some point we are likely to come up against the same challenge confronted by those active in the Greek solidarity movement: What do we do when some larger and more powerful actor, whether of market or state, proposes to multiply the impact of our exertions by joining their effort to our own? When a progressive city government, or even a FEMA, wants to "leverage" the power of grassroots initiatives by joining them into some kind of superstructure that is not under their direct, democratic control?

These are questions that anyone involved with the stewardship of a local mutual care effort, or really anyone at all who endeavors to *do something* about the Long Emergency on behalf of their own community, will ultimately face. And just as clearly, they are questions that individuals and communities will have to decide for themselves.

Based on what happened in Greece, though, what we can say empirically is that everyone who trusted in SYRIZA to deliver the goods got nothing, or worse than nothing. It may or may not be fair to paint all movements of the electoral left with this particular brush, but objectively that is what happened. Pragmatically, Greek solidarity activists would have been better advised to maintain their network of clinics and pharmacies and the profound investment in community capacity it represented. That way, whether a "radical left" national government succeeded, went down to ignominious failure or simply muddled along without any clear direction to speak of, people across Greece would still have options corresponding with their own needs and preferences, whatever those happened to be. At least, this is the deeper lesson for the Long Emergency: lifesystems must be designed so that they're as robust as possible to fluctuations of the underlying political or economic order, because fluctuation is all we are likely to know for the foreseeable future.

Beyond this, though, the Greek solidarity networks incorporated a recognition our own practice of care so urgently requires: that the upstream causes of whatever ill health we may suffer from are increasingly out of our control. Some of these causes are endemic and structural, consisting precisely in the "group-differentiated vulnerabilities to premature death" identified by Gilmore. Others have to do with the risks that are more broadly attendant upon living on a wounded planet: the insults bodies are subjected to when forced to labor in the spiking heat or breathe the smoke of distant fires, or the slow erosion of sanity caused by living with unreliable infrastructure.[145] We know that self-organized networks of mutual care can buffer us against these harms and offer refuge, especially for those most vulnerable to the interlocking and cascading conditions. But before any such thing can come to pass, enough of us need to perceive the necessity for it that we are willing to devote our own time, attention, energy and labor to making it real.

The Crisis pushed millions of previously more or less apolitical Greeks through a process that the great Brazilian educator Paulo Freire called "conscientization," in which people come to be aware of the interlocking systems of power that bind them.[146] "Radicalized" would not be too strong a word for what they experienced. And they were therefore willing to entertain radical approaches to the problems that confronted them: ways of organizing themselves that burst through the psychic guardrails of ordinary life; methods of caring for one another that bypassed the conventions of occupation, role and status; and means of collective self-empowerment that sustained them through their moment of greatest peril.

We know, from Katrina and Sandy, that acute climate shock can similarly radicalize people, opening them up to ways of doing things they never would have considered previously. The question now is whether sustained and chronic climatic disruption will produce a conscientization in quite the same way. The empirical evidence of Katrina and Sandy is: yes, they will. As the Long Emergency advances, leaving existing institutions increasingly unable to provide for our needs, it is these networks we will turn to—for our sustenance, for our healing, for our lives.

3

Collective Power

In the wake of Occupy Sandy, I often wondered if the practices that constituted the relief effort—and just as importantly, the values that animated it—couldn't be inscribed in our lives more permanently, developed into some more enduring infrastructure of care.

This was chiefly because a self-organized initiative had empirically proven itself more effective in delivering disaster relief than its top-down, command-and-control alternatives, and I couldn't help but suspect that the principle might extend to other contexts. But my curiosity was also driven by the way it felt to participate in the effort: helping to figure out how a random cluster of nonexperts might set up and run a high-tempo distribution hub was so much more rewarding than any of the work I'd ever done in ordinary late-capitalist life that I wanted everyone to experience something similar. I found myself more and more often imagining what it might be like if all of our institutions of governance were remade along the lines of the way we'd been doing things. What would that feel like? What new possibilities might open up if responsibility for far more of life was placed back where it belonged, in the hands of ordinary people?

One objection to this idea is that neither Occupy Sandy nor any of the other solidarity networks we've discussed so far were ever intended to be systems of universal, society-wide provision. They were emergency interventions, intended to suffice only for the duration of a sharp, unexpected departure from the ordinary. Even the Black Panthers' extensive program of self-organized community services was only intended to support Black survival "pending revolution."

In fact, people involved in mutual aid efforts, however heroic, have often remarked that they wished they didn't have to be. They're painfully aware of how contingent their offer is, how reasonable it is to fear that people in need will fall between the cracks and how much more dignified and comprehensive anything approaching true social provision would be. Here one thinks of the demand of Greece's autonomous clinics "that the state assume its responsibilities" for care of the community, or of Bobby Seale's virtually identical comments, forty-five years earlier and an ocean away, about shaming the government into upholding its formal obligations.[1] All of this is to say that self-organized care isn't always necessarily the way we might wish to do things in a better world, but in a state of exception it's what, and all, we have.

But what about when the excursion from the ordinary becomes permanent, when the organized abandonment of our communities starts to look a whole lot more like outright state failure? When the circumstances of the Long Emergency bite, how might we go about imagining not merely the stopgap provision of services, but an entire system of governance based on the same principles that underwrite the success of mutual care? Is it even possible to organize communities this way?

It's clear that any such thing would be extraordinarily difficult to achieve under the terms of political economy that currently condition our lives. Right now the necessary resources are for the most part allocated by systems that, whether they operate by logics of state or market, feel inaccessible to us. And they feel inaccessible because they *are* inaccessible: under the present dispensation, most all the decisions that matter are made by small groups of people operating out of sight of the public, in institutions that may not even in principle be accountable to the people whose lives they affect so dramatically.

But as David Wengrow and the late David Graeber argue in *The Dawn of Everything*, things have not always been as they are now.[2] In a great many times and places across the long reach of human association, in fact, they found that the decision-making institutions governing the allocation of resources *were* more accessible to ordinary people—more predicated on their active participation, more responsive to local need, less hierarchical. And of still greater relevance to our situation: that at least some societies actively adjusted how they went about organizing decision power, allowing them to flex in response to changing conditions in some quite subtle and sophisticated ways. The strong suggestion is that we can still choose to do the same.

And if there is any condition we might want our social and political arrangements to flex in response to, it is upon us now. The Long Emergency offers us an opening—a rupture in both the capacity and the legitimacy of the arrangements that now dominate our lives, and therefore a precious opportunity to rethink those arrangements. As I've defined it here, it consists precisely of a situation in which all of the institutions that conventionally structure our world have been stressed to the breaking point and must therefore be replaced by new ways of organizing the necessities of life.

But here a major difficulty arises. The trouble is that such moments of breakthrough can generally only be put to beneficial use by people who arrive at them with some concrete idea of what they want to achieve and how they intend to go about doing so.

What we need, then, is a theory to help us understand what kind of institutions we might want to develop if we are to reclaim the capacity to choose and to act in this moment of crisis. We need a theory of collective *power*, in other words, based on all the same qualities that animate mutual care and make it work. How might local governance work, what might it look like and how might it feel to engage with if it wasn't coextensive with government at all, but developed as an organic outgrowth of our own desire for self-determination? What steps might we need to take now if we wanted to get there?

Since the time of Kropotkin, a great many political thinkers have taken up the question of local power and how it may be developed outside the state; it's fair to say that this is a central concern of the left-libertarian tradition. In the past century, however, none that I am aware of has dedicated quite as much effort to exploring this question, in all its facets, as the curious, obstreperous, often infuriating American writer Murray Bookchin. The elements that appear and reappear in his conceptual tool kit, over forty or more years of published writing—the deliberative assembly, the autonomous polity and the confederation—are so well suited to the challenges of our moment that his lifework is worth exploring in some detail.

Murray Bookchin was born to Russian-Jewish immigrants in the Bronx in January 1921 and seems to have more or less immediately committed himself to an intensely politicized life, joining the Young Pioneers—the Communist Party USA's organization for children—at the age of nine.[3] It was neither the last political organization he would join nor the last he'd break with and denounce.

In fact, the list of groups Bookchin joined and positions he espoused over the course of his life is somewhat dizzying. By the time he was fourteen, the orthodox Stalinism of the CPUSA had already started to feel confining, and following Moscow's betrayal of the Republican cause in the Spanish Civil War, it came to repulse him. At this point he joined the Socialist Workers Party, but its Trotskyism proved no more congenial as a final ideological home for him. Over the course of the decades that followed—during which he worked in an iron foundry and on the line at General Motors, joined both the United Electrical Workers and the United Auto Workers and served in the US Army—he gravitated first toward a libertarian-socialist position and then, in 1958, a more explicit anarchism.

Even this, however, eventually cloyed for him, and in a series of blistering denouncements he declared himself no longer an anarchist, reconciled himself with at least local forms of electoral politics and finally moved to Vermont to put these ideas into practice. The strong impression one is left with, across this whole long series of arrivals and heated departures, is of someone perpetually searching for an institutional vessel for his intensely felt beliefs and perpetually being disappointed by what he found.

But at just about every step of his postwar ideological journey, he elaborated his commitments of the moment in print. His earliest published pieces appeared in a rather heterodox and ideologically diverse New York–based journal called *Contemporary Issues* ("A Magazine for a Democracy of Content"), and as the title of a 1952 article called "The Problem of Chemicals in Food" suggests, his concerns were ecological in scope from the very beginning. In this, Bookchin opened up a question that had never previously been treated as a valid area of concern for left thought: how shared prosperity might be achieved without pushing Earth systems past their safe operating limits.[4] In the 1968 essay "Post-Scarcity Anarchism" he went further still, imagining a politics of abundance in a time when fully automated luxury anything must have seemed still more science-fictional than it does now.[5]

Despite these rather considerable contributions, and some remnant currency in radical-ecology circles, it's hard to overstate just how marginal a thinker Bookchin had become by the final years of the twentieth century. And yet, with maximum improbability, the thought elaborated so laboriously in those books would turn out to be most relevant to the central global challenge of the twenty-first century and directly, indirectly or at least dialectically inspirational of its most forward-looking sociopolitical developments.

What did that thought consist of? Bookchin wrote a lot, usually in a state of high dudgeon at his many perceived adversaries on the left. Both his positions and his labels for them evolved, and while he was generally careful to note in later work just how they'd done so, this was not always clear to casual readers who encountered his writings out of sequence. This was especially so in the days before the internet came into widespread use, when a robust understanding of his beliefs could only be cobbled together by tracking down the evidence as it appeared across a scatter of indifferently distributed books. With the benefit of latter-day collected editions, though, and of internet resources like the Anarchist Library and Dana Ward's invaluable Anarchy Archives, it's possible to sketch the evolution of a series of interlocking concepts Bookchin called "Communalism" and "libertarian municipalism," as well as the broader project in which they were both embedded, "social ecology."[6]

Social ecology was a startlingly novel formulation, founded on two major insights. The first was Bookchin's recognition, even before Rachel Carson's 1961 *Silent Spring* had given the contemporary environmental movement its initial impetus, that the Earthly biosphere was in the throes of a profound crisis as a result of human action and headed for worse. He even predicted the specific form the crisis would take, warning as early as 1964—more than a decade, in other words, before the 1977 White House memo generally regarded as the first appearance in public thought of what was then called "the greenhouse effect"—that atmospheric heating driven by accumulations of carbon dioxide "may well rank among the most serious sources of future ecological imbalance and may pose major threats to the viability of the planet," "undermining the very capacity of the Earth to sustain advanced forms of life."[7]

Here Bookchin's clear, early articulation of what has since become universally accepted scientific consensus feels stunningly prescient:

> Since the Industrial Revolution, the overall atmospheric mass of carbon dioxide has increased by 13 percent over earlier, more stable, levels. It could be argued on very sound theoretical grounds that this growing blanket of carbon dioxide, by intercepting heat radiated from the earth into outer space, will lead to rising atmospheric temperatures, to a more violent circulation of air, to more destructive storm patterns, and eventually to a melting of the polar ice caps (possibly in two or three centuries), rising sea levels, and the inundation of vast land areas.[8]

Again, consider the unnerving clarity of vision it took to set these ideas in print months before Martin Luther King was awarded the Nobel Peace Prize, the Beatles played Shea Stadium, or American combat forces landed in Vietnam. The only aspect of Bookchin's 1964 framing that is in any way incorrect is the optimism of locating the melting "two or three centuries" from now.

It's Bookchin's second insight, though, that really gives his social ecology its continuing and acute relevance. This was that the planetary crisis was caused, in large part, by what he called the "social pathologies" of patriarchy, statism and capitalism, and could not be undone or reversed without first unwinding them. He understood, before virtually any of his contemporaries on the left, the causal link between our compulsion to dominate—especially as it was expressed in the capitalist project of unlimited growth—and the destruction of the ecosphere and therefore its capacity to support all Earthly life.

Marxist economics, with its theory of the "metabolic rift," offers some of the analytical insights you'd need to draw upon in order to reach a conclusion like this; the intersectional feminism of the Combahee River Collective others; and mainstream ecological science yet others again.[9] But social ecology is the first body of thought I am aware of that links the planetary crisis to the alienation we suffer as individuals and communities via their common causal factor of domination.

Where classical anarchism had always been defined by its revulsion for coercion and hierarchy, Bookchin now tied relations founded in these qualities directly to the question of our persistence as a species. If we wanted to survive, he argued, and to preserve the kind of healthy planetary ecosystem in which we might all thrive equally, we would have to undertake the work of reorganizing society and all its institutions so as to eliminate the possibility of domination—either of nature by humanity, or of any human being by another. This is a strikingly bold, integrative conception of power, especially given that it was first articulated in an era when the left was still largely given over to the machismo of national liberation, and it speaks directly to the ecological and intersectional concerns of our own moment like no other thought of the period.

To facilitate meaningful change, though, this theory of social ecology needs a corresponding form of concrete expression. Bookchin named this Communalism, with a capital C, in explicit allusion and homage to the Paris Commune of 1871. Communalism was designed around a set of "preconditions for human survival," among which were "the anarchist concepts of a balanced community, a face-to-face democracy, a humanistic technology and a decentralized society." Taken together, these would constitute nothing less than "a new politics structured around towns, neighborhoods, cities, and citizens' assemblies, freely confederated into local, regional, and ultimately continental networks."[10]

As expressed here, Bookchin's faith in the wisdom of ordinary people is profound. He evidently could not countenance the idea that when given the power to decide freely, anyone rational would opt for anything but cleanly powered, human-scaled, locally managed production that could be sustained over the long term. His clear supposition is that people empowered to make consequential policy decisions for themselves would ("naturally") choose to forgo the neocolonial megaprojects, the sweetheart deals and lobbyists, the expeditionary wars—in fact the whole grim architecture of extraction and exploitation that was tilting the entire atmosphere toward an untenable state. The assumption underlying his entire project, across decades, is that a free people organized on Communalist lines would organically tend toward distributional justice, achieved via what we'd now call a "circular economy."[11]

The locally scaled manifestation of Communalism was to be called "libertarian municipalism," a form of language Bookchin first started using in the early 1970s. (As always with Bookchin, his use of the word "libertarian" here reflects the older usage, in which it is more or less synonymous with "anarchist.") It was in and through this practice that Communalism proposed to "eliminate statist municipal structures and replace them with the institutions of a libertarian polity."[12]

So far as actually achieving this was concerned, libertarian municipalism "depends upon libertarian leftists running candidates at the local municipal level, calling for the division of municipalities into wards, where popular assemblies can be created that bring people into full and direct participation in political life."[13] Here Bookchin distinguishes between *government*, an "institutionalized association that constitutes a system for handling public affairs," and the *state*, which he remains enough of an anarchist to define as "a force for class repression and control."

The institutions of nonrepressive government are to be popular assemblies: participatory, deliberative venues where "citizens ... deal with community affairs on a face-to-face basis, *making policy decisions* in a direct democracy and giving reality to the ideal of a humanistic, rational society."[14] In fact, all the "management, plans, and regulations" necessary to the stewardship of a contemporary city would be "formulated democratically by popular assemblies." Where issues that transcend the narrow and particular interests of a given municipality arise, "the democratized municipalities should join together to form a broader confederation."

There are a few things we might want to note about all of this. The first is the improbability that significant numbers of "libertarian leftists" would vote, let alone contest office, in conventionally bourgeois elections. Beyond this, though, Bookchin never specifies how big his wards are to be, or what's supposed to happen if, once created, the people living in them show little inclination toward participation in popular assemblies. He fails to anticipate that many communities might prefer to define themselves by constitutive exclusion of the outsider, and never clarifies who does and does not count as a citizen for purposes of participation.

In fact, he displays an unusually strong, Enlightenment-derived faith in public reason (in both its senses of deliberative reasoning-in-public and of a public with the broad capacity for reason) that can be difficult to sustain for anyone who has been exposed to the various feminist and postmodern critiques thereof. He never convincingly explains why his decentralized confederal structures would necessarily be democratic ones, or why federated communities that *are* run democratically should necessarily be progressive or ecological in their commitments.[15] He has no real answer to capital flight and doesn't seem to have entertained the possibility that any polity that did succeed in organizing itself along Communalist lines might simply be contained, undermined, suppressed or annihilated—as indeed was the Paris Commune itself.

For all his blind spots, Bookchin's notions of social ecology, Communalism and libertarian municipalism offer a way of organizing our communities that is particularly well tuned to the rigors of the Long Emergency. And among all the aspects of this nested set of ideas, the most germane to us is the concrete practice at its core: the assembly.

What is the assembly? At its simplest, it is any group of people gathered to discuss matters of common concern and, when faced with the necessity of a decision, to choose among the courses of action available to them. If "democracy" in contemporary life so often gets reduced to the vote for one representative or indifferent choice over another, the participatory tradition of the assembly gives democratic values a far fuller and more robust expression. It is an immediate, concrete exercise of collective power, available wherever and whenever people come together in any number greater than a handful.

In the West, the formal articulation of participatory democracy begins with the 1962 Port Huron Statement of the fiercely idealistic Students for a Democratic Society, or SDS, which enshrined its authors' belief that "people should have a central role in determining those decisions that affect their daily lives."[16] But beyond some thought that "decision-making of basic social consequence be carried on by public groupings," and that these groupings have "the function of bringing people out of isolation and into community," the statement's authors offered no particular guidance as to how this might be achieved.

It is fair to say that a certain woolliness on the details was a broader failing of the era, a time when—as Francesca Polletta concludes, after having studied seven American movements that embraced the practice—even the most motivated "activists were making participatory democracy up as they went along."[17] So perhaps Bookchin can be forgiven for not outlining in any particular depth how he expected his flavor of public deliberation to function. But what's striking about Bookchin's advocacy for the assembly is that he sustains it uninterruptedly, from a time before Port Huron had even given a name to "participatory democracy," to an epoch in which most seasoned activists on the left had given the form up as hopeless. And this is largely because, wisely or otherwise, he was looking to a different set of antecedents than the SDS or the other activists of the generation immediately following him. Bookchin adduces proof of the assembly's superiority not as they did—from direct experience of its use as organizing, capacity-building or consciousness-raising tool in the course of the Civil Rights struggle—but from historical accounts of its practice in classical antiquity and colonial New England.

The notion that more or less densely-settled communities might be run on principles of broadly participatory decision-making has appeared in a wide variety of times and places across human history, from the medieval *folkmoots*, *þings* and *althings* of Northern Europe to the Haudenosaunee Confederacy of pre-Columbian North America.[18] As recent scholarship suggests, it may even have been present at the very dawn of urban-scale settlement, at the long-buried Ukrainian "mega-sites" of Maidenetske, Taljanky and Nebelivka—the latter, fully the size of medieval London by 3200 BCE, evidently comprised of "self-governing districts … with assemblies for decision-making."[19] Much of Graeber and Wengrow's book is dedicated to exploring this long and variegated history of deep political participation and what it may imply for our own choices.

But these are not the inspirations Bookchin draws upon in devising the tenets of his libertarian municipalism. Alongside his near-contemporaries Hannah Arendt and C. L. R. James, he looks instead to ancient Athens, the institution of the Ecclesia and the sovereign Greek ethical imperative of appearing before one's neighbors and peers in face-to-face deliberation.[20]

The monthly public assembly, the Ecclesia, does indeed appear to have been a carefully balanced and elaborately well-thought-out process, in which responsibility for decision-making in all matters of state was broadly distributed across the citizens of Athens. But for the contemporary reader, it's impossible to engage Bookchin's praise of it (or James's or Arendt's, for that matter) without stumbling at the very outset against a circumstance that ought to have been radioactively disqualifying for anyone claiming to be concerned with the expansion of human freedom: Athens was a slave state. Its vaunted "democracy" excluded an overwhelming majority of the population. In fact, only free male veterans of military service enjoyed the privilege of participating in the Ecclesia and, therefore, the other institutions of public deliberation.[21] In his article exploring the roots of participatory democracy, James mounts a bizarre, no-true-Scotsman defense of Athenian practice as not *really* constituting slavery as such, and for his part Bookchin does something very similar.

Fortunately, history offers more recent, somewhat less compromised examples of public deliberation that Bookchin could draw upon in his further development of libertarian municipalism—medieval Lombardy, the revolutionary sections of 1790s Paris, the anarcho-syndicalist Spain of the Civil War years.[22] But where he really seems to find the virtues of public reason epitomized is in the New England–style town meeting.[23] This is something he consistently extols across thirty years of writing, to the degree that he eventually moved to Vermont, where the town meeting survived as a living tradition, so that he could practice the technique full-time.[24]

For all this, it must be said that his understanding of the social, psychological and emotional dynamics of the assembly form was not particularly sophisticated—or anyway, not at least so far as that understanding was expressed in his published oeuvre, which conspicuously lacks the quality James C. Scott refers to as *mêtis*, or insight derived from hands-on, practical experience.[25] His many writings on the topic tend to consist, rather, of a repeated series of exhortations that the face-to-face assembly is the only "rational" and "moral" venue for collective decision-making, and that its superiority in these regards is sufficiently self-evident to recommend its widespread adoption.

That this was not universally considered to be a wise idea among people with more pragmatic experience of the form is something of an understatement; the historian Laurence Veysey wryly notes that, in "urging popular assemblies as the appropriate means for [the] day-to-day management of resources," Bookchin "unwittingly returned to the very device which had been clung to for so many wearisome years" during earlier upwellings of the utopian spirit in America, with dispiriting results.[26]

There are, of course, sound reasons why we might want to be wary of a naive or unconsidered practice of assembly. For Bookchin the process of collaborative truth discovery is something that takes place through deliberation in open assembly, always "according to the canons of *reason, reflection, and discourse* that uniquely belong to our own species."[27] You sense that he means for this to be radically inclusive and to affirm and uphold the capacities for rationality that are in principle enjoyed by all human beings. But as a guideline for something that is supposed to constitute the sole legitimate expression of collective will for all those living in a particular locale, this is woefully insufficient. Its insufficiency becomes especially evident in a complex, heterogeneous society.

Firstly, just because a process is formally open doesn't mean that it's actually accessible or inclusive, let alone welcoming. The composition of the deliberative group itself may feel as though it excludes the newcomer. It can be intimidating to offer one's opinion, especially in matters of controversy, and most of all for those who are not native speakers of the language in which the assembly is being conducted, or whose accent or customary mode of speech otherwise marks them as other. It may be practically difficult for people with any degree of speech or hearing impairment, sensory sensitivity or social anxiety to participate. And, of course, we might find ourselves unable to contribute should the place and time of assembly come into too much conflict with the obligations already imposed on us by work, family and the due care of the self.

Without very clear guidelines as to the rules that guide deliberation—limits on speaking time, for example, or the number of total comments made—the proceedings of an assembly may easily be dominated by the charismatic, the rhetorically gifted or simply those whose carriage and mode of self-presentation convey the fact that they are habitually used to being attended to. Any ambiguity in these procedures, particularly with regard to decision rules, may give the impression of a consensus that doesn't truly exist, or even be consciously exploited by the underhanded to advance some sub-rosa agenda of their own. Absent some degree of explicit, formal structure, an assembly process whose very reason for being is that it is supposed to be equal, open and noncoercive may wind up imposing its will on those who don't know how to read the prevailing currents of power, and, when it does, these dynamics will always break in favor of the elite groups and individuals who already enjoy that power.

And finally, the assembly works well where it is understood by all parties to be *the* assembly—that is, either formalized as a process of consensual governance, or consecrated by long-standing custom as the sovereign decision body of a given community. What does not work so well is when an ad hoc assembly is constituted of different people each time it meets, and participants, perhaps reasonably enough, decline either to be bound by the commitments of those who were there last week or to recognize decisions made in their absence.

Particular care needs to be taken when the assembly gathers in the open, in public space. The activist-scholar Alberto Corsín Jiménez tells a story about assembly participants in the main plaza of the Lavapiés neighborhood of Madrid having to negotiate with a group of recent immigrants who also wanted to use the plaza, reasonably enough, and were in the habit of playing loud music over their deliberations.[28] (It is notable that those immigrants evidently did not feel that the assembly spoke to or for them, or could.[29])

These were all points made resoundingly by a successive line of feminist critics whose work exposed participatory and deliberative forms of democracy to a powerful series of troublings: where Jo Freeman assailed the tacit power dynamics that persisted even in ostensibly "leaderless" and nonhierarchical activist groups, Nancy Fraser demolished the notion of a unitary public sphere, and Lynn Sanders noted that not everyone necessarily had the ability, the time or simply the inclination to participate deliberatively.[30] (For his part, Bookchin seems never to have taken this body of thought on board, even though aspects of it, notably Freeman's pivotal "The Tyranny of Structurelessness," had already appeared by 1970.[31])

Despite its pretensions to universality, then, the problem of the assembly is one of representative legitimacy. In order to be broadly perceived as valid, an assembly has to convene a threshold percentage of the population, and that number needs to be sufficient for it to practically enact its will. Kali Akuno of the Mississippi-based libertarian-municipalist initiative Cooperation Jackson is unusually specific in identifying that threshold, defining the assembly as "a body that engages at least one-fifth of the total population in a defined geographic area."[32] And this feels right: with one out of every five people in a community directly participating in discussions about its posture, priorities and future, their decisions undoubtedly bear a fair amount of weight. How legitimate is it possible to be, by contrast, if your "neighborhood assembly" of ten or twelve bodies occupies a single room, when right outside the windows you can feel the entire city breathe capital all around you, all the way out to its furthermost hinterlands?

Even when the necessary pains are taken to ensure that a given gathering in assembly is both genuinely invitational and consensually legitimate, there is one final consideration, which is whether it is actually dispositive. As suggested by the famous Atelier Populaire poster from the Events of May 1968 ("I participate, you participate, we participate ... they profit"), canny activists have always understood that "maximum feasible participation" is often a fig leaf for something else, a way of shedding unwonted legitimation on some preexisting agenda.

Neoliberal governments often deploy ostensibly participatory processes with the greatest possible cynicism, to lend the color of popular ratification to decisions that have already been made elsewhere: this is known as "consultation."[33] But the misapprehension that the assembly's role is essentially consultative is common enough, even among its radical advocates. For example, the late Jackson, Mississippi, mayor Chokwe Lumumba—widely known as a strong proponent of the form, and nobody's neoliberal—was comfortable characterizing the assembly as "a body where the people challenge government, ask government questions, get informed by government, and protest government when necessary."[34] But not, you will notice, as an institution that *supplants* government—in other words, not as a locus of power in its own right.

So what we're after isn't mere participation, or even the stronger claim on energy, attention and commitment represented by deliberation. To serve the end of collective power, the assembly can't simply be there to permit the therapeutic venting of grievances, facilitate a process of "consultation," or allocate some token wedge of the local council's annual budget. It must exist to *decide*, and its decisions must be dispositive over real resource.

Given that, the project of self-governance via assembly becomes something that is worth pursuing. If nothing else, the ability to participate in consequential decisions helps to shift the psychological locus of control, however incrementally, from external to internal. The world is no longer quite so much something that happens to you, and that you have no choice but to accept, but something you can intervene in, concretely and directly. The ability to act upon the world in this way is in itself palliative of the awful helplessness in the face of events that characterizes our time.

But it's also about something even larger than that. For the feminist philosopher Iris Marion Young, justice is more than merely a question of the equal distribution of goods. It is a condition in which "action, decisions about action, and provision of the means to develop and exercise capacities" are accessible to all.[35] This is why the practice of deliberative assembly isn't simply about getting together to vote for one or another among the options before us. In helping us build our capability for collective self-determination, and giving us a venue in which we might employ it, the assembly is, as directly as it is possible to be, concerned with the achievement of justice.

The question remains as to how any such thing might be practically implemented. In many cities, some kind of neighborhood-scale deliberative infrastructure is already there, in statute and practice both, and might be repurposed toward more substantive ends: in New York City, for example, David Harvey imagines "the revival of the now largely somnolent community boards as neighborhood assemblies with budget-allocation powers."[36]

This chimes with Bookchin's practically achievable "minimum program" for libertarian municipalism, which outlined a set of "steps that can be taken now include initiating ... municipalist movements that propose popular neighborhood and town assemblies—even if they have only moral functions at first—and electing town and city councillors that advance the cause of these assemblies and other popular institutions." But with even the elements of this minimum program requiring significant commitments of time and energy, any attempt at putting it into practice had to wait for a moment in which large numbers were primed to accept its logic.

That moment arrived at last with the new millennium, amid a set of circumstances in politics that are generally referred to as the "horizontal turn."

Though protest groups like ACT/UP, Earth First! and Critical Mass had pioneered its basic forms in the 1980s, we can roughly date the horizontal turn proper to sometime between the fall of the Soviet Union at the end of 1991, with its final discrediting of the Marxist-Leninist logic of command, and the breakout of networked organizing tactics into wide public visibility at the 1999 protests against the World Trade Organization in Seattle.[37] In between those events, and inspired above all by the 1994 Zapatista insurgency against the Mexican state in Chiapas, activists progressively abandoned traditional parties of the radical left in favor of flatter, "leaderless" organizing structures.[38]

This new way of coordinating collective action appears to have been first explicitly named as such in the practice of *horizontalidad* that emerged in Argentina in 2001.[39] And for the first time since the consciousness-raising groups of the mid-1970s, relatively small, nonhierarchical and self-organized groups returned to the center stage of political activism.

Rather than concentrating the power to decide in a single leader, or tightly sharing it among a party cadre, horizontalism distributed it across everyone motivated enough to show up and participate. Sometimes, the decision logic employed was the pursuit of full consensus, at others a simple majority vote. But materially, this looked much the same, wherever on Earth you happened to encounter it: people gathered in a rough circle, often in a courtyard, clearing or public plaza, visibly and volubly discussing the matter before them. (If the universal symbol of leftism in the era of national liberation was the Kalashinkov raised in a clenched fist, its truest emblem in our own is undoubtedly the cheap and ubiquitous knockoff Monobloc chair, visible in depictions of such gatherings from Bogotà to Kampala to Berlin.[40])

To be sure, much of this was made possible by the diffusion of newly affordable networked communication technologies, principally text messaging and, a few years later, the smartphone with its microblogging and secure-messaging apps. But horizontalism was more than a matter of information-technical innovation. The horizontalist generation developed a new attention to mood, affect and subjectivity in deliberative gatherings. By the time of the WTO protests in Seattle, activists were already using an array of hand signals to convey the sense of a meeting, from enthusiastic assent to vehement objection.[41] Assemblies increasingly came to draw upon a repertoire of techniques that simply did not exist in the West at the time of the Port Huron Statement, taking inspiration from Indigenous practice and especially the Zapatista notion of a "world which contains many worlds."[42]

By 2011, those who occupied the squares had ready to hand

> a rich and growing panoply of organizational instruments—spokescouncils, affinity groups, facilitation tools, break-outs, fishbowls, blocking concerns, vibe-watchers and so on—all aimed at creating forms of democratic process that allow initiatives to rise from below and attain maximum effective solidarity, without stifling dissenting voices, creating leadership positions or compelling anyone to do anything which they have not freely agreed to do.[43]

These elements of horizontal practice constituted a lightweight, portable kit of parts that was broadly available at moments of social or economic rupture, and such moments came thick and fast as the second decade of the new century dawned.

Across the Arab world, from Tunisia to Bahrain, conspicuously young populations finally lost patience with the absolutist oppression of elderly despots and the foreclosure of their life chances that went along with it. The *indignados* of Spain, like the Aganaktisménoi, were responding to a different set of pressures: their aspirations for a better life had been sanded away to nothing by the years-long recession gripping Europe's southern tier, often brutally exacerbated by austerity programs of the sort imposed upon Greece by the Troika. And in the United States, millions could no longer quite escape the sense that somewhere along the way, the American dream had become the sole prerogative of an absurdly wealthy few; this tiny sliver of the population, having reaped stratospheric profits from the financialization of just about everything, now left everyone else to a grim destiny of casualized employment, equally precarious housing and debt service drawn out unto the grave.

What united significant numbers of people in all these places was the common sense that their future was being stolen away from them in real time, without their having had the slightest say in the matter. And they responded in much the same way: with a demand for *¡Democracia real ya!* ("Real democracy now!"). This demand was most visibly expressed in a wave of occupations that broke out spontaneously at Tahrir Square in Cairo in January 2011, at Puerta del Sol in Madrid and Syntagma Square in Athens in May, at Zuccotti Park in the financial district of downtown Manhattan in September and, somewhat later, at Gezi Park in Istanbul. This was the global coming-out party for horizontal praxis known as the "movement of the squares."[44]

For many participants, myself included, this tide of protest constituted the first time in our lives that our subjective experiences of the world were reflected in mass political action of any sort. We had grown tired of being told that politics would only ever amount to the choice of the least-worst option and that the best we could ever expect to achieve was the most tepid and incremental sort of reform. On some level that was deeper but harder to articulate, we'd wearied of never seeing our dissent from the bland late-capitalist consensus depicted, or even acknowledged, anywhere in public life. So for us, the wave of occupations felt like a sudden irruption of jubilee time. From Zuccotti Park itself to Dame Street in Dublin, the predominant mood in every protest camp I was able to visit in the fall of 2011 was a kind of infectious glee or delight that this should be coming to pass at all.

It's highly tempting to understand the "new municipalist" wave that broke out during 2014–15, then, as in part an attempt to bottle the euphoria of occupation and extend the logic that had guided the occupation of the squares to a pursuit of lasting local power.

Consciously or otherwise, new municipalism exploited the opening of the Occupy moment to draw upon the massive surge of people radicalized by their experience of austerity in the post-2008 period and with their energy attempt an enactment of the late-Bookchinian project. Though there never seems to have been any intention to articulate anything like a "standard municipalist policy agenda"—any attempt to do so would be "contrary to the decentralized, autonomous nature of the movement"—city-scale movements of highly similar sensibility sprouted up on six continents in the years following 2011, virtually none of them affiliated with a pre-existing political party.[45] Broadly concerning themselves with housing justice, "the feminization of politics" and countering the invasion of local economies by venture capital–funded Silicon Valley platforms like Airbnb and Uber, they broadly thought of themselves as "new municipalists."[46] And what they applied to their contestations of local power was the horizontal process and the assembly form they had learned in the squares.

This was the critical moment at which large numbers of people moved from protesting the neoliberal conditions under which they lived to actually *doing something* about them. With varying degrees of success, each of these movements now tried to adapt the "minimum program" of libertarian municipalism to the real-world challenge of winning a citywide election. If we suspect that this neo-Bookchinian approach to power might truly offer up insights that help us endure the Long Emergency together, it is this moment of transition from theory to practice we will need to consider most closely.

Though large-scale efforts pursued new-municipalist strategies in places from Valparaíso to Zagreb, it is the major cities of Spain that traveled furthest down this road. During the long, drawn-out years of austerity that followed the particularly sharp Spanish financial crisis of 2008, Madrid, Barcelona, Zaragoza, Cádiz and A Coruña each gave rise to an organic movement espousing municipalist values, organized not as a traditional political party but as a "confluence." In setting themselves the project of winning citywide power, these confluences—Ahora Madrid, Barcelona en Comú and their peers—collectively began to generate for the first time an experientially informed body of thought about what municipalism is, how it works and what it does on the ground.

"Confluence" is a difficult-to-translate term in Spanish municipalism, used to describe what might elsewhere simply be called a "platform." As was emphasized to me any number of times during my travels in Spain, confluences are precisely *not* coalitions of parties. The primary point of distinction seems to be that a coalition is a temporary, tactical coming-together of existing entities that continue to maintain their own distinct identities (e.g., a labor union, an NGO, a social movement) as they work together toward a given end. By contrast, a confluence is an in-gathering of *individuals*—in principle, even the same individuals who might have been mobilized by a coalition among the parties to which they belong—organized under a new identity and committed to a process of self-definition by assembly.

Partisans of any existing formation were free to join the confluences, but they had to do so as unencumbered individuals. "Nobody could participate in the gatherings in representation of other collectives, associations, or institutions such as political parties and unions … Everybody was a bare participant and had to speak on her own behalf."[47] In Spain, the language used to explain this, even by ordinary activists, can be uncannily high-theoretical; the word chosen to describe this logic by just about every street-level Ahora Madrid participant I met was "molecular," as if they'd just that moment put down a dog-eared copy of Deleuze.

Neither a social movement nor quite a political party, then, the confluence offered distinct strengths and weaknesses. One clear strength was its rootedness in the daily experience of specific neighborhoods, which gave it both legitimacy and a means of staying abreast of evolving conditions that conventional parties did not have access to in quite the same way. Frequent *asambleas populares* kept the confluence grounded, counteracting what might otherwise be its tendency to abstraction and "making sure that it is constantly aware of the realities within which it lives."[48] They also performed a search function

—sweeping the horizon, in effect, helping the confluence as a whole discover emergent matters of concern that might otherwise abscond from its awareness. These might in turn reflect common or even citywide struggles and therefore prove effective as issues to organize around.

Another strength enjoyed by the confluences was their broad power to convene. Bookchin's libertarian municipalism had refused both a conventional class analysis and the politics of identity as organizing principles, regarding them as invidious and prone to the creation of power-squandering fissures.[49] Prefiguring Graeber's brilliant rhetorical maneuver in positioning Occupy as an appeal to "the 99%," its bold, implicit gamble was that the alienations and dislocations of late capitalism would eventually be painful enough that they would be experienced by virtually everyone in a society and could be mobilized as such.

In the wake of 2011, this actually appeared to be the case: both the *asamblearismo* of the squares and the new municipalism of the confluences aimed to speak to, and therefore politically activate, people who were not currently affiliated with any existing party or movement. The numbers and enthusiasm of their public meetings spoke vividly to the success of this strategy.

But even at this point, it was not obvious how that passion might be transformed into actual power. This speaks to a feature of the confluences which in truth was probably both a strength and, in certain lights, a weakness. Utterly uninterested in imposing a disciplined uniformity of belief among members, the confluences always supported a robust diversity of viewpoints, and this extended to the theories of change held among their most committed activists. In Spain, this disagreement was, again, conducted at an unusually high level of abstraction. It was generally articulated as the tension between a "Laclauian" faction and a "Negrian" one.

At issue between them was nothing less fundamental than the question of how popular power can most readily be developed and exercised. One tendency within Ahora Madrid, broadly associated with the national left-populist party Podemos, committed itself to establishing radical democracy along the ambitious lines suggested by Ernesto Laclau and Chantal Mouffe.[50] This involved the pursuit of institutional state power and the attempt to leverage it toward the "counterhegemonic" transvaluation of all the values operating in everyday late-capitalist life.

The opposing tendency, with roots in the left-libertarian Traficantes de Sueños bookstore and publishing house, held to the contrasting theory of "constituent power" developed by the Italian autonomist Marxist Antonio Negri, and later elaborated with Michael Hardt.[51] This body of thought turned its back on the seizure of institutions and placed its faith instead in the continual becoming of the multitude itself, conceived as such.

Though the confluence form unquestionably drew its original energy from a distinctly Negrian surge in the plazas and the neighborhoods, it's tempting to read the evolution of Spanish municipalism as a gradual eclipse of the Negrian perspective by the Laclauian. In Madrid and Barcelona both, this was accelerated by the practical realities associated with victory and the assumption of electoral office.

In his 1996 book *Aramis, or the Love of Technology*, the late French sociologist Bruno Latour describes a process that unfolds any time a technology works its way from abstract idea to realization, a double articulation he refers to as "recruitment" followed by "translation."[52]

In order to establish purchase in the world, a project needs to attract partners, which might be individuals, institutions or even material objects. This is what Latour calls *recruitment*, and it's just as true of political projects as it is of technical ones. A political platform running a candidate for local office, for example, will need to recruit door-to-door canvassers, volunteers to post on social media and people willing to work the phone banks. If their proposition involves deliberation in assembly, they'll require facilitators of assemblies, spaces to hold them and some way of recording and storing the minutes of each. They'll need to attract designers, printers, videographers, drivers and, of course, funders to shoulder the financial burdens of all this activity. Depending on the operating environment, they may even need street medics, or people strong and confident enough to provide security. And most obviously of all, they'll need to recruit votes.

Recruitment is vital in order to advance any nascent project. But each new actor recruited apprehends what they've encountered a little bit differently, and the project is slightly modified by the very act of their recruitment. This is *translation*. Sometimes, the alterations required to recruit one partner to the project are intolerable to another, and one or another of them drops out.

For our purposes, there are two particularly salient qualities of translation. The first is that it is low fidelity. There is always some degree of conceptual slippage involved, every time a new actor is recruited to the effort. And the second is that this process is iterative: it repeats every time some new component is added to the mix. Repeated enough times, like some material-semiotic game of Telephone, it can result in the thing that finally hits the streets bearing little or no resemblance to what was originally imagined. It has evolved by drift.

This is exactly what happened when the libertarian municipalism imagined by Bookchin in the 1980s was translated into the "new municipalism" practiced in the main cities of Spain, post-15M.[53] What is municipalism? The answer would depend on who you asked and when you asked them. And a good deal of friction inheres in the fact that there's necessarily a mismatch, a profound one, between the way municipalist assemblies worked in the squares and neighborhoods and the way municipalist civic administration was compelled to operate.[54]

This was, of course, recognized quite clearly by the people involved: as Barcelona en Comú communications manager Marina López told the *Guardian* in 2016, a year into their first administration, "The difference with being in power is there are two parallel processes—ours and the institutional one, and they don't work in the same way or [at the] same speed."⁵⁵ The affects generated by each, the skills they called upon, even the kinds of people they spoke to were all different from one another. According to activists who were there, there was even a palpable difference in tone and tenor between the original neighborhood assemblies of post-15M Barcelona and the formally similar gatherings later convoked by Barcelona en Comú in power.⁵⁶

So it's not an exaggeration to say that parts of municipalist theory were sawn off to fit. The notion that policy might continuously be developed in deliberative assembly fell by the wayside—in Madrid, spontaneous neighborhood assemblies were no longer taking place by the time the citywide municipalist confluence Ahora Madrid was forged, while those in Barcelona had largely dried up by the fall of 2012.⁵⁷ And what of the allegedly "crucial" distinction between policy development and administration by recallable councils? Similarly, nowhere to be found: following the municipalist victories in both cities, administration proceeded much as if any other insurgent candidacy had taken City Hall. As central as they may have been to the process of governance envisioned by Bookchin, these practices were immediately shed by actually existing municipalism in its 2015 Spanish manifestation. Indeed, one longtime activist quit Ahora Madrid at the very moment of its ascension to power "because the project had changed so much in the process of winning the election, that they no longer recognised it as the radical, horizontalist, prefigurative project they originally joined."⁵⁸

Other issues were caused by a misperception of how much power the city government had to make change. Bookchin had always taken pains to distinguish between local *electoral* politics and the larger domain of *parliamentary* politics. The position he seems to have been reaching for in his late phase was that, of all the forms of statecraft, the one we encounter at the municipal level is the most accountable to ordinary citizens, the easiest to participate in directly and the least unclean. He therefore winds up defending the legitimacy of participation in local forms of elected government, if only with the intention of one day disassembling them from within, and arguably this is the point at which his transition out of anarchism is complete. This is a rather nuanced position, but there's nothing that's particularly unclear about it: participation in local government is acceptable to the convinced municipalist, while that in the regional or national state remains beyond the pale.

As is so frequently the case, however, this seemingly crisp and clear distinction in principle evaporates on contact with reality. For one thing, it's often not so very clear just where "local government" begins and where it ends. In Spain, for example, municipal governments don't enjoy the power to levy taxes or even necessarily to allocate budget as they see fit. So when Ahora Madrid came to power, they were broadly unable to enact those aspects of their agenda that required any significant capital investment to speak of. The power to affect Madrileños' lives in most of the ways that signified simply resided at a higher level than any amenable to the kind of face-to-face neighborhood democracy Bookchin imagined. At this point a Laclauian position starts to seem reasonable.

The need to wrap a complicated and unconventional proposition in the body of a single individual took its toll, as well. In Barcelona the municipalist candidate, Ada Colau, had come out of housing activism, had a movement history and enjoyed a longstanding reputation for daring on the local left, but in Madrid the only name put forward that was acceptable to all factions (see: recruitment and translation) was a local magistrate named Manuela Carmena. Carmena was broadly respected for her incorruptibility but otherwise had no particular identification with the municipalist moment—and in time, this would tell. Ahora Madrid's activists had banked on her serving willingly as the "empty signifier" called for in Laclauian theory, a blank screen onto which voters could project whatever they wanted. And furnished with this invitation, the voters went ahead and did just that. Indeed, the range of things that people projected onto Carmena was notable above all for its cringeworthiness, with graphics circulating in the run-up to the election unabashedly portraying her as Batman, Angela Davis, Princess Leia, Che or, most curiously of all, Maria von Trapp from *The Sound of Music*, twirling in an Alpine meadow with an AR-15 assault rifle gripped in each hand.[59]

This surge of enthusiasm carried Ahora Madrid to victory in the elections of May 24, 2015, albeit as a minority government supported by the conventionally socialist PSOE (Spanish Socialist Workers' Party). As things turned out, though, not merely did Carmena refuse to be anybody's blank screen, neither did she govern as much of a municipalist. On the day after being installed in Madrid's City Hall, in the Palacio de Cibeles on the Paseo del Prado, she told her electorate, more or less in so many words, that as Manuela Carmena was who they had voted for, they would now be governed as Manuela Carmena saw fit. Those who had declared themselves not so much *asambleistas* or *Madridistas* as *Manuelistas* were closer to the mark than they knew. (So much for the fine Bookchinian theory of delegated and revokable power.)

Finally, Ahora Madrid found out the hard way that, unlike their partners in the PSOE or other traditional political parties of clear tendency and long standing, a municipalist confluence formed relatively recently is not likely to have significant knots of longtime supporters distributed throughout the administrative apparatus. Even in a best-case scenario, upon acquiring the keys to City Hall, a newly elected municipalist administration would still have to tutor the civil servants who actually run things on the day-to-day in relatively new and unfamiliar values, priorities and processes—and that costs time, energy and political capital. And this, of course, presupposes that bureaucrats share a certain degree of sympathy with the newcomers and are willing to try new ways of doing things. In administrative departments that are *not* favorably disposed to the incoming administration, it will be greeted instead as such interlopers generally are: with foot-dragging, malingering, work-to-rule strikes and so on.

In the end, Madrid and Barcelona both managed to see their confluences into power: Ahora Madrid under Manuela

Carmena until 2019, and Barcelona en Comú with Ada Colau for two full terms, until finally going down to defeat in 2023. Both cities objectively got "municipalism." But whether that municipalism was libertarian in any meaningful sense was another question entirely.

In his later writing, Bookchin staked everything on a wager that municipalists could successfully occupy the local state, consolidate whatever power inhered in it and use that power to catalyze further transformations of democratic expression. On this theory, their time in office would be dedicated to building a series of participatory counterinstitutions that might then go on to seed libertarian values and practices at every level of city life, driving a deeper, longer-term transition toward Communalist life. In short, municipalist candidates would "become Mayor to abolish the position of Mayor."[60]

Perhaps too much was lost in the process of translation that all ideas must undergo as they make their way toward realization, but nothing of the sort happened in Spain. What libertarian municipalism was stripped of, as it made itself palatable to the Spanish electorate in the heady season of 2015, was just about everything that made it distinct as a political tradition. Most of the features that might have commended it to us as a way of contending with a hot and dangerous future—the power it restored to neighborhood-scale actors, the connections it drew between the exercise of that power and broader movements toward ecological care, and more—fell away like a discarded husk.

Some of the measures called for in the Ahora Madrid platform were eventually enacted during the Carmena mayoralty, notably an audit of public expenditures, a freeze on evictions, gender parity in appointments and a reconsideration of certain boondoggle megaprojects associated with the previous administration. Beyond that, though, Ahora Madrid could not possibly bear up under the hope Madrileños had invested in it, and Carmena was defeated by the right-wing Partido Popular at the 2019 elections. The hugely popular traffic-calming measures introduced in central Madrid under Carmena were immediately reversed upon the PP's resumption of power, evidently largely out of spite and/or the desire to be performatively pro-car, not because the change of policy produced any measurable benefit whatsoever.[61]

Barcelona fared somewhat better in this regard. Although a high-profile effort to bring the city water supply back under public ownership was eventually defeated in the Spanish Supreme Court, Barcelona en Comú did manage to establish a municipal renewable-energy provider (as well as a low-cost funeral company), remunicipalize home care, retrieve a number of kindergartens and domestic-violence shelters from private providers and perhaps bring to heel some of the overtourism and short-term rental custom that had threatened to render life in the core neighborhoods of Barri Gòtic and El Raval untenable for locals.[62]

I do not mean to minimize the importance of these and municipalism's other accomplishments in Spain, particularly for those who continue to enjoy them on a daily basis. They are real. But clearly they fall far short of substantiating the claims Bookchin had made for his libertarian municipalism, and neither do they offer anyone much of a recipe for *doing something* about the conditions of the Long Emergency. If one of municipalism's failure modes is outright defeat, then, another is clearly victory of the sort achieved in Barcelona and Madrid: governance hard to distinguish, in the end, from that of a more or less entirely conventional social-democratic administration, lacking most or all of the participatory-deliberative features Bookchin insisted on as essential.

Indeed, the amount of recruitment and translation necessary to contest City Hall almost seems to justify the anarchist critique of the later Bookchin: on the available evidence, it certainly seems that to engage electoral forms of democracy at all is already to be watered down and recuperated, at such a high cost in effort that nobody involved retains enough energy to try again later.

So if we conclude, in the end, that the state is not amenable to being reclaimed in this way, this is not driven by some misguided quest for ideological purity.[63] It's simply pragmatic. By subordinating itself to the conventional rhythms of representative politics—the pendulum swings of sentiment, the tendency of nominally redistributive parties to accommodate local business interests so as to prevent capital flight, the erosion of the tax base and above all the possibility of defeat—the ostensibly mighty municipalist wave of 2015 produced few if any lasting policy accomplishments. Worse yet, there was no wholesale subjectivation, radicalization or activation of the broader public, nor were institutions created or allocated persistent sources of funding during the period in which confluences enjoyed control of the local state.

These sharp lessons suggest that the later Bookchin was wrong, to which there are two possible responses. The first—and in Spain, this is what the Laclauians of Podemos eventually went with—was to argue that local power could not be sustained without the overarching, protective penumbra of the national state, which should therefore be contested robustly through the usual electoral means. Having seen power at the city scale slip through their fingers, activists of this conviction saw no other way to accomplish the counterhegemonic transformation of subjectivity they so desired than by reorganizing themselves to win national elections.

But this seems to neglect the fundamental lesson of defeat at the ballot box: power that is developed through electoral means can evaporate that way, too. Everything you built can be wiped away in a heartbeat, the moment a sufficiently motivated opponent is sworn into office.

Happily, though, there remains another approach to building popular power, one that is less vulnerable to the shifting opinions of the electorate. This is not to say that it is in any way undemocratic: if anything, its interpretation of democracy asks a great deal more of the people than simply showing up to vote every few years. It is in every way less conventional, more interesting and harder to achieve than electoral victory, but ultimately, I think, has much more to teach us about the future. It started from the widespread conviction that to think in terms of the state was already a mistake, in a place called Rojava.

*

There has been a profusion of names for what happened in the breakaway cantons of northern Syria following the 2014 withdrawal of the Damascus regime, and that profusion is frankly bewildering. Roughly contemporaneous, and to all appearances equally authoritative, sources refer in English to the Democratic Federation of Northern and Eastern Syria, or the Federal Democratic System of Northern Syria, or the Autonomous Administration of North and East Syria (AANES). Most of us know it, more simply, as "Rojava."

With a population of somewhere between 2.5 million and 5 million, and persisting in some form from July 2012 to the present, Rojava appears to be modern history's largest-scale and longest-running example of a place where order was achieved in the absence of a state, where decisions of real material consequence were made by ordinary people sitting in assembly.[64]

This is already extraordinary enough. But what is still more extraordinary, and what particularly commends it to us in our time of troubles, is that the people of northern Syria achieved this with their world on fire, amid circumstances of the most terrible devastation. And what is most extraordinary of all is that so little is known about it outside the region, even now. It's hard to credit that the efforts of millions of men and women over a decade or more can simply be made to disappear from history, but this increasingly appears to be the case. If we want to recover the knowledge they won at such a high cost and see what lessons we might be able to learn from their experience, perhaps it's best to simply start from the first weak signals that reached the West.

Starting toward the end of 2014 and picking up speed all through the year that followed, word began to filter out to the outside world that there was something astonishing happening in Kobanê, Afrîn and Cîzire, the three provinces of northeastern Syria. The most improbable stories started to emerge: of an ecosocialist society blossoming on what seemed like the most inhospitable of soil, even amid the all-consuming chaos of an exceedingly brutal civil war; of a revolution "rooted in the theories of Bookchin and the practice of the Zapatistas," and a society sufficiently committed to gender equity that it required every town, village and hamlet to elect male and female co-mayors;[65] of a fierce, all-female militia called the YPJ, which had helped to defeat the puritan jihadis of Daesh in open combat and in so doing rescued tens of thousands of captive Yazidi women from being sold into sexual slavery.

Much as with the movement of the squares, and then Occupy Sandy—but still more so, because it seemed so much more ambitious and larger in scope—each new dispatch from Rojava arrived as an explosive expansion of what felt possible, and you couldn't read the slightest thing about it without wanting to jump and rave for the joy of it all. In an article published just about immediately after crossing back into Turkey, the anthropologist Mick Taussig described the incredulity he felt at what he'd seen in Kobane: "Sometimes words fail you. Names are not enough. Anarchist? Feminist? You have to be kidding."[66]

Since at first blush few places on Earth would appear to be less hospitable to the rise of an ecological, feminist, libertarian-socialist society than this war-scarred wedge of northern Syria, all of this requires a good deal of explanation. In order to place what happened in Rojava in its proper context and understand the process by way of which this miracle came to be, we need to reckon with the singular figure of Abdullah Öcalan and understand how the work of a deeply obscure American thinker came to fructify the thought of a Kurdish rebel languishing in a Turkish jail.

Born in eastern Turkey in a year variously estimated to be 1946, 1947, 1948 or 1949, Öcalan was Kurdish, a member of an ethnic minority distributed in a powerless scatter across the four national territories of Iran, Iraq, Turkey and Syria. At the point at which he co-founded the Kurdish Workers' Party, or PKK, in 1978, Öcalan was by all accounts a fairly conventional Marxist-Leninist and thought of the Kurdish struggle in the terms of national liberation that were common to the era. In this early phase, the declared aim of the PKK was to establish a homeland for the Kurdish people, a Kurdistan on the entirely conventional lines of the Westphalian nation-state.

Outlawed and branded a terrorist organization by the Turkish state, for the next two decades the PKK was forced to operate out of more or less clandestine sanctuaries in Syria, with Öcalan himself reportedly living in a safe house in Damascus for much of the period. Following his CIA-facilitated 1999 capture in Nairobi, however, Öcalan was spirited away to the Turkish prison-island of İmralı in the Sea of Marmara, where he remains imprisoned as of this writing, and this is the moment at which everything began to tilt.[67]

Spared execution only by virtue of Turkey's hopes for eventual accession to the European Union and denied access to his lawyers for more than a decade now, he has remained on the heavily guarded island fortress in all but total isolation. In the interest of allowing him to prepare an adequate legal defense, though, his jailers did grant the prisoner access to books—"hundreds," including works by Braudel, Foucault, the Zapatistas' Subcomandante Marcos and the midcentury German feminist and sociologist Maria Mies.[68] And among those hundreds of titles were some written by Murray Bookchin.

There is no public account of just how Bookchin's writing got to Öcalan in the first place, or which books specifically were part of the tranche he had access to; the only one mentioned by name in the correspondence between the two is the 1992 *Urbanization without Cities*.[69] The entire matter remains something of a puzzlement: again, Bookchin was hardly top-of-mind in radical circles in 1999, and indeed, Bookchin himself appears to have been somewhat mystified by the development. (His daughter Debbie, a prominent municipalist activist in her own right, relates that upon receiving correspondence from the jailed PKK leader, her then eighty-three year-old father turned to her in evident bemusement: "Apparently the Kurds have been reading my work and are trying to implement my ideas."[70])

Yet to hear Öcalan tell it in his introduction to *Democratic Confederalism*, it was these works that guided his pivot from garden-variety Marxist-Leninism to the confirmed antistatist he became.[71] If the connection between Bookchin's thought and the actually-existing new municipalism of 2014 and thereafter was somewhat cloudy, in Rojava the influence was direct and unambiguous.[72]

It must be said that *Democratic Confederalism* breaks no particularly new ground intellectually, but that is not to detract from its considerable merits as a work of synthesis. Öcalan, in essence, caught Bookchin at a point in his development before he had renounced anarchism, and took him at his word. It's this antipathy to the form of the nation-state that underlies Öcalan's striking refusal to call for the establishment of a "free Kurdistan" and instead work toward the development of a confederal, nonstate society.

More strikingly still, his writings unhesitatingly locate the origin of all oppression in the gender relation, arguing that neither social justice nor ecological balance will ever be possible until women collectively claim the power denied to them through the past several thousand years of patriarchy. This, indeed, was so central to his thought that "the fundamental principle of democratic socialism inside the Kurdish freedom movement is referred to as 'killing the male.'"[73]

This marked turn away from Marxist orthodoxy led Öcalan to reject the idea of a "necessary passage through stages of [historical] development" and to dedicate himself rather to the project of building "radical democracy in the here-and-now."[74] Having already reorganized the PKK to counter its increasing centralism and bureaucracy, starting in the 1990s, he now proceeded to imagine what an entire society might look like if subjected to the same sort of transformation.[75] Based on his reading of Bookchin, Öcalan concluded,

> A free life cannot be established by using the same tools that are used to enslave society, nature, women, and everyone else ... [P]ower and state structures must be totally replaced with entirely different methods, and we should not, as many revolutions have done in the past, fall into the temptation

of using the very weapons of the system that would corrupt
our revolutionary goals.

Öcalan proclaimed the democratic confederal system at
Newroz, Kurdish New Year, 2005, initially giving it the unfortu-
nate (and swiftly rethought) name Koma Komalên Kurdistan.[76]

What is proclaimed, however, does not just automatically
come to pass, and the establishment of the nonstate Kurdish
society Öcalan dreamed of had to wait for the necessary conditions to come into being. Those conditions arose, for better
or worse, amid what is by common reckoning among the
bloodiest and most bitter of all contemporary conflicts: the
civil war that broke out in Syria in 2011.

For those not already immersed in the region's shifting political, religious and ethnolinguistic crosscurrents, this chaotic,
fractally complex, multi-way struggle can be almost impossible
to understand. In its roughest outlines, though, the civil war
pitted the nominally Ba'athist, ethnically Arab Assad regime
in Damascus, supported and supplied to this day by Russia,
against a "Free Syrian Army" supported by Turkey; the jihadi
Salafists of Daesh (better known in the West as the Islamic
State of Iraq and Syria, or ISIS); and a Kurdish-led coalition
eventually organized as the Syrian Democratic Forces, or SDF.
By the end of 2011, the progress of these multiple insurgencies forced the Assad regime to triage its remaining resources,
contracting to the rump regions where it felt itself to be on
firm ground. This very much excluded the country's northern
tier, where the Kurdish rebels increasingly demonstrated that
they could capture and hold territory—and it left Daesh their
primary antagonist.

Known in the West primarily for a series of gruesome decapitation videos and equipped with scriptural justification for an
extensive armature of practices that included ethnic cleansing,
slavery and the establishment of rape camps, Daesh made a
highly clarifying foe for the nascent Rojavan revolution. The
recruitment pitch seems obvious, most particularly for the

region's women, faced with a choice between forced "marriage" to a Salafist slaver or taking up arms and throwing in with the autonomous, all-female militia of the SDF, the Women's Protection Units, or YPJ. The ranks of the YPJ swelled.

At Mt. Sinjar on the Iraqi border, where Daesh had slaughtered entire Yazidi villages and hounded tens of thousands of survivors into the baking hills, and then during the 2014–15 siege of Kobanê, the Kurdish-led coalition revealed itself to be an effective fighting force. Supported by United States airdrops of weaponry and supplies, as well as US airstrikes in direct support of combat operations, the combined militias drove Daesh from Kobane by late January 2015, smashing its fighting formations and setting the survivors to disorganized flight.

The ground was now clear for the transformation that Öcalan had first committed the PKK to at Newroz 2005. In the three cantons of Kobanê, Afrîn and Cîzire, this took the form of an umbrella Movement for a Democratic Society, known by its Kurdish acronym TEV-DEM, and a series of institutional innovations that drove the practice of democratic confederalism down to the hamlet level.

What eventually became clear in the months that followed was that Democratic Autonomy, the theory of collective life Öcalan had derived from his reading of Bookchin, had been operationalized in Rojava and somehow made real at the largest scale. Instead of an ethno-national homeland, what the insurgent Kurds of northern Syria had set themselves to building was a society without a government, built on autonomous cantons and neighborhood assemblies and dedicated to gender equity and repair of the ecosystem.

In the West, such ideas tend, still, to be regarded as the province of deeply unserious people—"luxury beliefs" only suitable for the spoiled young, or others privileged enough not to know the pressures of exigency. In Rojava, they were put into concrete practice, often by people for whom privilege might mean having an intact roof on the building in which they were sleeping that night. "I don't know if you will believe me when I say I could physically feel the revolution," said the sociologist Dilar Dirik, upon her arrival:

> "How does one feel freedom on a body?," you may rightfully ask. But ... as soon as I stepped on Rojavan soil, suddenly, I breathed freely for the first time in my life. And though I found myself in one of the most dangerous places in the world, I felt safer than ever.[77]

Dirik was not alone in feeling that the people of northern Syria had achieved something exceptional. To paraphrase Sartre's famous comments about Che Guevara, the autonomous citizens of this new Rojava—and especially those fighting in the ranks of the Kurdish militias, the YPG and YPJ—struck me from the moment I first read about them as the most fully realized human beings of our time. As revealed in interview after interview, their choices and actions seemed fully aligned with their beliefs, in a way that very few of us ever get to experience.[78] Their understanding of domination and what it requires of those who would unwind it was direct, complete, unclouded. And despite the brutality of their war and the sorrow of their circumstances, it was hard for me not to envy them a little. They had been beset by something terrible, and they were *doing something* about it. Beyond the general inspiration of knowing that such things are still possible, it's this specific quality of having been forged under maximum pressure that commends Rojava to us now as a guide to fruitful conduct in the Long Emergency.

Rojava made good on Bookchin's proposal that larger polities be divided into political units compact enough that they might be governed effectively in regular, face-to-face assembly. This step appears to have been taken on pragmatic grounds, after the neighborhood councils that had initially been established proved unable to contain everyone who wanted to join them. The sense that this sudden clamor to participate was the irresistible upwelling of something far too long suppressed is palpable, even through secondhand accounts:

By the spring of 2012, hundreds of thousands of people were flocking to the neighborhood meetings, eager to participate, in numbers far greater than the venues could accommodate ... Clearly the neighborhood unit was just too large. So to allow all residents to represent and organize themselves, the [revolutionary administration] created a new level in the cities' council structure: the commune, at the level of the residential street.[79]

The commune completed the architecture of open, democratic decision bodies operating at every scale of Rojavan public life, from each canton itself down to each cluster of households. "Decentralized administration and differing needs and circumstances between the three cantons" meant that the details of its implementation have varied over time and from place to place across the AANES, but some suggestive numbers can be offered.

The city of Qamişlo, for example, was initially divided into six districts, each of which was further subdivided into 18 communes of 300 residents apiece; in the countryside, a single commune might suffice for a whole village.[80] By 2016, there were some 530 communes in Afrîn, and 620 in Cizîre.[81] These units became the basic cell of the Rojavan revolution, simultaneously its fundamental enabling condition and its message.

In principle, each commune organized under TEV-DEM was supposed to be relatively self-sufficient, hosting a production cooperative that generated enough to provide for its own needs as well as affording some degree of trade between neighbors. Under this system, it was the commune's general assembly that apportioned the necessities of life among residents—fuel, bread and so on—and also where decisions about the day-to-day running of the community were made.[82]

Each commune was also furnished, wherever possible, with a range of committees corresponding with the administrative functions of a city government, from the ideology committee, which handled the operation of educational institutions, to the peace committee, charged with the maintenance of public safety. In scale and function, these were roughly parallel to the neighborhood assembly working groups of Spanish municipalism. They were, however, able to achieve what the working groups could not—not merely offering neighbors a venue in which they could make decisions for themselves but actually furnishing them with the tools necessary to enact the results.

The commune structure allowed Rojava a degree of creativity in the management of everyday challenges that exceeded anything Bookchin had imagined, or for that matter anything ever deployed at scale in the West. There were three particular features of Democratic Autonomy that seem as though they were significantly enhanced by the system of local assemblies: its centering of women's voices; its pursuit of justice, both civil and criminal; and its ability to integrate the disparate, mutually wary ethnic and religious communities of Syria's northern tier.

Taken together with its antistatism, it is the deep commitment to feminism that gave the Rojavan experiment much of its shimmeringly improbable character (and in turn furnished the Western media with their most enduring image of Rojava, the fighters of the YPJ).

I have never come across a fully satisfactory explanation as to just how and why the commitment to gender equity became so deeply entwined with the Kurdish revolution. The equality of women seems to have been there all along, as both abstract value and practical method, informing all phases of the PKK's struggle since at least the 1987 founding of its first all-female body, the Union of the Patriotic Women of Kurdistan (YJWK). Even beyond this, though, as Dilar Dirik makes clear in her invaluable study *The Kurdish Women's Movement*, everything we have come to understand as "Rojava" would be unthinkable without accounting for the utter centrality it placed upon women's voices, perspectives and experiences of the world.[83]

The Rojavan theory of feminism is called "jineology," from *jin*, the Kurdish for "woman," and for better or worse, in practice it follows tenets first laid out by Öcalan in his 2003 manifesto, *The Sociology of Freedom*.[84] These were predicated on both a fairly traditional gender binary and a comparable degree of essentialism, Öcalan holding that women were "biologically more compassionate and empathic than men, had more 'emotional intelligence' and were closer to nature."[85] If it is bracing enough to read a political figure with such widespread influence opine that "a movement for woman's freedom should strive for anti-hierarchical and non-statist political formations," it is just as disappointing to read in the same breath that this is "because hierarchy and statism are not easily compatible with woman's nature."[86]

It is fair to wonder whether any jineology framed in this way can easily accommodate the post-Butlerian understandings of gender current on the Western left. But Öcalan is not Rojava, and jineology as it was interpreted by Rojavan women inclined away from such raw essentialism: Dorşîn Akîf, an instructor at the Women's Academy in the Cîzire town of Rimêlan, explained in 2015 that "Concepts of men and women aren't biologistic—we're against that ... Of course we believe that gender is socially constructed."[87] (Even friendly Western observers may not have grasped the depth of thought often involved in the day-to-day working-out of jineology, though, prevented by their own prejudice from seeing its sophistication. As the late David Graeber put it, "It never occurs to them that people in Kurdistan might be reading Judith Butler too."[88])

Whatever its weaknesses as theory, jineology was hugely effective in practice. The mixed TEV-DEM communes implemented "the feminization of politics" rather directly, in the form of the distinctive dual-mayor structure, the mandate that each committee be at least 40 percent composed of women, and above all in the mass participation of women in direct self-determination. But Rojavan women also had access to their own dedicated communes, organized under the auspices of the Rojava-wide confederation of women's organizations Kongra Star, and these went further still.[89] If jineology figured women as "the oldest colony," the reorganization of women's life around their own communes can be understood in part as a literal process of decolonization, ejecting the oppressor from the territory it had so long exploited and undertaking the reclamation of an all-but-forgotten sovereignty.[90]

Parallel, women-only governance structures were set up by Kongra Star in each commune, with veto power over any decision that bore on the girls and women within their ambit. Participation in these councils was high, on average fluctuating between 50 and 70 percent, and in some neighborhoods regularly reached 100 percent of the adult female population.[91] Kongra Star also sponsored the establishment of a Mala Jin, or House of Women, in each district, as both an institution and a physical "place where women can turn for assistance, support, mediation, advice, and protection."[92]

But it was the assemblies where the real alchemy happened. Their invitation to discuss, debate and decide transformed what had been strictly private, familial affairs—often enough hidden out of a misplaced sense of shame—into matters of public concern, whose resolution the whole community was thereafter accountable for. The widely circulated images of fiery young YPJ fighters provided the world with one image of Rojavan women no longer willing to bear the yoke of patriarchal oppression in any of its aspects and prepared to defend their bodily autonomy at all costs.[93] The women's assemblies gave it another. These images were not nearly as widely reproduced, but what they depict is in its own way every bit as vivid and moving: headscarfed women, generally a few years older than their opposite numbers in the YPJ, gathered by the dozen in their cheap Chinese Monoblocs in one dusty courtyard after another, visibly determined to assert themselves as the agents and protagonists of their own lives.

The commune structure also lay at the heart of the Rojavan approach to public safety and the resolution of conflict.

In most larger Rojavan population centers, there was an armed security formation called the Aşayîs, which along with responsibility for countering jihadi or Turkish attempts at sabotage took on some of the functions of police; as "many" residents frankly explained their situation in 2014, "without the Aşayîs, none of us could live here."[94] But wherever possible, both disputes between neighbors and more serious breaches of public order were handled locally and consensually, through the mediation of peace committees. Katherine Finn, an Irish barrister who observed the Rojavan justice system in operation in May 2018, noted that this "legal system mirrors the political structure, which is to say that there are fora for resolution of legal problems from street level upwards."[95]

At the most local level, peace committees were composed of anywhere between five and ten members elected from among the residents of a commune, with the usual provision that at least 40 percent of them be women. (In the parallel women's committees organized under Kongra Star, specifically charged with responsibility for domestic and other forms of patriarchal violence, they were entirely composed of women.) These were empowered to investigate and redress whatever breaches of the peace arose in their commune's immediate locale. Their basic tool was mediation.

In such a mediation process, the members of the peace committee—none of whom needed to be legally qualified, many of whom remained untrained by anything except experience—gathered an alleged perpetrator, their victim and any witnesses in a series of informal conversations, which ordinarily took place in homes or other noninstitutional locations. There they would collectively attempt to determine what had taken place and what, if anything, could be done to repair it. Perhaps the most unfamiliar aspect of this is that it does not rely upon the adversarial framing common to Western systems of jurisprudence, in either common-law or Napoleonic varieties: there is neither prosecutor nor defense. The emphasis is placed, rather, on consensus and on a collaborative search for measures of redress and rehabilitation that can be agreed to by all parties.

The range of measures for redress available to peace committees was both extensive and creative. It included imprisonment, as a last resort, but more often involved a range of sanctions tailored to the specific situation, most of which were aimed at keeping the offender in the community in some way. These included

> a period of education, lasting until the trainers are convinced that the person has changed; work in a cooperative or public service; exclusion from the commune; social isolation—for some people the hardest [punishment] of all; boycott, if the convicted person has a shop; temporary relocation to another neighborhood; and exclusion from some public rights.[96]

Beyond its moral decency, this desire to avoid imprisonment wherever possible speaks to one of the key benefits of this sort of restorative practice for collective resilience: when an offender can be rehabilitated locally, the community retains access to their energy and whatever skills they might have to offer, and the fabric of family and neighborly relations remains to a greater or lesser degree intact.

Should the members of a commune- or neighborhood-level peace committee for whatever reason not be able to achieve agreement, they were able to invoke a larger-scale form of public safety administration, known as the "justice platform." These convened anywhere up to 300 people to hear cases, drawn from "related communes and councils, civil society organizations [and] social movements," and were considered to be the final arbiter short of the formal court system.[97] Due to their size, these more often resorted to a majority-vote-decision rule than the strict pursuit of consensus, but the spirit in which proceedings were conducted was the same: the search for a resolution that all parties could live with. This is the assembly writ large—the assembly with real dispositive power over life, chartered and undertaken with all the high seriousness of any courtroom anywhere.

The turn to such relatively informal methods of jurisprudence wasn't simply an artifact of the civil war, some field expedient turned to out of desperation. As with jineology, the commitment to restorative justice precedes the revolution in Rojava, and its techniques had been practiced in Kurdish communities on both sides of the Turkish-Syrian border for many years. In 2011, a member of the legal committee in the Kurdish-majority Turkish town of Gewer told a visiting team of German researchers that, under Democratic Autonomy as it was practiced there, "We don't lock people up and then release them fifteen years later. Instead we try to effect a fundamental transformation in the person and then reintegrate him."[98] This chimes with the Mala Jin organization's account of its own conflict-resolution work, a decade later: "We build peace in the society, we are neither [civil] nor criminal lawyers. The goal ... is to avoid taking the case to the court."[99]

The AANES was and is by no means a prisonless LeGuinian utopia. It has maintained a prison system throughout its existence, which at one point held some 2,700 civilians and 11,200 Daesh prisoners of war, as well as a far larger network of detention camps for as-yet-untried Daesh fighters and their families.[100] But there does seem to have been a concerted, consistent effort to rethink criminal jurisprudence in such a way as to divert people from ever entering this system. And though, as we've seen, there were police units in Rojavan society, they appear to have conceived of their role differently than any public safety department we're likely to be familiar with.

Graeber gives us a sense of just how differently, in his account of a December 2014 visit to an Asayîs training academy:

> Everyone had to take courses in nonviolent conflict resolution and feminist theory before they were allowed to touch a gun. The co-directors explained to us that their ultimate aim was to give everyone in the country six weeks of police training, so that ultimately, they could eliminate the police.[101]

In the West, police, prison and other institutions of the carceral state maintain such a hegemonic hold over our imagination that we can scarcely even conceive of ways in which the ends of public safety might be pursued that do not make recourse to them. Our experiments with restorative justice are just that: tentative, underfunded, small in scale. As yet, the infrastructure to underwrite a consensual jurisprudence barely exists for us, and it certainly has yet to be embedded in community safety institutions with broad purchase, even given the widespread revulsion with policing that has broken out in the post–Black Lives Matter, post–Sarah Everard moment.

By distinct contrast, Rojava remains the only contemporary polity I know of in which restorative practice was not part of an experimental or diversionary program intended to reduce loads on the conventional criminal justice system. It *was* the system. By distributing the capacity to de-escalate conflict, preserve public order and protect both individuals and communities across the entire social field, Rojavan practice developed ways of securing justice appropriate to a free people, and its methods and insights remain available to call upon in other times and places where there is no state.

Finally, Rojava appears to have devised a social architecture that was, at least in certain times and places, successfully able to recruit participants from a wide variety of Syria's famously fractious factions and communities. In part, this seems to have been due to perceptions among the part of the population that did not throw in with Democratic Autonomy that a better quality of life was being enjoyed by their peers.[102] As a Kurdish Peshmerga fighter not affiliated with the SDF told Dilar Dirik, admiringly, "We see what their table looks like, we see how they eat. They don't own anything for themselves."[103]

But the embrace extended to other religious and ethnic communities, as well: not merely Kurds, that is, but also the Alawite and other Arabs, Armenians, Circassians, Druze, Syriacs, Turkmen and Yazidi living in the three liberated cantons. Although Democratic Autonomy originated among Kurds, in practice its village-level institutions were open, and participation in them seen to be so beneficial, especially for women, that members of other ethnic communities either enlisted in them directly or formed their own equivalents. As Silvan Afrin, an economist from the city of Dêrîk, described her local assembly, "It's an open meeting, where people in the neighborhood talk about their problems, and everyone comes, Arabs, Kurds, Syrians, everyone."[104]

It's certainly possible to overstate the case, but this remarkable ability to attract members of communities figured as other, and integrate them individually and collectively in a process of shared self-determination, stands out in a time that otherwise seems hell-bent on atomizing us along every conceivable fracture plane of identity. The lesson appears to be that if you can build something that tangibly improves the scope of agency experienced in daily life, people will flock to it, whatever reservations they may hold.

This is part of what gets missed when Rojava is narrowly understood as a Kurdish achievement. A pattern of life that did, indeed, begin among the Kurds of northern Syria was effective enough in expanding their exercise of freedom that it appealed to members of other communities—and it was expressed through an institutional design that was open and capacious enough to welcome everyone who felt it spoke to them. Another way of describing this is as an insistence that there is no necessary contradiction between the work of survival, the work of care and the work of justice.

For now, all of this seems moot. At some point during a call with Turkish president Recep Tayyip Erdoğan on October 6, 2019, a circuit closed somewhere in the wet congeries that serves Donald Trump as a brain, and under the impression that it was somehow a projection of strength and resolve, he did exactly what Erdoğan wanted of him: he ordered that the US special forces that had hitherto afforded Rojava an umbrella of deterrence be withdrawn. This was an unmistakable signal that the fate of the Kurds was no concern of the United States, and it effectively transformed Syria's northern tier into a free-fire zone.[105] Two days later, under the cover of airstrikes and artillery barrages, Turkish forces rolled across the border, and the Rojavan experiment was effectively nipped in the bud.[106]

Afrîn had already been lost to the Turks at the beginning of 2018. Now much of the remaining territory of the three original cantons was converted to a thirty-kilometer-wide "safe zone" carved up between Turkish and Russian forces, the contours of which were agreed to without any Syrian participation to speak of, at a meeting between Erdoğan and Russian president Vladimir Putin held barely two weeks after the former's call with Trump.[107] A Turkish campaign of assassinations and drone strikes aimed at destabilizing the AANES continues to the present, as well as the hugely destructive diversion of water from the Syrian reach of the Euphrates.[108]

Life in Rojava goes on, as best it can. But hemmed in by great-power games, the realpolitikal necessity of cooperation with the Damascus regime, and the unremitting hostility of its neighbor to the north, Rojava no longer seems to have the organic capacity to continue its development of Democratic Autonomy.

As different as they surely were, and for all the distance that separates the ends they came to, the throughline that connects new municipalist Spain with revolutionary Rojava consists in people *doing something* about conditions of life they had come to find intolerable. In considering the practical lessons of both, the original insight bound up in Bookchin's social ecology still feels substantially correct: that there is a profound relationship between the microscale and the macro-, between the means of politics and their ends, between ordinary people gathered in assembly to discuss the problems they face and the fate of the ecosphere they belong to.

In Rojava, the popular assembly finally surpassed the "moral functions" it had been limited to at its maximum extent in municipalist Spain, and opened at last onto actual power. In the apportionment of daily necessities, in the restorative work of the peace committees, in the development of women's capacities, it was the venue in which questions of real consequence for everyday life were decided. But this appears to have been possible only because of the power vacuum left by the withdrawal of the Syrian state, amid the devastation and anguish of civil war. There was in practical terms no government in northern Syria following the Assadists' withdrawal to Damascus and, until the establishment of the councils, very little in the way of functioning governance, either.[109] And this meant that the abstractions of Öcalan's *Democratic Confederalism* could be translated into a set of facts on the ground with relatively little in the way of slippage.

What happened in Rojava during the years immediately thereafter is still the preeminent example of what people do to care for themselves when the emergency in their lives becomes permanent. Its power to inspire remains undiminished. But if circumstances amounting to abject state failure are the sole material conditions under which anything like Democratic Autonomy becomes possible, it may not be a practically useful guide to surviving the particular future we face. Until and unless we experience that failure for ourselves—and, inshallah, nobody again ever should have to face what the Syrian people have endured—the Rojavan experience may not offer us much insight into action we can take in our own circumstances.

We still need a way of caring for ourselves that is true to the possibilities and constraints of our own situation, that can be put into practice around and in the shadow of the state (as well as outside it entirely, should that come to pass). We still need to discover a way of organizing collective power that does not rely upon the shifting winds of electoral sentiment, that lets people establish meaningful control over resource by themselves and for themselves, without waiting for the approval of anyone else.

I am convinced that, with its conceptual architecture of Communalism, confederalism and libertarian municipalism, social ecology is a strong part of the answer to these questions. But Bookchin devised this body of thought at a time when the planetary crisis had not yet advanced to a critical stage. In the terms we would use now, it was a strategy of mitigation, intended to drive the decarbonization of production and therefore help to maintain Earth systems within their safe operating limits.

In our moment, those systems have already exceeded the parameters of their normal variation—the bounds they've fluctuated within for all the time since the Eemian interglacial period 125,000 years ago. The ecosphere, by definition, no longer operates in the way it has for much of the time we have walked the planet. The time for mitigation has passed. So we now need to weigh a question Bookchin never had to consider: Can practices inspired by his social ecology and Communalism function as strategies of *adaptation*? We need to discover if, and how, they might be translated into terms we can use, and whether they are tools we can rely upon as we make our way together amid the desperate seasons of this harsh new world.

4

Beyond Hope

And so we find ourselves at a moment of decision. What can we do now, to make our way through the terrifying set of conditions we've inherited? What choices are available to us?

We can buy less, and that more locally, in the hope that in aggregating and responding to our purchase signals, the market will commit itself, permanently and worldwide, to a low-carbon production pathway.

We can vote, in the hope of electing legislatures and governments committed to real climate action and able to see their policies enacted as binding law.

We can protest, in the hope that legislators will note and heed the will of their constituents, and that governments and transnational bodies can be pushed toward a more aggressive defense of the planet, whether they were elected or not.

We can engage in civil disobedience, in the hope that we can convince enough of our fellow citizens of the lateness of the hour, and that they, too, will be motivated to *do something*.

We can engage in the sabotage of extractive industries, in the hope that their calculus of return on investment can be shifted, and that shareholders will tire of plundering the Earth for so little in the way of gain.

We can work toward the revolutionary seizure of power, in the hope that we will succeed in time to take meaningful action on climate, and that our success will inspire other would-be insurgents to undertake and accomplish the same, everywhere.

We can entrust our fate to technical means, in the hope that someone somewhere will invent a way of safely decarbonizing the atmosphere, or reflecting the sun's heat back to space, or stabilizing the ice sheets where they are, or really all of that.

Each of us is free to commit to any of these courses of action, or—at the risk of some incoherence—even all of them at once. They are all based on a self-consistent theory of change of one sort or another. But despite their superficial differences, all of these strategies share some deep qualities in common. They are all indirect: they leave you moored in your life, standing by, doing nothing to develop your own capacities. They act with delayed effect: however long they take to work, we can be reasonably sure that it is not soon enough. They are wildly contingent on the coordinated efforts of others, depending on the energy, conviction and incorruptibility of human beings beyond our reach or ability to influence, and their capacity to cooperate with one another at scale.

Finally, there's no guarantee that any of them will *work* or even produce any measurable results at all. You could invest every iota of your life energy in any of these strategies for change for the rest of your days on Earth and move the needle on climate not at all.

This leaves us with one final possibility. We can *act*—directly, immediately, locally, without waiting for the state or any other institution to undertake our defense. What might that look like?

In her wonderful social history of squatting on New York's Lower East Side, *Ours to Lose*, Amy Starecheski tells the story of the electricity-generating stationary bicycle set up on the sidewalk outside C-Squat on Avenue C, which supplied power to a bank of phone chargers during the extended outages that followed Superstorm Sandy.[1] The entire community gathered around the chargers, at first simply to top up their phones, but later simply because that's where the people were. Over these days and weeks, the sidewalk in front of C-Squat was the most obvious place for people experiencing a sharp, sudden disruption of their way of life to seek out useful information, the comfort of fellowship and vital material support.

Here in microcosm is a model for the kind of community infrastructure we will need to see us through the Long Emergency: when the grid goes down or the water from the pipes isn't safe to drink, there ought to be a place close at hand where we can attend to these material needs ... that is *also* a place where we might seek the strength, insight and reassurance of others in the same straits.

As the unfolding reality of Earth system collapse increasingly intersects with the organized abandonment of our communities, and the complex systems we rely upon for the maintenance of everyday life prove to be far more fragile and contingent than we'd ever understood them to be, many of us will have more and more need of settings like this. What I believe our troubled times now ask of us is that we be more conscious and purposive about creating them in our communities—each one provisioned against the hour of maximum need and linked with others in a loose, confederal network. I call them "Lifehouses."

The fundamental idea of the Lifehouse is that there should be a place in every three- or four-city-block radius where you can charge your phone when the power's down everywhere else, draw drinking water when the supply from the mains is for whatever reason untrustworthy, gather with your neighbors to discuss matters of common concern, organize reliable childcare, borrow tools it doesn't make sense for any one household to own individually and so on—and that *these can and should be one and the same place*. As a foundation for collective resourcefulness, the Lifehouse is a practical implementation of the values we've spent this book exploring.

There's a kind of positive externality that emerges from organizing things in this way, as well. As we've seen, one of the problems that always vexes those of us who believe in the assembly, and similar deeply participatory ways of managing our communities, is that these types of deliberation are often a hard sell. Most of us are exhausted, for starters. Our lives already hem us in with obligations and prior commitments, situations that require our presence and undivided attention.

We may not always have the energy or the wherewithal to travel very far to "participate," even if we're convinced in the abstract of the value of doing so. If the place of assembly is right in our immediate neighborhood, though? And we happen to be going there *anyway*, to charge a phone, pick up the kids, return a borrowed dehumidifier, or simply seek shelter from the heat? Then the odds that any one of us will get meaningfully involved in the stewardship of collective services increases considerably.

Just like the phone chargers on the table outside C-Squat, think of the infrastructural provisions as the "killer app": the compelling proposition that pulls people into the Lifehouse. But the deep value is in the other voices we encounter there.

Lifehouses would be most useful if we thought of them as places to help us ride out the depredations of neoliberal austerity *now*, as well as the storms to come. This means furnishing every cluster of a hundred or so households with access to a structure that's been fitted out as a shelter for those displaced from their homes, a storehouse for emergency food stocks and a heating-and-cooling center for the physically vulnerable. It should be able to purify enough drinking water, and generate enough electric power, to support the surrounding neighborhood when the ordinary sources of supply become unreliable. And it should be staffed, on a 24/7 basis, by volunteers who know the neighborhood and its residents well and have a developed sense for the matters that concern them most.

That way, when the moment strikes, there's no need to organize makeshift distribution sites like the tent in Malik Rahim's driveway, or hope that the parish church has a rector sympathetic enough to offer up their space. Both the physical facilities and the social networks to support a robust local mutual care effort are already in place. Indeed, that care effort is at this point the merest extension or intensification of what people are already doing in their everyday lives.

The value of such a place extends past the material to the social, psychic and affective. If a Lifehouse can be somewhere to gather and purify rainwater, the nexus of a solar-powered neighborhood microgrid and a place to grow vegetables, it can also be a base for other services and methods of self-provision —a community workshop, a drop-in center for young people or the elderly and a place for peer-to-peer modes of care like the "hologram" Cassie Thornton derived from her experience of the Greek solidarity clinics to latch on. It can be all those things at once, provisioned and run by the people living in its catchment area.

If mutual care needs a site, and so does collective power, then that site should draw out and strengthen the connections between these ways of being in the world.

It is imperative in this that we avoid any suggestion of planning or pre-defining something that must emerge organically from people's own priorities and decisions. *Everything* important about this idea must be worked out in practice, in the light of local experiences, local struggles and local values. But in what follows, I'd nevertheless like to set out some of my own thoughts about the things a Lifehouse ought to do and be.

At the outset, though, I should probably set some expectations about what Lifehouses *cannot* achieve.

It's clear even in these early days of the Long Emergency that the scale of devastation involved in many climate-driven events will often be so extreme that no community hub will be able hold its own. There is no suggestion here that (for example) any facility will help a community survive sustained wet-bulb temperatures above 35°C (95°F) if it is unable to maintain its own cooling, or shelter people from the total destruction of a runaway wildfire, or do anything at all for them if it is submerged beneath rising floodwaters.

Not every community Lifehouse, further, will be able to provide for each and every circumstance it might be confronted with. It's obviously hard to purify enough rainwater to drink when there hasn't been a drop of precipitation for months, or to grow anything unaided in soil that's been depleted of its fertility over decades. However resourceful people may be, there will inevitably be times that they need tools, medicines or equipment that simply cannot be procured or produced locally. In part, this is why we cannot imagine the Lifehouse as something that stands alone. Each one needs to be linked with others in some confederal structure, so they can distribute some of their burdens across the network in moments of acute pressure and in this way bear up under what might otherwise be an intolerable load.

But even that fails to address the central reservation some who are otherwise sympathetic to the idea may hold. A Lifehouse, even a large-scale network of Lifehouses, is not the revolution. It cannot directly hold to account any of the actors we know are responsible for our peril. It can do nothing overt to prevent the larger forces of market and state from continuing to dominate the world and in doing so desecrate it. Our commitment to build the Lifehouse may even dovetail uncomfortably with the premise, if not the conclusion, of an argument we know the extractive industries are preparing to foist upon us—that it is too late to stop the planet from heating and therefore that there is little enough sense impeding them in their pursuit of profit. And for this reason alone, the idea will not be acceptable to many who think of themselves as belonging to the progressive tradition. All a Lifehouse can ever do is give people a space in which they might realize a vision of social ecology, tending to themselves and the planet by practicing and experiencing solidarity, mutual care and self-determination.

In the fullness of time, this may itself prove to be a form of slow repair and, should it propagate widely enough, a healing of the damage done. But in any timeframe we will live to see, any Lifehouse will, at best, remain what scholars of these things call a "heterotopia of resistance": a space organized outside, apart from and in opposition to the main currents of a society.[2] Establishing such spaces may or may not help to advance the grander vision of ecological accountability and justice we cherish, but I think we will be very glad to have recourse to them when the moment of need arrives.

It probably does need to be said in so many words, though, that despite the inherently global nature of this crisis, just about everything about the discussion that follows concerns actions we take in our own backyard.

When everything goes sideways, we're largely compelled to make do with the resources in our immediate vicinity. But there's a good argument to be made for continuing to organize and work locally, too. At this most granular scale, it ought to be possible for us to reassert at least some control over our conditions and to witness the results of our efforts.

That "witness" is vital in ways that aren't simply about functionalist assessment. In dark times, we need to be able to see the impact of our actions to keep despair at bay. We need to feel like there's some more or less direct gearing between the choices we make together and the concrete extension of shelter to those in danger. We need, in other words, to feel our power. That only really becomes possible when the questions we are deciding involve things that are close at hand.

If we do want to organize a Lifehouse in our community, the very first question we'll be confronted with is where we intend to house it. It will have to be a place where people can safely gather in numbers, maybe not the assembly of "one-fifth of the total population in a defined geographic area" specified by Cooperation Jackson's Kali Akuno, but not too far short of that, either. Beyond sheltering those people from the elements, it should be able to physically support the services and provisions they require when everything else fails them.

In many neighborhoods, there will often already be a building or physical site that organically serves many of these functions. This is the neighborhood's naturally arising Schelling Point, or node of unconscious coordination.[3] Whether house of worship or union hall, high school gym or public library, it will be where people in the surrounding streets instinctively turn for safety and aid in times of trouble.

For example, consider the 51,000-odd church buildings scattered across England, each of them located at the heart of a town, village or urban parish, and each generally built to abide across the centuries. In a time when the profession of Christian faith is in precipitous decline, many of these buildings have neither an active congregation to care for them nor meaningful links to the lives unfolding all around them. They face abandonment, decrepitude and eventual collapse, even as the human communities they're embedded in still have want of the sanctuary they once offered. Many of these structures would make exceptional Lifehouses—it's easy to imagine them restored to new purpose with solar panels shading the wonky gravestones, and perhaps a cluster of direct air capture units huffing away out back.

Even in places where no such stock of abandoned churches exists, though, there will likely be solid options available for recuperation. Just about every neighborhood that has become a sacrifice zone under the ordinary circumstances of organized abandonment has one or more underutilized structures perfectly suited to use as a Lifehouse. Think of commercial premises that can't be leased profitably, or a school in a catchment area depopulated of school-age children. These structures belong to the category spatial researcher Samaneh Moafi calls "negative commons": having been discarded because they've lost all utility as either capital or the state reckon it, they become available for collective use almost as an afterthought.[4] They are there to be grasped and made use of.

A Lifehouse needn't even be a conventional building per se. In a time of violent and unpredictable hazards, there is some logic to implementing the idea as a cluster of lightweight, rapidly demountable structures like those erected by the radical architectural practice raumlaborberlin on the site of a rainwater retention pond at Berlin's former Tempelhof airport.[5] This complex, Floating University, has been designed to accommodate a wide range of climate conditions. All of the structures that comprise it are built of cheap commodity materials like scaffolding tubes, timber frames, sheet plywood and straw and can be reconfigured very nearly at will as programs and requirements shift.[6] Floating University therefore evolves with the seasons and changing uses and remains able to function as a gathering place whether the ground beneath is fully flooded or parched to the point of cracking. Given even a few days' warning, the components of a Lifehouse organized along these lines might be broken down and moved to a safe location, or even laid by to wait out the danger in suitably hardened storage onsite.

Raising new structures any more substantial than those making up Floating University, though, will become increasingly difficult to justify over the years to come, on the principle that the least damaging building is the one that's already built.[7] The enormous quantity of carbon released into the atmosphere in any conventional construction process offers a very strong argument for reclaiming the structures that already exist, at or close to the psychic heart of the places in which so many of us live, as homes for community resilience hubs. There will, of course, be neighborhoods where there are no such abandoned structures—but these, virtually by definition, will be places where a robust market for land continues to function. Such communities don't have acute need for the things a Lifehouse does. They would appear to already be adequately cared for by the market, and most likely prefer it that way. The rest of us, though? We will increasingly want somewhere we can come together to care for ourselves and for one another, and to decide from among the courses of action available to us.

In some cases, it may be possible for a community to form a special-purpose land trust or the like: some legal instrument that would let it buy a derelict school or house of worship legitimately, refit it as a Lifehouse and build up a reserve fund for the upkeep, maintenance and repair that will surely be necessary. But gaining access to underutilized or abandoned structures, and occupying them over any meaningful period of time, will often mean summoning the courage to operate outside the bounds of law. Elaine Brown explains how this worked for the Black Panthers: "If we wanted to open a clinic, we took over a piece of property, we didn't pay rent. We would run an electrical line from wherever, didn't pay for electricity. We'd go to the hospital and just steal supplies."[8]

I know that many of us struggle with such fearless directness of action, often for excellent reason. There are no upsides to getting your life tangled up with authority, for any of us, and the consequences of having done so can easily drag on for years even where they are not immediately lethal. But the Long Emergency has a way of clarifying the stakes of inaction. The derelict middle school on the avenue is unambiguously worth more *tonight*, as a shelter for bodies at risk, than the land beneath it is to some sovereign wealth fund far across the sea at some abstract time to come. At moments like this, when all that stands between people in desperate need and the possibility of their rescue is a pair of bolt cutters, the moral force and the practical necessity of breaking the law are in complete alignment.[9] All that's required of us is that we summon the courage to act.

The mutual aid slogan has it that "audacity is our capacity."[10] The French Jesuit (and philosopher) Michel de Certeau suggests that the powerless must always "vigilantly make use of the cracks that particular conjunctions open in the surveillance of the proprietary powers," which is really another way of saying the same thing.[11] There's no question that *our* particular conjunction produces the kind of lapses in oversight Certeau is talking about, and will continue to, in near-endless profusion. What we now need to determine is whether they will be wide enough to smuggle our lives through intact.

Being able to draw upon the resources of a properly outfitted Lifehouse has surprisingly deep implications. A community that is able to house, feed and care for its members, furnish them with clean water to drink and generate enough power to heat or cool them will find that it is broadly robust to the consequences of decisions made elsewhere. It is effectively autonomous.

This is not the same thing as autarky, or total self-sufficiency, which is in any event never truly achievable. But a degree of self-reliance in these matters does afford a community significant room for maneuver in a world that is otherwise defined by the constraints it imposes. Become resourceful in these specific ways, and the ability of others to place limits on your freedom of action is sharply circumscribed. You can participate in larger networks or decouple from them at will, without affecting your underlying capacity to provide for your neighbors.

The technical term for this architecture of connection is

"distributed," and it's the least familiar of the three basic ways to organize a network.[12]

We all know what *centralized* institutions look like. From schools to hospitals to companies large and small, they're all around us, in both public and private spheres, and have been all our lives. In a centralized architecture, all information flow between one local node and another is forced to travel through a controlling authority that sits at the hub of the network. This is the way hierarchical, command-and-control organizations like FEMA or the Red Cross are structured, and it makes them very slow. Information from elements at the network edge has to travel all the way to the center before decisions about posture and commitment can be reached. As we saw with the Black Panthers, this kind of network topography is acutely vulnerable to a decapitation attack: destroy the central node, and all of the others are cut off from one another, utterly unable to learn anything about another's condition or coordinate their activity in any other way. (We say of such networks that they have a "single point of failure.")

The obvious alternative to a centralized organizational structure might seem to be one that is *decentralized*, and this is certainly the term that's most often used in political contexts to describe nonhierarchical arrangements of power. But there's some ambiguity in this, stemming from the different ways in which network theorists and people who talk about politics use language. Not all decentralized networks preserve the features of robustness, resiliency and local autonomy that best suit a federation of Lifehouses.

In hard times, then, what we're really after is a *distributed* structure, in which independent capacity and decision-making authority reside in every local node in the network, and each is free to connect with any or all of the others, on a horizontal, peer-to-peer basis.

This means that nobody involved ever has to wait for guidance or permission from above to act: when emergent conditions arise, people have all the tools, skills and resources they need to respond locally. It's not particularly efficient: in fact, there is by definition maximum redundancy and duplication of effort in a network of this sort. But there is no single point of failure. Individual nodes or the communication links between them can be disrupted or even destroyed, without damaging any other node or the resilience of the network as a whole. This quality makes a distributed topology very well suited to a time of widespread volatility, and it's what commends it to us for the organization of our Lifehouse network.

What if something happens to the Lifehouse itself, though? Why not distribute its functions around the neighborhood, so there's no single point of failure? It's an excellent point, and people may want to consider doing just that. But there does come a moment at which the benefits of dispersion are outweighed by its disadvantages, and in this case the upsides of being together feel like they are worth the risk of concentrating our life-critical assets in one place.

The seemingly abstract distinction between the various kinds of network, and the implications of each for local autonomy, become much easier to understand when we consider a concrete case, like the supply of electric power. This is the most basic infrastructural good a Lifehouse will need to furnish—not just to run a bank of phone chargers, like the bike outside C-Squat, but to maintain the refrigeration of food, the operation of medical devices and, still more so, the relatively narrow range of conditions in which bodies can be sheltered from climatic extremes outside.

Technically, the North American power grid is decentralized. There are only indirect links between the two major and three minor interconnections that constitute it, each of which is itself composed of multiple system operators protected by any number of failsafes, cutouts and backups. But at any level experienced by ordinary consumers, the network is a centralized, hub-and-spoke affair. Electricity is generated at one place, far away, and brought to each individual client through an elaborate and vastly reticulated infrastructure of substations, long-distance transmission lines and trunk cabling.

When a single transmission line falls to overload, storm or sabotage, all the clients on the far end of the break are left without power.[13] When the link that gets severed is a true single point of failure, or when more than one cut is involved, the entire regional grid goes down. And when it does, it may be weeks, even months, before power is restored, as some communities learned to their sorrow in the aftermath of hurricanes Katrina, Sandy and María.

For the most part, we only liminally understand just how deeply we rely on stable, continuous electric supply. It's a classic example of an infrastructure that works silently in the background to sustain us and that we never value or even notice until it fails. Let the power be cut, though, and we lose lighting, refrigeration, air conditioning, connectivity and the ability to charge all the devices that constitute the material basis of modern life, all at once. The second-order effects of a power outage for other infrastructures can be every bit as severe and just as long-lasting: after 2017's Hurricane María, for example, 87.9 percent of the cell towers in Puerto Rico remained offline for three weeks or more.[14]

This makes it essential that power supply to a Lifehouse be robust to the kind of grid failure that now occurs routinely in the wake of major weather events. The classic solution is for each site that requires uninterrupted electric service to purchase and run its own gasoline- or diesel-fueled generators instead of relying upon mains power from the grid. When Common Ground realized that it was "vital to keep radios, fans and lights on in the hot days and nights" of a Louisiana autumn, for example, it was just such generators that allowed them to keep their operations going.[15] (Demonstrating that what distinguishes a decentralized from a distributed network is often a matter of scale and perspective, each generator was itself the hub of a local constellation: Common Ground "would set one up in one backyard and run extension cords to multiple houses.")

Generators may well have been "the only sources of power for months in the Seventh and Ninth Wards, as well as the coastal areas" hit hardest by Katrina (as indeed they were for weeks in those parts of the New York area struck hardest by Sandy, or much of Puerto Rico after María). And they are, unquestionably, a distributed power solution that liberates anyone who has one from total reliance on the grid. But as a way to power the activities of a Lifehouse, generators are far from ideal. Each one is a point source of pollution. All but the most recent models are disruptively loud. They're not designed to operate continuously over days or weeks. Above all, they depend on reliable access to stocks of refined fuel, which is the true brake on their ability to underwrite local autonomy.

Here is where distributed, renewable power sources like solar, wind and small-scale hydro truly come into their own. These are quiet enough for people to live and work in close proximity to them—in the case of photovoltaics, they are all but silent. They are nonpolluting and make no further contribution to emissions once built and installed. But most important, their fuel supply cannot be disrupted or deliberately interdicted. This makes renewables ideal as measures of last resort, as was seen during the savage self-destruction of Yugoslavia in the 1990s, when the residents of the besieged Bosnian town of Goražde built hydroelectric generators from salvaged car alternators and washing-machine drums; dropped into the Drina River to spin, these guaranteed a modest flow of current, sufficient anyway to charge batteries.[16] This quality of robustness will prove essential in the extended volatility of the Long Emergency.

Ideally, then, each Lifehouse serves as the hub of a local microgrid, linking together some combination of solar panels, wind turbines and micro- or pico-hydro generators scattered across the neighborhood, sited wherever they make the most sense.[17] This wouldn't have to shoulder all the same burdens as a permanent off-grid installation but merely generate enough supply to support environmental control, refrigeration and connectivity at times when the grid was unavailable. The model here would be the forty-one microgrids Resilient Power Puerto Rico installed on the island between 2017 and 2022, each one stewarded by a local mutual aid organization and collectively responsible for "over 200 kW of power generation now managed through community leadership."[18]

Resilient Power's broader effort follows in the footsteps of Casa Pueblo in Adjuntas, a democratically run community organization whose headquarters has been solar-powered since 1999. When María knocked out the power in Adjuntas, Casa Pueblo's solar microgrid survived fully intact, allowing the headquarters building to serve as an "energy oasis" where locals were able to recharge life-critical equipment like respiratory therapy machines, as well as phones or tablets.[19] Here is the most robust, real-world proof of the Lifehouse concept possible: in the midst of calamity, a self-organized, autonomous local group used free power from the sun to shelter and care for those imperiled by the storm and its consequences. The experience of post-María Puerto Rico is unequivocal on this point. Locally and democratically managed microgrids give each community that operates one power over power itself and therefore all the capacity to protect life that flows downstream from it.

If the ability to generate electric power is best distributed down to the neighborhood level, then so is at least some ability to feed people. In ordinary times, we can imagine a Lifehouse operating just like the People's Free Food Program did—or, for that matter, any contemporary community food bank still does—with volunteers hustling up donations of canned food, day-old baked goods and produce past its sell-by date from local merchants. But where the Lifehouse really comes into its own is as a source of collective nourishment when those usual channels of supply are unavailing.

For those who have never experienced real deprivation, it can seem odd to worry much about widespread hunger: if there is one thing late capitalism seems to excel at, it is keeping up a cornucopian flow of cheap calories. But the daily news is full of worrisome signals about the world food supply, even in conditions well short of the 2°C heating regime we currently seem to be headed for by century's end.

In the same week of July 2023, for example, the Modi government banned the export of all varieties of white rice save the basmati that Indians tend not to eat, after record-breaking rains destroyed most of a year's crop, while Russia stepped up its interdiction of the Ukrainian wheat and oilseed supplies some 400 million people worldwide depend on.[20] As improbable and frankly dystopian as it seems, we now genuinely need to consider scenarios in which the staple crops that feed most of humanity have failed, the extended supply chains that bring us the better part of our diet have been amputated by war or embargo, or both of these things are true at once.

Not every community will be equally vulnerable to this kind of supply-chain disruption. But in the existing ecology of places like the UK, food cannot be grown in quantities sufficient to support the full dietary needs of the present population, even using the entire agricultural capacity of the land. What's more, the ability of any urban site to make up for shortfalls in imported food is inherently constrained, hemmed in by poor or contaminated soil, by limited sunlight and above all by insufficient area. So the contribution any Lifehouse will ever be able to make is at best thought of as something supplemental to other sources of supply, even if every flat roof, community garden and allotment available were to be turned over to full-scale production. We will have to be very clever about developing a distributed capacity based on the widest possible variety of high-density production techniques, from vertical farming to aquaponics and fungiculture.

It would be easier if adequate nutrition were simply a matter of providing people with some threshold amount of calories. Worldwide, the minimum daily energy requirement of the human body is typically met through cereal crops—staple grains like wheat, rice and corn—that are straightforward enough to grow in the sort of plots we're contemplating. But protein is equally essential to the maintenance of bodies, and that's somewhat more challenging to produce in dense urban environments.[21]

Self-described "ecomodernists" look to the emergent technology of "precision fermentation" to provide us with the protein our bodies require.[22] They look forward to a day when the land area now dedicated to cattle and poultry operations can be returned to wildness and all our needs can be met by bioreactors racked in clean, low-footprint city-center facilities. At first blush, this scenario seems ideally suited to a world of Lifehouses. But beyond being as yet utterly unproven as a source of palatable protein at scale, precision fermentation is *proprietary* technology—some private actor's intellectual property, to be licensed as the owner sees fit. It is nutrition conceived as tech start-up, leaving enthusiasts no other option than to trust that the Silicon Valley mindset will have better results when applied to industrialized food production than it has in any other context.

A pronounced (and, in my opinion, entirely appropriate) skepticism about this has tended to push people to the opposite extreme. The influential farmer and agroecologist Chris Smaje, for example, argues that the push toward industrial synthesis of food is dangerously wasteful of time we don't have, and that a return to "agrarian localism" is necessary if we want to feed ourselves adequately in the times to come. This would involve a mass flight from the cities and return to the land, where "the work awaiting the new agrarians is clear—growing food and [fiber], building shelter [and] producing a modest livelihood from the local ecological base."[23] Smaje glosses this as a way to "unleash ordinary people and trust them to start developing local food systems in which they make themselves part of a renewable local ecology."[24]

The reason I don't reject Smaje's vision out of hand is the same reason I trust the mutual care efforts we've previously discussed: they both turn on a fundamental faith in our capacity to organize the fulfillment of our needs on our own behalf. But while the approach Smaje recommends certainly ticks more of our boxes—it's labor-intensive, it's based on robust and well-assimilated technologies and it derives all of its necessary inputs of energy from the sun, at zero cost—it's not at all clear that comprehensive deurbanization and a mass return to the land would be achievable anywhere (let alone desirable: this scenario has little enough appeal even for those of us not haunted by visions of being "sent down" in the Cultural Revolution, or of the neo-medieval peasantry grimly working the blasted and barren terrain in the final, awful segment of the 1984 nuclear-war drama *Threads*).[25] I think it's a reasonable bet that whatever else happens, most of us will continue to live in densely settled urban places, even amid the worst conditions of the Long Emergency. And if we're not talking about buying our protein from the precision-fermentation merchants, that means a scenario in which we produce our food either directly, through relatively energy-intensive vertical farming methods, or through exchange with federated agroecological communities in our arable near-hinterlands.

There is, of course, no reason why a Lifehouse might not enjoy close relationships with one or more such farming communities. Recent academic research suggests that some version of this is already achievable—in the United States, for example, 90 percent of the population could feed themselves entirely on crops grown within a hundred miles of where they live, even now.[26] But best of all would be for each Lifehouse to supplement whatever food it might secure through such exchanges with local production, as a hedge against all other eventualities coming to pass.

That this is at all a realistic prospect turns on the possibilities opened up by newly available techniques of vertical farming, which allow growers to cultivate crops indoors, in hydroponic racks that are stacked as densely as space and lighting considerations allow. These are designed to maintain the ideal microclimate for the chosen crop and can yield continuous production cycles year-round—of staple grains, as well as leafy greens and vegetables.

At Tampines Block 146 in Singapore, for example, a variety of rice optimized for vertical-farming conditions has been grown since October 2021.[27] It takes roughly four months to produce each rice crop there, in a six-story structure made of cheap twin-wall plastic and commodity scaffolding racks much like the ones raumlabor used at Floating University. It would be boundlessly unwise to hang too much of our planning for a difficult future on this one pilot installation, but as a proof that calorie crops can be grown under controlled vertical conditions using open-source techniques, the implications for Lifehouse-based indoor agriculture are reassuring.[28]

Again, though, self-reliance means finding ways to produce protein locally, as well as cereal crops or vegetables. The community technology advocate Karl Hess experimented with basement trout farming in the Adams Morgan neighborhood of Washington, DC, in the 1970s. But despite the "five pounds of fish per cubic foot of water" his group managed to produce in a typical setup—each yielding "three tons annually at costs substantially below grocery store prices"—this sort of high-density aquaculture doesn't seem to have caught on.[29]

By contrast, where Hess's group had rejected chickens out of hand as being "too noisy" for city-center contexts, the years since have seen a certain hipster resurgence of interest in backyard coops, and the art of urban chicken-keeping is now well developed. But the options now available extend much further than either trout or chicken. High-density, controlled-environment techniques lend themselves to the production of plant-based, mycological or even insect-derived proteins, which can be cleverly combined in closed-loop ecosystems. The Singapore vertical-farming facility, for example, feeds the biowaste it generates into a local black soldier fly farm, whose protein-rich larvae are in turn used to feed tilapia for human consumption.

More conventional, less energy-intensive agriculture always remains a possibility, as well, wherever the constraints of space, soil quality and sunlight permit. There may even be benefits to combining distributed solar power generation with distributed food production. Not merely do well-placed solar panels not compete with biomass for available sunlight, they offer growing crops the dappled shade that protects them from overheating or desiccation while, for their part, photovoltaic panels derive an efficiency boost from the moist microclimate of growing things.[30]

This allows us to conceive of Lifehouse plots as "agrivoltaic" installations that harness these mutually beneficial qualities for increased agricultural yields and enhanced power output both. A limiting factor here is the continuing widespread availability of solar panels, whose photovoltaic cells are mostly still manufactured in China and come to consumers elsewhere via the same perilously extended supply chains that held up so poorly during COVID-era disruptions.[31]

Growing food has never been easy under any conditions, and crops fail (or simply fail to thrive) for all kinds of reasons, both predictable and unforeseen. In a time strewn with virtually unlimited hazards to agriculture, from soil salinization to violent winds, achieving any meaningful yield to speak of will clearly require massive investments of a community's time and effort. The ultimate justification for Lifehouse-based agriculture, though, consists not in the argument that it is the easiest or most energy-efficient of all possible ways to organize food production—it clearly is not—but that it is one of the few ways that communities might improve their odds of continued access to complex diets when long-distance supply chains collapse.[32]

The prospect is one of a tight, efficient loop: whatever is successfully grown in the beds and racks of a Lifehouse can be offered immediately in the associated co-op or food bank, used in the kitchen to make hot meals with, or perhaps traded with others in the regional network. For Smaje, this may look like just another desperate, rearguard "attempt to rescue a high-energy, high-capital urban consumerism that can't and shouldn't be rescued," albeit one with more of a horizontalist and communitarian spin than is usually the case.[33] I'd prefer to think of it as an attempt to strike some workable balance between the naive techno-optimism of the ecomodernists and the isolationism of rugged-individualist homesteaders—and preferable, in any case, to a scheme centered on the decantation of billions into a countryside as unprepared to greet them as they are to understand it.

And beyond that, there's something inexpressibly wonderful about an environment where things are alive and growing, in a

world that is in so many ways designed for the scaled production of death. As far back as the late 1960s, activist-architects
like Street Farm proposed that cities could be places where a
"profusion of sprouting, breathing, photosynthesizing, living
things surround and entwine human dwellings."[34] There's no
reason why Lifehouses couldn't be devised with this sort of
vision in mind—and in ways that were not possible in any
earlier time, as well. The Street Farmers meant this as a way to
fend off ecocatastrophe, but it also happens to be a reasonable
tactic for enduring it once it's arrived: an intact canopy is a
self-organizing, carbon-negative infrastructure with shading,
temperature-lowering, air-filtering and bioremediating qualities,
as well as a home and thoroughfare for other living things.

If a Lifehouse-based program combined these qualities with
a longer-term restoration of urban soil, via the "do nothing"
agricultural techniques made famous by Masanobu Fukuoka's
book *The One-Straw Revolution*, people under pressure of
ecosystemic collapse might find that they could simultaneously
feed themselves well and care for other forms of life, and leave
the Earth better off for their having done so.[35]

But, perhaps, for the most rudimentary or rigorously natural
forms of agriculture, all of these notions of local energy generation and food production depend crucially on specialized
physical hardware of one sort or another. So the final element
of autonomy any Lifehouse will need to consider is how it
might produce a greater proportion of these material necessities locally. How can we plan for conditions under which the
wind turbines, aquaponics tanks or cargo-bike components so
critical to the community's ability to feed and care for itself
can't simply be ordered off the internet?

One way would be for each community to develop some
capacity for "autonomous production," or what the theorist
Jason Adams glosses as "local production for local use, outside
the bounds of the wage-labor system."[36] In concrete terms, this
turns on access to a workshop furnished with a usefully broad
range of machine tools and equipment, from drill presses to

TIG welders to sewing machines, ideally co-located with other facilities in the Lifehouse itself.

The primary factor preventing a community group from assembling such a workspace from scratch is plainly cost. Even the basic tooling for a digital fabrication studio—say, a laser cutter, a computer numerical control (CNC) milling machine and a few 3D printers—involves expenses that may run well into the tens of thousands of US dollars, and there are very, very few neighborhood groups willing or able to front that kind of money without a clear, immediate, tangible and pressing justification. The maintenance of some abstract capacity for material autonomy is not nearly enough—and of course, by the time the need for autonomy becomes pressing, it may be too late to do anything meaningful to achieve it.

The answer may lie in the volunteer-run workshops that already exist in most big cities, which rather uninvitingly tend to be called "makerspaces," "hackspaces" or "fablabs."[37] The typical makerspace already sports most of the machine tools we're interested in, particularly as regards digital fabrication, and is operated by a membership that's passionate (or in most cases, frankly evangelical) about what can be done with them. Although there aren't nearly enough of these workshops in existence to furnish each neighborhood with its own autonomous production capacity, they do constitute a version of this resource that's available to draw on right now.

Just as important, the global maker community nurtures within its membership the hard-won knowledge of how to use these tools safely, efficiently and well. And that knowledge tends to drive a set of politics that are broadly consonant with the aims of a Lifehouse network. In municipalist Madrid and Barcelona, the so-called "hackers" were key players in the confluences, bringing with them not merely their facility with hardware but all their ideas about the intellectual commons and free access to tools and information.[38]

The instinct for mutual aid runs deep in the community, as well. During COVID, members of makerspace collectives around the world worked long hours to churn out 3D-printed face shields and the low-cost, DIY air-filtration units known as Corsi-Rosenthal boxes.[39] And perhaps most pointedly of all for our purposes, we have the example of an "intercultural fablab" called Habibi.Works "implementing self-aid since August 2016" at the Katsikas refugee camp in northern Greece, where members drawn from the camp's thirty nationalities bring its fabrication capacity to bear on the challenges they face in their lives as asylum seekers.[40] The values of open access, solidarity and self-reliance held by so many in the maker movement make them obvious as prospective partners in any Lifehouse-based production workshop.

The vast enthusiasm for the power and potential of digital fabrication on the part of some makers has occasionally led to a misreading of community needs, or really a failure to engage local people, understand their priorities and place production capacity at their disposal. This was the case in Barcelona in 2013, when academic researchers opened a fablab on the former site of a food bank in the impoverished Ciutat Meridiana district without first having secured any real buy-in on the part of their new neighbors.[41]

It would be an understatement to say this was poorly received: residents of Ciutat Meridiana even briefly occupied the fablab in protest, and it was clear that what they were protesting was the insult to their autonomy every bit as much as it was the loss of their food bank. As the counterexample of Habibi.Works suggests, not nearly every makerspace will be so oblivious to local need or sentiment, but it's reasonable for anyone thinking of setting up such a thing to ask deep questions about just who might constitute the "community" in their "community production workshop."

It's not a bad idea, then, for anyone interested in setting up such a thing to think about how they might open lines of communication with their local makerspace and its membership now—both to explore any natural affinities that might exist and to address questions of access and inclusion. The nascent workshop can only benefit from the insight of those most familiar with these tools and techniques of fabrication, who understand best what they can and cannot do. And with many makerspaces facing perpetual difficulty in organizing accessible commercial space, there may be real benefit in proposing they rehome their activity on the site of a newly opened Lifehouse.

A Lifehouse outfitted in this way will not be able to produce anything particularly elaborate: most of the high-complexity physical artifacts on which any real independence is predicated would exceed the near-term fabrication capabilities of even the best-equipped collective workshop. (Photovoltaic panels are perhaps the most obvious case in point, but there are any number of other examples.) But even the most rudimentary local production capacity will nevertheless help a community secure more of what it needs, in more of the amounts required, for longer into any period of supply-chain disruption. And this would be particularly useful with regard to components needed for the maintenance or repair of other life-critical systems.[42]

The years of techno-utopian hype about digital fabrication technologies like 3D printing have tended to obscure that, at base, these are just relatively simple ways of making relatively complicated things. And in a time of unpredictable access to the material things we rely on, it's this unglamorous, easy-to-overlook wherewithal for autonomous production that will ultimately underwrite any community's capacity for mutual care and the shelter of bodies in need.

There is an additional point that needs to be made about all the technologies a Lifehouse relies upon, whether for generating power, providing for its nourishment, maintaining its own physical capacities, or addressing any other of its needs: that all of these means are themselves vulnerable to entropy and decay. As any number of off-grid homesteaders and back-to-the-land communes have learned the hard way, when such life-critical systems do break down—and they will break down—and the capacity to repair them fully and restore them to service does not exist within the community, the margin of survival becomes very thin indeed.

What is best of all, then, is to rely wherever possible on ways of doing and being that are robust to disruption because they are fundamentally simple and hardy. These are what I call "technologies of permanent recourse." They are tactics developed in and for hard times and circumstances, that broadly remain available to us even under significant stress. They aren't based on finicky high-maintenance components, don't have lots of external dependencies, do not rely on the persistent availability of an extended supply chain and can largely be built up and repaired from those resources we already have ready to hand.

They favor electromechanical means over electronic ones, mechanical means over those, and passive, organic ones wherever feasible, and can therefore tend to be labor-intensive, as opposed to capital-, equipment-, energy- or computation-intensive. They can be turned to surprisingly sophisticated ends, including refrigerating food and filtering enough drinking water for a neighborhood.[43] Above all, they aren't owned by anybody: the methods underlying them are literally common knowledge.

The next best thing, where some particular piece of equipment is required, is for it to be something that can be salvaged from the everyday environment at little or no cost. Common Ground was exemplary in this, from their first lashed-together distribution hub to the UHF radio network they built from gear that "most would consider obsolete junk."[44] But more broadly this is a thread that connects many of the sites and efforts we've considered, from the knock-off Monoblocs that dot the courtyards of Rojava to the cheap scaffolding and commodity plywood that raumlaborberlin uses in its structures.

What commends such artifacts to us in the Lifehouse scenario isn't simply about the benefit we derive by further leveraging the sunk carbon costs of their production, though that is certainly a consideration. It's not even fundamentally about their low cost, ready availability or robustness. It's about a secondary quality that emerges from these primary ones, which we might follow the Roman Catholic priest and social philosopher Ivan Illich in thinking of as "conviviality."[45]

Convivial tools derive a good part of their appeal from the fact that they can be tinkered with. Like an old bicycle or a waterwheel, they can't be damaged too badly by experimenting with them, and at worst, if you should happen to destroy one in an attempt to adapt or modify it, you ought to be able to scavenge others of the same sort and start all over again. Even better, they educate people in how to use them, tending to be organized in modular subsystems that, if not quite self-explanatory, yield a diagram of their functioning to a little patient investigation.

Because tools like these lower the risk of looking foolish, or of wrecking something delicate, expensive and irreplaceable, not simply the technically inclined but a greater proportion of the Lifehouse community will be comfortable engaging with them. And this open and unintimidating quality is what pushes any truly convivial system past formal accessibility toward active invitationality. Under such circumstances, competence with the systems that undergird common life ceases to be a matter of a jealously cultivated exclusivity and is instead broadly distributed throughout the community.

And when the need for maintenance or repair arises on some piece of infrastructural equipment that is *not* convivial, as Illich defined it, let alone based on a technology of permanent recourse, we might put some thought into how we can better leverage the community's existing base of knowledge. Here Karl Hess offered the notion of a *community skills inventory*: a way to compound individual resourcefulness by surfacing it and making it more widely available.[46]

You write code, your neighbor repairs furniture, the woman down the street does a little plumbing—but, as things stand, none of you has any idea of the capabilities that reside right in your immediate vicinity, or in what permutations your skills might be combined. A shared skills inventory repairs this gap in a community's understanding of itself and what its members can do. And better still, it points toward the possibility of cross-training, so the most critical skills are distributed across the entire community, and no one person has to bear the weight of being the only trained medic or mechanic or beekeeper around. In this way a Lifehouse doesn't merely rely on the abilities of the people in its surroundings, but can help to develop them, too.

Equipped in these ways, a Lifehouse community has everything it needs to carry out programs of mutual care and in this way take a first vital step toward self-determination. But the full expression of local autonomy involves the exercise of collective power: each Lifehouse must be free to decide its policies and its trajectory through the world for itself. Following the practice of the earlier movements we've discussed, it seems natural that the means of doing so would be the assembly.

Amid the dashed hopes of those movements, though—from the sputtering-out of 15M, Occupy and the similar Nuit Debout protests in France to the utter wreckage of our dreams for Rojava—the cringe factor clinging to any discussion of the assembly is real. There's a curiously libidinal quality to this rejection: we seem to reserve a special portion of hate for those things especially that we once thought might lead to our liberation, because they didn't turn out to work immediately and on the spot. The assembly form is no exception to this principle, which makes proposing it as a means of self-determination well suited to the Lifehouse context even more daunting than it might otherwise be.

But so far as I'm concerned, the assembly remains the technology of permanent recourse par excellence. It is always there in potential, any time more than two or three of us gather—a set of possibilities that remains available whenever we need to discuss matters of common concern and decide together what to do about them. If the Long Emergency is always something that first confronts us in our immediate physical surroundings, any effort at building up shelter from degree zero will necessarily involve something along these lines. Our fate will turn on a small-scale politics of deliberation conducted among neighbors, based on the capacity to assess, propose, debate and decide.

Here "resourcefulness" might mean nothing so much as refining our capacities to listen, to empathize and to hold space—all qualities, as it happens, that are practiced and developed in the assembly. So for all the funk of earnest futility that has settled onto the form, it's worth picking it up, dusting it off, seeing how it can be made to work.

That requires some careful thinking about what does *not* work. It seems to me, first of all, that the assembly has been stuck with Bookchin's "moral functions" for quite some time, and that this is a major part of why so many of us tend to find it unappealing. The various national citizens' assemblies that have been convened to debate climate policy furnish an excellent, if pungent, example of the moral-functions trap.[47] These mobilize the most extraordinary draughts of goodwill and sincerity, but they have yet to inspire any legislative or regulatory action to speak of, anywhere. This leaves participants, for all their exertion, with no more traction on events than if they had done nothing at all.

There is, therefore, a profound mismatch between the intense intellectual and emotional effort required by this way of showing up in the world and the payoff it generally yields. I can't imagine that many of us, exposed to the intense time and energy pressures of late-capitalist life as we are, will cheerfully devote our evenings to hammering out consensus on positions that are destined to remain symbolic, "consultative" or "advisory." And it further seems natural that anyone who did, nevertheless, invest their precious life energy in such a process would sour on it—permanently and rightfully—when whatever consensus they'd so carefully crafted in this way came to be disregarded in its entirety by those with actual power.

There is a way out of this trap, though. The obvious way to resolve this mismatch, and rescue the assembly from its own irrelevance, is *for it to have power over how it disposes of its own organic resources*, so that there is a direct connection between the decisions we make together and what we can see happening in the world around us. This is the fundamental condition for our own effective use of the assembly. It cannot be symbolic, or therapeutic, or merely a way of taking the community's temperature on a given question. It actually has to have meaningful authority over allocations of resource.

And this is precisely what the Lifehouse offers. What the newly established neighborhood assembly will have direct, unambiguous control over is everything that attends the management of a community resilience-and-resourcefulness hub: all the inputs it requires, all the resources it generates and all of the questions that arise in the course of its daily operation.

If there's limited space at the Lifehouse, is it needed more for storage or shelter? If there's limited energy, is it best spent trying to find a more suitable space, or establishing a workshop or a vegetable plot at the existing one? If there are funds to spend, should they be used to buy seeds or machine tools? Should anyone, for that matter, be paid for their services to the Lifehouse, or should it remain a purely voluntary effort? Can someone who's violated the social contract in one way or another be asked to leave the building, or even permanently barred from using its facilities?

Deciding questions like these, with immediate, visible, material consequences, is real in a way that an advisory citizens' assembly hammering out consensus on matters of national policy cannot ever be. It is to implant self-determination in a form not a million miles different from that practiced by the communes of Rojava in the heart of our own civic life.

And though we must say it very quietly, any sufficiently dense network of communities self-managed in this way begins to look like the first subtle stirrings of a nonstate society, organized from the bottom up. "Quietly," because the truth is of course that many, and perhaps most, of those who use the Lifehouse and its services will be interested in no such thing. They'll just want somewhere they can turn to for aid, care and comfort when the moment of maximum crisis has found them alone and vulnerable.

But what if there's less distance between these two perspectives than we think? Reflecting on the wave of local mutual aid efforts that arose during the COVID lockdowns, the anarchist researcher Shane Burley observes that "[w]hat was so remark-able" about them was that for the most part they "did not come out of radical or political communities; they were just people looking to survive by caring for one another."[48] This suggests that in a great many places on Earth, a healthy, Kropotkinian instinct for solidarity remains close to the surface, even after so many years of marination in the neoliberal mindset, and will indeed well up spontaneously given the right circumstances. Perhaps, then, among all the other living things growing there, a Lifehouse can also incubate this new vernacular, the emergent common sense of a world to come.

Whatever form a Lifehouse takes, it cannot simply be a bubble of safety, secured for its own inward-turned membership but disconnected from neighboring streets and the city and world beyond.

There are several good reasons why we might want to con-ceive of the Lifehouse, from the very beginning, as one node within a larger network. Unless deliberately linked to one another, each is individually vulnerable, whether to shortfalls of its own capacity to provide, disruptive circumstances it simply cannot contend with, or, most distressingly of all, the intentionally destructive acts of hostile parties. But there is also the question of what insularity does to the culture of any group of human beings.

Organized only with reference to itself, a Lifehouse will have a hard time escaping a condition the science-fiction writer and critic Brian Aldiss famously derided as the "cozy catastrophe," in which a blithe and favored few continue to enjoy bourgeois comfort in isolation while the world offscreen chars to cinders all around them.[49] And the idea of a Lifehouse that offers refuge to a lucky few, but in doing so fails a far larger number of others, feels like a contradiction in terms, if not an affront to the very set of values that motivated its creation in the first place.

Most of these problems go away, or at least bite with con-siderably less force, if each local, autonomous refuge were to be joined with others in a loosely linked federation, coupled via some common infrastructure that cradles and sustains them all. But here we get into some practical trouble. You *can* begin organizing a Lifehouse in your neighborhood right now, without waiting for anything or anybody else. What you can't do is assume that anyone else, anywhere, will be motivated to do the same thing. And that makes it very difficult to discuss the prospects for a network among and between such local initiatives in any but the vaguest terms. About all we can practically do, for the time being, is articulate the kinds of qualities useful for such a network to have.

I think we can reasonably assume that any effort we make to shelter our own community against the turbulence of the Long Emergency will have strong resonances with similar efforts unfolding in parallel elsewhere, at least some of which will be motivated by values highly congruent with the ones we hold. Whenever we should happen to encounter the representatives of such an effort, it's worth exploring whether these affinities are close enough to permit mutual exchange and collaboration, in the way that the Greek solidarity clinics circulated information about the methods, techniques and protocols they relied upon.

We might look to examples like the endlessly impressive Mutual Aid Disaster Relief network in the United States, which aims to forge links between radical grassroots resilience and recovery groups (and offers guides covering everything from trauma counseling to bioremediation to help them in their efforts). Or the annual Fearless Cities events, which connect activists and initiatives from around the world who are working toward local power in the new-municipalist tradition.

But hovering behind that rather obvious thought is the suggestion of a closer coupling, which becomes especially salient if we intend our labors of care and sustenance to yield fruit at anything beyond neighborhood scale. Should we propose to organize life in ways that prefigure the large-scale mechanisms of decarbonized cooperation and exchange that any post-Emergency world will necessarily be founded on, we will need to identify those who share our longer-term goals and join with them in a framework capable of purposive, coordinated action.

This conception of the relationship between the local and global appears to have been first articulated in political terms by the Paris Commune of 1871. Kristin Ross, its most gifted English-language biographer, tells us that the "Communal imagination operated on the preferred scale of the local autonomous unit within an internationalist horizon," a way of thinking about social being that left "little room for the nation, or, for that matter, for the market or the state."[50] "Under the Commune," Ross tells us, "Paris wanted to be not the capital of France but an autonomous collective in a universal federation of peoples. It did not wish to be a state but rather an element, a unit in a federation of communes" that was global in scale.

If this sounds familiar by now, it should: it's an early articulation of the line of thought that was later developed by both Murray Bookchin and Abdullah Öcalan. We tend to understand Bookchin's libertarian municipalism and Öcalan's democratic confederalism as having to do with a neighborhood-scale politics of autonomous communes and assemblies, but this is to neglect the overarching structure that both Bookchin and Öcalan explicitly imagined sustaining such local efforts. In fact, the degrowthist writer Aaron Vansintjan argues that libertarian municipalism, definitionally, "is not decentralized localism" at all, and is "only possible at scale, extending beyond the individual municipality to form a network of autonomous, but collaborative, settlements."[51]

What might such a collaboration involve, restated in the terms most relevant to a Lifehouse? The easiest to imagine is a mesh of affiliated, mutually reinforcing projects loosely joined at the scale of a city, much in the way discrete relief efforts in Red Hook and the Rockaways and the Lower East Side all flew the banner of Occupy Sandy. Perhaps, as well, Lifehouses might be linked by shared technical infrastructure in the manner of Decidim, an open-source deliberative platform originally developed by and for Barcelona en Comú that was thereafter adopted by other municipalist groups.

Beyond that point, we're compelled to think in terms—a joint charter, nested councils, a common identity?—that can only really be worked out in practice by those directly involved, in response to their emergent needs and desires. Speaking only for myself, though, I like to imagine a maximum program of confederation working something like the exclaves or outposts of a nonphysically contiguous, distributed, nonstate society—a Lifehouse archipelago draping the habitable regions of the Long Emergency world in the possibility of refuge.

At the very least, we can imagine local efforts connected by an armature that sustains them whenever conditions threaten to overwhelm them. At such moments, we might want to invoke mutual aid in the sense of the term more usually understood by emergency responders, as a formal standing agreement by way of which communities agree to share resources with one another in times of acute local need. When a crisis of this sort requires something that exceeds our own capacity—whether specialized equipment or anything else that draws on means or numbers beyond those we happen to have on hand—such an agreement would allow us to request assistance across the lines that formally cleave one Lifehouse from another. And like any other such request, it is immeasurably easier if the parties involved already exist in some kind of relationship with one another.

Being connected to a broader network of Lifehouses also opens up the prospect of knowledge sharing between them. Again, per Elisavet Hasa, it was the diffusion of hard-won practical insight across the Greek solidarity clinics that allowed them to persist for even as long as they did. Hasa points out that it wasn't just skills or process diagrams that circulated through the Greek solidarity network, but inventories as well: detailed lists of all the tools, devices and items of furniture that between them constituted the workings of a functioning alternative healthcare infrastructure, right down to the disposal bins.

A similar practice surfaced in municipalist Madrid, in the form of the *intercambiadero*, an online database of the different tools, resources, materials and infrastructures kept by the activist projects in the network, "from garden hoses and wheelbarrows to shovels, sanders, or computer servers."[52] We know that any such bill of parts can never constitute refuge in and of itself without being animated by sustained, concerted effort. But it amounts to an instruction manual for the achievement of collective dignity, and it's easy to see how an inventory of this sort might nevertheless furnish irreplaceable insight for anyone wanting to organize a Lifehouse in their own community but doesn't have the first idea where to start.

There's another facet, as well, to what Vansintjan suggests about the necessity of federation. The greatest threat facing (or presented by) any Lifehouse is the case where it is either consciously captured by an identitarian group of one sort or another or is simply dominated from the start by a homogeneous local population. In either event, it will feel unwelcoming and exclusionary: "for" some people, but not others. At its worst and most intentional, this can harden into the kind of reactionary localism epitomized by the Greeks-only kitchens organized by the fascist Golden Dawn or, at a larger scale, the off-grid redoubts white nationalists dream of establishing in secessionist Cascadia.[53] But even short of circumstances like those, it's not hard to imagine how something that thought of itself as a "community resilience hub" might nevertheless come to conceive of the community it served in fundamentally defensive terms. Such "Lifehouses" would be armored, inward-facing, hostile to the newcomer—and therefore anathema to every value upheld by the efforts we've explored in these pages.

Confederation is the remedy for this tendency and perhaps even the sole way of practically countering it over the long term. We've already explored some of the material advantages a Lifehouse derives from membership in a confederal superstructure of some sort. The way to prevent local hubs from sliding into exclusionary defensiveness is by reframing those advantages as *privileges*: in order to enjoy them on an ongoing basis, local Lifehouses would have to maintain consensual standards of openness and invitationality. Beyond the sincere conviction of its members, this is the only factor that might keep a Lifehouse in any way inclined in that direction from collapsing into reactionary localism, and for that reason it feels absolutely essential to me that such values be articulated and affirmed at the level of the whole network.

Beyond such basic commitments, that each Lifehouse will necessarily reflect distinctly local values is entirely as it should be. But in any linked structure of more than three or four such communities—let alone one we might imagine extending to the continental or even global scale—there will be a point at which the desire to uphold particular local values comes into tension with those espoused by the federation as a whole. There must be some way to address this tension that allows a broader community to flex and that prevents it from shattering at the first sign of principled divergence. Here I want to introduce the notion of the *pragma*: a local agreement or adaptation allowing groups to reconcile their observance of some overarching principle with whatever shim or fudge factor in implementation is necessary to meaningfully enact that principle locally.

The pragma is best thought of as additional information about how things are done locally that does not constrain anybody else within the network. A Lifehouse where people are predominantly vegan, for example, might wish to enunciate that value as a pragma. A Lifehouse in which many people are in recovery, similarly, may wish to adopt a pragma discouraging or even forbidding the on-premises use of alcohol or other drugs. The point is to manage divergences of commitment or belief short of the point at which local groups holding them would be forced to defederate from a larger network, or be defederated.

Aren't people already doing this all the time? Of course they are—tacitly. The whole point of articulating such adaptive measures as pragmas, though, is to make this process explicit, so as to function as a relief valve for at least some of the pressure that so often leads to factionalism and splitting on the left. Instead of forcing the entire network to observe (say) the tenets of BDS and running the risk of having the whole thing fracture and come undone, there is nothing to prevent a local Lifehouse from choosing to do so collectively, as a pragma.

In this way, local Lifehouses can maintain whatever principles they like, so long as they don't come into direct conflict with those espoused by the network as a whole. Your Lifehouse observes Ramadan? Wishes to forgo the use of products or services based on so-called "AI"? Asks for a 1 percent tithe from businesses operating in its catchment basin? Go ahead and do that. Who, after all, has the standing to tell you how your community should show up for itself? But do it as a pragma and in this way preserve the benefits of acting as an autonomous element within a larger articulated whole.

If we want to build ourselves a refuge against the hard times to come, then, at least one way of doing so seems clear. We don't have to imagine the revolutionary seizure of state power, or some deus ex machina event that wipes the slate clean and allows us to begin anew. All we need to imagine is a meshwork of Lifehouses spanning the land, each one a place where people come to avail themselves of sanctuary, restoration, sustenance and solace, each one managed and governed by the people who use it. If this is in some ways an ambitious vision, it's also one that is comparably modest and achievable. Amid all the anguish of our great undoing, it sketches the improbable outlines of something extraordinary: a wildcat infrastructure of care, drawing on the best that is in us, to shelter the most vulnerable among us, at the very moment we need it.

But in order for any of this to come into being, someone still has to be the first to act.

In her great novel of "ambiguous utopia," *The Dispossessed*, Ursula K. Le Guin has her protagonist, the heterodox physicist Shevek, form a "syndicate of initiative" with his partner and a few allies at just such a moment of decision.[54] The members of a syndicate of initiative speak for no one else. They act only in their own names, guided solely by their own assessment of the moment and what it requires. They take upon themselves the full responsibility for acting and remain accountable for their choices in the face of opposition that seeks to undermine everything they endeavor to achieve. But what they do redefines the parameters of the situation they contend with.

There is a curious parallel between the choice Shevek and his syndics make and that made by anyone who undertakes some program of mutual care outside the state. The first moments of any project along these lines are always fraught with risk, and in such moments it's easy to be dissuaded by the daunting weight of all the forces aligned against success.

But here I want to invoke what I earlier described as "the great secret of Occupy Sandy," a quality that we know from the testimony of people involved is something it shared with Common Ground, the Greek solidarity clinics and the communes of Rojava above all: taking initiative in this way feels wonderful. Taking concrete action in defense of our communities —*doing something* about the situation we find ourselves in and exercising collective power over it—is reparative in itself and a specific for the numbing dread that otherwise gnaws at us in this time of storms. It can even help us manage the helpless, corrosive rage occasioned by the cruelty and injustice of this Emergency, or the terror we feel at the thought of our pending nonexistence.[55]

If we have reason to expect that a surging sense of joy and reconnection is what awaits us at the culmination of our effort, that ought to be enough to see us through the difficulties of its inception. Or enough, anyway, that we're able to show up for ourselves and for all those who need us.

So let us organize our own syndicates of initiative and together build the Lifehouse. Let's start with what is closest at hand, build outward from there and link our efforts with those of the others who have set themselves the same task. Let's let go, finally, gratefully, of all our vain hope for the future and use that energy instead to undertake the work—the necessary work—of care, of repair, of survival.

There is just one final thing to say about the Lifehouse and whatever promise it may hold, which is that the powerful generally cannot tolerate and will not simply let people pursue even the humblest projects of autonomy and self-determination.

Across the centuries, popular attempts at self-reliance and self-definition have been assailed wherever and whenever they have appeared, by state and nonstate actors both. But everything history teaches us about the fate of such initiatives since the days of the Paris Commune suggests that the state constitutes by far the greater threat to their existence.[56] What brought the Commune to its abrupt end, after a mere seventy-two days, was the same thing that has so often doomed the ventures in self-governance that followed: exogenous state violence. From Vienna's Karl-Marx-Hof in 1934 to Barcelona in 1939 to Rojava in 2019, in fact, just about any time a space has emerged in which even modest numbers of people have managed to organize the necessities of life on their own initiative, those spaces, those people and all their hopes have been crushed by force of arms.[57] It may well be that all of these experiments might sooner or later have succumbed to their own internal tensions and contradictions, but we'll never know that—because what actually cut them short was the armed might of the state.

In our time, of course, most liberatory projects fall well short of any point at which they might even remotely constitute a threat to power or capital of the sort that was posed by Communard Paris, Red Vienna or revolutionary Barcelona. But to ensure that this remains the case, a thoroughgoing program of preemptive harassment is directed at anything that might constitute a kernel of insurgent counterpower, most especially so if the actors involved are in any way racialized or marked as other.

Nothing is too petty in this respect. No radical effort is too small, local or unassuming to escape hostile notice, and no activity so self-evidently benign that some attempt will not be made to disrupt it—not even feeding the hungry. FBI agents circulated ginned-up kompromat to San Francisco businesses in a largely successful attempt to "impede their contributions to [the Black Panther Party] Breakfast Program."[58] City building inspectors, accompanied by police, threatened the volunteer staff of the youth-centered nonprofit Chicago Freedom School with fines of up to $1,000 a day for "preparing and serving large quantities of food without the proper retail food establishment license," because they bought pizza for teenagers who'd been tear-gassed while protesting the murder of George Floyd.[59] The Houston Police Department continues to cite Food Not Bombs activists, issuing fines amounting to an unsupportable $23,500, for the sin of furnishing free meals to the homeless.[60] The State of Georgia indicted activists protesting the "Cop City" police training center in South River Forest under the Racketeer Influenced and Corrupt Organizations act, characterizing each tranche of reimbursement for kitchen supplies among them as "an overt act in furtherance of the conspiracy."[61] It probably shouldn't surprise us when agents of the state harness every institutional, regulatory and legislative means at their disposal to undermine alternative projects and seal off the spaces in which they might grow. But what still retain a capacity to astonish are the spite and psychic smallness with which they so often go about doing it.

When harassment won't suffice, the state has other means of disruption available. From the Earth Liberation Front and Animal Liberation Front in the United States to the long infiltrations of activist communities in the UK, it is clear that even the smallest, most ineffectual or harmless radical groupuscules will be penetrated, compromised and seeded with agents provocateurs.[62] This extends to mutual aid initiatives with an overt politics. One of the earliest members of Common Ground—so trusted, indeed, that between January and April 2007, he served as its director of operations—was an FBI informant.[63]

And sometimes, indeed, the means of disruption are raw and lethal. Let a community assert any degree of territorial control or show any sign that it intends to subsist outside capital permanently, and it will swiftly find itself a community marked for elimination in one way or another.

This is neither hyperbole, nor paranoia, nor an inflated sense of the significance of such efforts. More than one Lower East Side squat was set ablaze under mysterious circumstances and allowed to burn to the ground as officers of the city's department of Housing Preservation and Development stood by.[64] In Philadelphia in May 1985, the Black separatist group known as MOVE was massacred, their whole neighborhood burned down around them. And any student of the Black Panthers can tell you what happened to its emergent generation of leaders: Bunchy Carter was set up for assassination. Fred Hampton and Mark Clark were murdered in their beds.

This will toward elimination is now bolstered by technological capacities the state never had in the time of the Panthers. These include spyware to eavesdrop on a target's conversations and map their social connections; automated facial recognition that tracks individuals of interest, even amid large crowds; anomaly-detection algorithms that allow an operator to detect and characterize patterns of behavior in similarly large datasets and in this way anticipate the emergence of protests; and the first tentative steps toward deployment of lethal autonomous systems on the borders—all gleefully vended by the grubby NSO Groups and Palantirs of the world.[65]

Much of this technology, inevitably, is hugely overhyped and will never work in the ways touted. But enough of it already does that any state equipped with it will enjoy the prerogative of isolating potential cells of dissent or resistance at the threshold of emergence and either preempting their formation or otherwise disrupting their ability to act effectively. As to what constitutes "dissent or resistance" in the mind of the state, we know that the symbols of Extinction Rebellion and Greenpeace, as well as YPG/YPJ insignia and the green-and-black flag of ecoanarchism, have appeared in a visual guide to extremist groups circulated by Counter Terrorism Policing in the UK.[66] Despite later caviling by that organization and attempts to withdraw the materials in question, they undoubtedly represent the way our efforts at mutual care and the development of collective power will be perceived by many within the state security apparatus.[67]

All of this might seem a million miles removed from our talk of Lifehouses, with their humming microgrids and verdant gardens. But as the pressures of the Long Emergency intensify and the competition for resources tightens, I think it's a fair bet that the attempt to furnish care will itself attract the kind of violence that was previously lavished only on (actual or perceived) threats to the dominant order. And while the state may always constitute the preeminent threat, it's by no means safe to assume that this violence will be coming from the state alone.

This will particularly be the case wherever someone extends care toward refugees, asylum seekers, or other individuals or communities marked for othering and exclusion. Any gesture in this direction is sure to attract the rage of local fascist or ethnonationalist formations, just as Golden Dawn physically attacked free clinics, social centers and refugee camps during its years of greatest influence in Greece.[68] Some of these formations, like Golden Dawn itself, will even claim that some kind of ecological consciousness justifies their assaults on whatever infrastructure exists to shelter the weakest and most vulnerable.[69]

If a mutual care effort manages to persist for long enough in holding any space at all, the odds are that someone somewhere will eventually be moved to oppose it by force. So long as it confines itself to the more stereotypically feminized aspects of care work and social reproduction, that effort may—*may*—be tolerated. But even then, there are no guarantees: even something as beloved and broadly supported in the community as Occupy Sandy was attacked, and whoever was responsible in that case was perfectly willing to firebomb a church. If the broader prospect we face is one of grinding twilight wars and unrelenting, wanton cruelty at all the interfaces where the habitable zone meets the world in flight, that cruelty will surely extend to the very spaces, and providers, of shelter. We can already see it happening.

So even in the case that, against all odds, we are actually able to create Lifehouses and in them make common cause against the future bearing down upon us, our efforts can't end there. The implacable truth is that such communities must organize and prepare to defend themselves, or stand by in helpless acquiescence as they and everything they love are made to perish from the Earth.[70]

Concretely, this is a dreadful, heart-stopping prospect and cannot be regarded with anything remotely like equanimity. But history is uncompromising on this point, and it is something that everyone embarked upon the politics of care must ultimately reckon with. This is the grim thing, the lesson of Golden Dawn and COINTELPRO, of Daesh and the vigilantes of Algiers Point: there is little point in sheltering bodies from the undirected chaos of the storm if you are not also prepared to protect them from those who specifically mean to do them harm.

Conclusion

At the end of the world, plant a tree.
                    —*Musnad Ahmad*, hadith 12491,
                          as reported by Anas Ibn Mali

In the last, peri-apocalyptic chapter of David Mitchell's 2014 novel *The Bone Clocks*, the provisional government entity responsible for the apportionment of misery in an Ireland at the end of its tether is called, simply, Stability.[1] Its armed convoys bring the monthly ration of food, and its sullen teenage conscripts help themselves to the local produce, and the local women, as compensation for the salary that no longer comes. Stability is resented. It is clumsy, unjust and heavy-handed. It achieves its barely ceded legitimacy through force of arms. But it manages to keep the peace and the calories flowing, however minimally in either case, and for that the townspeople of Kilcrannog accede to its oafish rule with something approaching gratitude.

There's a canny understanding in Mitchell's act of imaginative framing: the name he gives this occupying force captures what desperate people are desperate for when beset by insurmountable crises on all sides—and equally, implies all the many precious things they are willing to trade away cheaply, if only granted that one thing they can be certain of. It almost doesn't matter what flavor of politics nominally guides Stability in its attempts to assert control over a reality become ungovernable, and Mitchell doesn't bother to specify. In the state *in extremis* it administers, everyone but those lucky few closest to the center (or able to grow for themselves) goes to bed hungry, and that hunger speaks louder than any prior belief or commitment.

Stability offers some ground to stand on. It constitutes some assurance, however illusory, that tomorrow will be much like today in the ways that matter, or enough like today to make plans, anyway. If it sacrifices a few complainers and malcontents to keep the broader peace, well: you know what they say about eggs and omelets—and better still if the breaking of eggs happens somewhere safely out of sight. We should never underestimate the appeal of a promise like this when everything's gone maximally sideways.

Stability will be the fundamental value proposition of a certain kind of politics in our time of undoing, and we need to reckon with just how seductive it will prove to be for too many of our neighbors in the global North. For them, the overriding instinct will be to press on, to avoid confronting any of the increasingly blatant asymmetries of access to care that characterize our world, just so long as someone promises to preserve the rudiments of a comfortingly familiar way of life. And they may even succeed at securing some measure of continuity for themselves—but only by shedding increased turbulence and suffering onto others, as if to say: there's only room enough for us on this lifeboat.

Such massive failures of empathy and simple human decency are, of course, repulsive. But there is nothing inherently wrong with stability itself. All living things require some degree of consistency in their environment if they are to endure past their first moments of existence. If the word has taken on a tinge of conservatism, that is only because what the powerful so often wish to stabilize is a situation of injustice. The far deeper challenge is how to protect and extend those situations in which people manage to cast a penumbra of care and comfort not merely over themselves but over everyone they can reach who stands in need of it.

Each of the projects in this book, in their own way, have tried to do just that: carve out a period of space and time in which desperate people could be sheltered from the press of need long enough to find their feet and, eventually, their voices. Very often this involved arranging the most basic provisions of physical safety, bodily sustenance and medical care for people to whom those things had been denied. The Panthers did it for the poor Black communities bypassed, or at very best patronized, by the Great Society. The volunteers of Common Ground and Occupy Sandy did it for themselves, in neighborhoods brought to the ground by heavy weather—as did the Greek solidarity clinics, in a land undone by nothing more material than a few fatal paragraphs in a loan agreement.

If care is what sustains our capacity to exist at all, though, what sustains care is the exercise of power. In a world where the maintenance of a high standard of comfort for a very few seems to require that virtually everyone else be deprived of any control whatsoever over the circumstances of their being, any ability to grasp resources and direct them toward the care of those in need requires that we reassert our claim to that control. The Spanish municipalists aimed to extend the ambit of self-determination to an entire city, and the Kurds of northern Syria across a territory every bit the size of a smaller nation-state. Murray Bookchin dreamed it at the scale of the entire globe: a confederal mesh of autonomous communities spanning the planet, in which free people might bring the metabolism of their collective being back into line with the cycles and rhythms of a thriving Earth.

What I've tried to evoke, in my account of each of these cases, is the sense of collective power as a positive pressure, pushing outward against the chaos and night. Wherever communities exercised this power, they were able to establish an envelope, however fragile or temporary, inside of which the injured might catch their breath and restore themselves—and therefore regenerate their organic capacity to endure, to resist and to create.

It has never been easy to achieve this, anywhere or at any point in history, and we know that wherever someone has attempted to do so, that attempt has most often been resisted with force. But what was never easy becomes sharply more difficult still in a time of unending storms. It will often feel as if everything is conspiring against our ability to care, feed and protect ourselves, and maintain the lifesystems that sustain us against a world ruled by death.

It increasingly seems that if there is going to be any rescue at all, it's going to be that which we devise on our own, together, largely unaided by anyone or anything else.

There is a certain compensation in this.

Conversations about decarbonization policy or carbon-credit markets or stratospheric aerosol injection, after all, offer agency solely to a narrow technical and managerial elite. They center only particular kinds of knowledge, even though the policies being discussed stand to affect every living thing on the planet. They're not detached from our experiences of the world under heat, precisely, but they take place at too many removes for those experiences to really weigh in considerations. (It's hard to imagine anyone who might have struggled ashore from a foundering raft, say, or charred half their body after falling to a searing sidewalk, seated around a table in those air-conditioned conference rooms.)

So far as virtually every one of us is concerned, these strategies to rescue the world involve decisions made by other people, and we may or may not even be informed about them until they're fait accompli. Bizarrely, they don't propose any role for you and me, other than that we carry on doing as we always have. All they ask of us is that we continue to consume, continue to live in isolation from one another, continue our complicity in the churn that gave rise to the storms to begin with.

But the kind of conversations we will need to have if we propose to build the Lifehouse are different. These conversations will take place with, among and between people directly exposed to the conditions of the Long Emergency, who will be directly affected by whatever decisions are made. They will engage each and every one of us, draw on our whole capacity as living beings and necessarily result in novel approaches to knowing, doing and being. I can tell you from personal experience that something extraordinary begins to happen when people discover what it feels like to be sustained by their own efforts in this way. Their sense of what is doable, so impoverished through the long neoliberal twilight, expands to encompass new horizons. And we know from the testimonies of so many who were there what that feels like—again, it feels like *healing*, accompanied by a massive upwelling of *purpose*, *power* and *possibility*. If ever there were anything that might help us overcome the deer-in-the-headlights paralysis otherwise so endemic to our time, it consists in this. We can number it among the few, precious gifts of the Long Emergency that has otherwise taken so much from us.

But there is a flip side, as we know there must be. As anyone who has ever undertaken the care of another knows, the work it takes to stabilize a situation on the edge of chaos often seems overwhelming—the more so when the need for it is sustained indefinitely. The work of mutual care in the Long Emergency will be constant, and it will never end. It will unavoidably exact a toll from everyone who undertakes it. There's no way around this: at some point, everyone who energetically commits themselves to the effort of repair will experience depletion, exhaustion and burnout.

We know, too, that these things invariably fall most heavily on those who work hardest to push back the night. You might expect that people who were so attuned to what the care of body and soul requires, and so boundlessly dedicated to the restoration of others, would not forget to replenish themselves. But all the people I know called to this work most urgently also seem to be those who tend to beat themselves up because they can never do enough. And it's true. There will always be someone who needs them and always someone they cannot reach.

What I want to say to them is this: it's not anyone's job to reach every last one of the billions of human beings imperiled by our time of Emergency, nor are you betraying them by remembering to take care of yourself. There are relatively few things I have ever taken to heart from the Jewish ethical tradition which is my birthright. Among them, though, are a few lines attributed to a rabbi named Tarfon who lived around the end of the first century of the current era, later bound into the compilation of oral wisdom known as the Pirkei Avot: "It is not incumbent upon you to complete the work [of repairing the world], but neither are you at liberty to desist from it."[2] I have always found Tarfon's charge electrifying, possibly because it is both bracing and comforting, and I continue to turn to it for strength in difficult moments.

In context, I interpret Tarfon to mean that we keep organizing, even if what we're doing often feels like little more than shifting drifts and piles of washed-up flotsam around the terminal beach. We keep doing the work, come what may. We make such shelter as we can, for as many as we can, for as long as we can, and when we are asked, we do what we can to help others make shelter themselves. This work is what we have, it is all we have and it is all anyone can ask of us. As difficult as all of this might be to accept, internalizing it affords us one final gift, which is the gift of clarity.

So, no: protest marches will not save us, nor will any political party. Blockchains will not save us. Meatless Mondays will not save us. UBIs will not save us. Greta will not save us. Central bankers will not save us. Mindfulness will not save us. Mass timber will not save us. Voting will not save us, but neither will not voting. Vertical farming will not save us. A World Congress of Mayors will not save us. Blowing up pipelines will not save us. Carbon credits will *definitely* not save us. Green New Deals will not save us. Cyanobacteria will not save us. Cargo bikes will not save us, not even electric ones. "Precision fermentation" will not save us. Painting roofs white will not save us. Airships will not save us. AI will not save us. Nothing that any billionaire does will save us. If anything at all is going to save us, *it will have to be us*. "Who will build the ark?" the late Mike Davis famously asks.[3] The only possible answer is that we will, together.

Thus, perhaps, the strangely affirmative character of a life so close to the precipice. There is so much to do, so many who need what we have to offer. The darkening landscape before us is lit by the flashing certainty that there is nowhere else we were meant to be but here, nothing higher or more important we will ever do than this. And it is gathered here, in the ruin and wreckage of all our hopes for the future, that we might finally learn what it is to know care—for ourselves, for one another and for the wounded Earth that cradles us.

at Newington Green, September 2019–September 2023

Acknowledgments

My debts to Nurri Kim are too many and profound to list, or even try to characterize. In so many ways, she is my very own Lifehouse. All I can do is thank her, with my infinite love, and hope to be the same for her for all our days on Earth.

Leo Hollis trusted me to deliver, during long stretches of radio silence that would have driven any ordinary editor to apoplexy. It cannot have been easy. I hope he feels that the results repay the effort. My thanks also to the copyediting team of Jeanne Tao and Jeffrey Klein, whose commitment, attention to detail and indulgence of my idiosyncrasies is greatly appreciated.

In my conception of the Lifehouse, I acknowledge a profound psychic debt to the six "Visions" illustrations Clifford Harper produced for *Undercurrents* magazine in the mid-1970s, depicting, respectively, a "Collectivised Garden," a "Basement Workshop," an "Autonomous Housing Estate," an "Autonomous Terrace," a "Community Workshop" and a "Community Media Centre," all repurposed from vernacular British housing typologies, and all explicitly running on renewable solar and wind power. Clifford's visions continue to resonate and to inspire, and it would please me to no end for people to discover his work through reading about it here.

After seeing my original Mastodon post on the Lifehouse, a friend named Gregor May pointed me to a few tantalizing paragraphs he had spotted in the course of his own archival research. These appeared on page 34 of the *Whole Earth Catalog* for March 1970 under the caption, "Some Ideas on the 'Lifehouse' Concept," and were attributed to an organization out of Palo Alto called ecology action (complete with groovy lowercase orthography). Per ecology action:

> The lifehouse is a neighborhood community center set up in your own home, where help and information on the starting and running of food co-ops, gardens, sidewalk trees (among many other related things) can be found ... Eventually, the lifehouse concept will, hopefully, result in the "community of San Francisco" being run by its citizens on an ecologically sound basis ... The will to do something about your own survival is the most important thing. The lifehouse will provide an opportunity for all of us to be involved in exercising our will to survive.

If, like so many other steps we might have taken to protect the climate, the best time to have put this idea into practice was a half-century ago, perhaps the original framers would nevertheless be heartened to know that people keep coming up with it.

While any errors of fact, interpretation, emphasis or taste you may trip over are, of course, my sole responsibility, this book that is substantially about community would have been impossible had I not been sustained, challenged and encouraged by a community of brilliant thinkers and doers. To lift a line from a book I know I read in adolescence, but which otherwise failed to make much of an impression on me: I am glad you're here with me, here at the end of all things.

I am once again grateful for the insight, solidarity, support and energy furnished, in various ways, by Jabari Adisa, Javier Arbona, Jon Ardern, Timo Arnall, Markus Bader, Rev. Chris Ballard, Fay Ballard, Debbie Bookchin, August C. Bourré, Tanya Byrne, Greta Byrum, Elisabeth Calderón Lüning, Deb Chachra, Brendan Cormier, Alberto Corsín Jiménez, Aimee Meredith Cox, Cansu Curgen, Nicholas de Monchaux, Dilar Dirik, Cory Doctorow, Christina Dunbar-Hester, Nick Durrant, Dominic Evans, Christopher Fahey, Simone Ferracina, Carrie Friese, Daisy Froud, César García Sáez, Andrey Goncharov, Sarah Grant, Avsar Gurpinar, Suzi Hall, Clifford Harper, Elisavet Hasa, Owen Hatherley, Eric Höweler, Tom Igoe,

Margaret Jameson, Gaby Jeliazkov, Olalekan Jeyifous, Priya Jha, Matt Jones, Erin Kissane, Janette Kim, Olive M. Kim, Justina Kochansky, Laura Kurgan, Laurie Laybourn-Langton, Chris Lee, Anthony Leone, Sophie Lewis, Enma López Araujo, David Madden, Azadeh Mashayekhi, Adrian McEwen, Justin McGuirk, Michael McQuarrie, Ana Méndez de Andés, Anna Minton, Samaneh Moafi, Oli Mould, Leila Nachawati, Tamara Paris, Dan Pfiffer, Leigh Phillips, Benedetta Piantella, Alison Powell, Babak Rahimi, Padmini Ray Murray, Kristien Ring, Carla Rivera Blanco, Tod Robbins, John Robinson, Ahmet A. Sabancı, Fred Scharmen, Dubravka Sekulić, Dianna Settles, Shiri Shalmy, Natalia Smirnov, Easton Smith, Stavros Stavrides, Ninni Suni, Cordy Swope, Alice Taylor, Matthew Thompson, Simon Gareth Thorpe, Fran Tonkiss, Joe Trellick, Sophia Tu, Shan Vahidy, Christina Varvia, Brenda Vértiz, Frank Vial, Glenn Wallis, Eyal Weizman, Ines Weizman, Darren Webb, David Wengrow, Daniel Wolpert, J. Meejin Yoon, Jillian C. York, and everyone I worked alongside in ACT/UP Philadelphia, at the Berkeley Free Clinic and at 520 Clinton. I owe a particular debt of gratitude to my steadfast Mildmay Chums David Madden and Dubravka Sekulić for enduring my primordial drafts, late-night rants and consistently iommic taste in music. Thanks also to Billy Smith and Cheyenna Layne Weber for helping me ensure the accuracy of certain details of the text.

This book was written to the sounds of Aluk Todolo, Barn Owl, Bismuth, Bong, James Cleveland and the Angelic Choir, Current 93, Deafheaven, Deathprod, Earth, Ex Eye, Gazelle Twin, Godspeed You! Black Emperor, Hildur Guðnadóttir, Lee Hazlewood and Nancy Sinatra, Krallice, KTL, Lankum, Lingua Ignota, Frank London and Jon Madof, Masada, MMMD, Muslimgauze, Nadja, Nature and Organisation, Panopticon, Planning for Burial, Phurpa, RAKTA, Emma Ruth Rundle, Ben Salisbury, Scarcity, Senyawa, She Drew the Gun, Sleep, Songs: Ohia, the Staple Singers, SubRosa, SUNN O))), Swans, Thou, the Clara Ward Singers, White Hills, Windhand, Wolves in the Throne Room, Wrekmeister Harmonies, Year of No Light, Zeal and Ardor and "Life on Earth" by Hurray for the

Riff Raff (the version with Preservation Hall Jazz Band, over and over again). Biomechanical recalibration by Phil Cavell at Cyclefit, London. When in Helsinki, Adam Greenfield enjoys Kulttuurisauna, Hakaniemenranta 17. Support your local independent bookshop.

YOU WANT IT DARKER.

Notes

Introduction

1 National Oceanic and Atmospheric Administration, National Centers for Environmental Information, "Monthly National Climate Report for October 2012: Sandy Storm Surge and Wind Summary," November 2012, ncei.noaa.gov.

2 My own contemporaneous account of Occupy Sandy, including a detailed description of how the 520 Clinton relief hub worked, can be found in "Preliminary Notes to a Diagram of Occupy Sandy," posted on my blog on November 21, 2012. speedbird. wordpress.com.

3 Sharon Lerner, "How Sandy Saved Occupy," *American Prospect*, November 27, 2012; James West, "What Happened to the Money That Occupy Sandy Raised?," *Mother Jones*, June 18, 2013.

4 "Red Cross Recovery Efforts to Help Sandy Survivors," American Red Cross, December 19, 2012, redcross.org.

5 "Energy Transition Will Move Slowly over the Next Decade," Economist Intelligence Unit, December 1, 2022, eiu.com.

6 J. David Goodman, "Suspicious Fire Chars Part of Brooklyn Church," *New York Times*, December 23, 2012.

7 Rebecca Solnit, *A Paradise Built in Hell: The Extraordinary Communities That Arise in Disaster* (New York: Viking, 2009).

8 Charles E. Fritz, *Disasters and Mental Health: Therapeutic Principles Drawn from Disaster Studies*, Historical and Comparative Disaster Series No. 10 (Newark: University of Delaware Disaster Research Center, 1996).

9 John P. Clark, *The Impossible Community: Realizing Communitarian Anarchism* (New York: Bloomsbury, 2013), 214.

10 Cassie Thornton, *The Hologram: Feminist, Peer-to-Peer Healthcare for a Post-Pandemic Future* (London: Pluto Press, 2020), 4.

11 From a phone interview conducted with an unnamed Occupy Sandy volunteer, August 23, 2013, in Eric Ambinder and David

M. Jennings, *The Resilient Social Network* (Falls Church, VA: Homeland Security Studies and Analysis Institute, September 30, 2013).

12 Clark, *Impossible Community*, 214.

1. The Long Emergency

1 Aine Fox, "Shapps Admits Rail Network Cannot Cope with Extreme Heat as Track Hits 62C," *Independent*, July 19, 2022; Kit Malthouse, "Heatwave Response," *Hansard*, Commons, vol. 718 col. 963, July 20, 2022.

2 The reading for June 8, 2023; it has come down marginally since, as it tends to on a seasonal basis, but the general trend is upward and accelerating. You can see the current reading at co2.earth/daily-co2.

3 Graham Caswell, "The Window for a Livable Future Is Closing, Warns IPCC," Green Central Banking, February 28, 2022, greencentralbanking.com.

4 Intergovernmental Panel on Climate Change, *Climate Change 2022: Impacts, Adaptation and Vulnerability* (Cambridge, UK: Cambridge University Press, 2022).

5 Jeff Tollefson, "Earth Is Warmer Than It's Been in 125,000 Years," *Scientific American*, August 9, 2021.

6 Intergovernmental Panel on Climate Change, *Climate Change 2022*.

7 Chi Xu et al., "Future of the Human Climate Niche," *Proceedings of the National Academy of Sciences* 117, no. 21 (May 4, 2020).

8 Cormac McCarthy, *The Road* (New York: Alfred A. Knopf, 2006).

9 Eamon Barrett, "Taiwan's Drought Is Exposing Just How Much Water Chipmakers Like TSMC Use (and Reuse)," *Fortune*, June 12, 2021; Willy Shih, "Severe Winter Weather in Texas Will Impact Many Supply Chains beyond Chips," *Forbes*, February 19, 2021.

10 Thiemo Fetzer, "Subsidising the Spread of COVID-19: Evidence from the UK'S Eat-Out-to-Help-Out Scheme," *Economic Journal* 132, no. 643 (April 2022).

11 David Wallace-Wells, *The Uninhabitable Earth: Life after Warming* (New York: Tim Duggan Books, 2019).

12 Alan Buis, "Too Hot to Handle: How Climate Change May

Make Some Places Too Hot to Live," Ask NASA Climate, March 9, 2022, climate.nasa.gov.

13 Daniel J. Vecellio et al., "Evaluating the 35°C Wet-Bulb Temperature Adaptability Threshold for Young, Healthy Subjects," *Journal of Applied Physiology* 132, no. 2 (February 2022).

14 David Wallace-Wells, "The Mysteriously Low Death Toll of the Heat Waves in India and Pakistan," *New York Times*, July 14, 2022.

15 Sarah Toy, "Streets Are Getting So Hot They Are Causing Serious Burns," *Wall Street Journal*, July 26, 2023.

16 Syed F. Saquib, Joseph T. Carroll and Paul Chestovich, "Seasonal Impact in Admissions and Burn Profiles in a Desert Burn Unit," *Burns Open* 5, no. 2 (April 2021).

17 Jorge Vega et al., "A 5-Year Review of Pavement Burns from a Desert Burn Center," *Journal of Burn Care and Research* 40, no. 4 (July/August 2019).

18 Jack Healy, "Scorching Hot in Phoenix: What It's Like to Work in 115 Degrees," *New York Times*, June 20, 2021.

19 Chunwu Zhu et al., "Carbon Dioxide (CO_2) Levels This Century Will Alter the Protein, Micronutrients, and Vitamin Content of Rice Grains with Potential Health Consequences for the Poorest Rice-Dependent Countries," *Science Advances* 4, no. 5 (May 23, 2018).

20 Ibid.

21 Nicky Driedonks, Ivo Rieu and Wim H. Vriezen, "Breeding for Plant Heat Tolerance at Vegetative and Reproductive Stages," *Plant Reproduction* 29, nos. 1–2 (June 2016). There is special promise, as well, in an emerging wave of agricultural crops and techniques adapted for hotter, drier environments, ultimately inspired by long-standing Indigenous lifeways of the American desert Southwest. See Gary Paul Nabhan et al., "An Aridamerican Model for Agriculture in a Hotter, Water Scarce World," *Plants People Planet* 2, no. 6 (November 2020).

22 Jean-François Bastin et al., "Understanding Climate Change from a Global Analysis of City Analogues," *PLOS ONE*, October 16, 2019.

23 Allison M. Thomson et al., "RCP4.5: A Pathway for Stabilization of Radiative Forcing by 2100," *Climatic Change* 109, nos. 1–2 (November 2011).

24 Allianz SE, "Megacities Exposed to Flood Risk," December 8, 2015, allianz.com.

25 Stephane Hallegatte et al., "Future Flood Losses in Major Coastal Cities," *Nature Climate Change* 3, no. 9 (September 2013).

26 Geert Jan van Oldenborgh et al., "Attribution of Extreme Rainfall from Hurricane Harvey, August 2017," *Environmental Research Letters* 12, no. 12 (December 13, 2017).

27 Eric S. Blake and David A. Zelinsky, *National Hurricane Center Tropical Cyclone Report: Hurricane Harvey, 17 August–1 September 2017* (National Hurricane Center, January 23, 2018).

28 Hallegatte et al., "Future Flood Losses."

29 Christopher Flavelle, Jill Cowan and Ivan Penn, "Climate Shocks Are Making Parts of America Uninsurable. It Just Got Worse," *New York Times*, May 21, 2023.

30 C40 Cities Climate Leadership Group, "How to Adapt Your City to Sea Level Rise and Coastal Flooding," C40 Knowledge Hub, February 2022, c40knowledgehub.org.

31 Michael Oppenheimer et al., "Sea Level Rise and Implications for Low-Lying Islands, Coasts and Communities," in Hans-Otto Pörtner et al., eds., *The Ocean and Cryosphere in a Changing Climate* (Geneva: Intergovernmental Panel on Climate Change, 2019); United Nations Department of Economic and Social Affairs, Population Division, *The World's Cities in 2018: Data Booklet* (United Nations, 2018).

32 Intergovernmental Panel on Climate Change, *Climate Change 2014: Impacts, Adaptation, and Vulnerability* (Cambridge, UK: Cambridge University Press, 2015).

33 See "TPC Camp," in Charley Hailey, *Camps: A Guide to 21st Century Space* (Cambridge, MA: MIT Press, 2009).

34 Christopher Flavelle, "How the Government Is Failing Americans Uprooted by Calamity," *New York Times*, July 23, 2022; Andreas Seibert, *From Somewhere to Nowhere: China's Internal Migrants* (Zürich: Lars Miller Publishers, 2008).

35 Ricardo Martén and Camillo Boano, "Checkpoint Urbanism: Violent Infrastructures and Border Stigmas in the Juárez Border Region," *Urban Studies* 59, no. 3 (February 2022); "Greece: Violence against Asylum Seekers at Border," Human Rights Watch, March 17, 2020; Border Violence Monitoring Network, *Systematic Human Rights Violations: Border Violence, Pushbacks and Containment in Ceuta and Melilla* (August 6, 2021).

36 The United States Customs and Border Protection agency, for example, claims a zone of jurisdiction extending 100 miles from any land or maritime territorial boundary. As of 2018,

65.3 percent of the American population lived within this zone. Tanvi Misra, "Inside the Massive U.S. 'Border Zone,'" CityLab, May 14, 2018, bloomberg.com.

37 "Sea-Watch Ship Aurora Detained on Fabricated Grounds," sea-watch.org, August 21, 2023.

38 "The Pylos Shipwreck," Forensis, July 7, 2023, counter-investigations.org.

39 As this posture was dubbed by Theresa May, then Home Secretary of the United Kingdom, in a world-historical instance of saying the quiet part out loud. James Kirkup and Robert Winnett, "Theresa May Interview: 'We're Going to Give Illegal Migrants a Really Hostile Reception,'" *Telegraph*, May 25, 2012. See also Liberty, ed., *A Guide to the Hostile Environment: The Border Controls Dividing Our Communities—and How We Can Bring Them Down* (London: Liberty, May 2019).

40 Chris Rumford, ed., *Citizens and Borderwork in Contemporary Europe* (New York: Routledge, 2009); Chris Rumford, *Cosmopolitan Borders* (London: Palgrave Pivot, 2014).

41 So are shootings among civilians. "Estimated risk of firearm incidents increased almost monotonically with higher temperatures … even moderately hot temperatures were associated with higher risk of shootings." Vivian H. Lyons et al., "Analysis of Daily Ambient Temperature and Firearm Violence in 100 US Cities," *JAMA Network Open*, December 16, 2022.

42 John O'Loughlin, Andrew M. Linke and Frank D. W. Witmer, "Effects of Temperature and Precipitation Variability on the Risk of Violence in Sub-Saharan Africa, 1980–2012," *Proceedings of the National Academy of Sciences* 111, no. 47 (November 25, 2014).

43 Marshall Burke, Solomon M. Hsiang and Edward Miguel, "Climate and Conflict," *Annual Review of Economics* 7 (August 2015).

44 Damian Carrington, "Lack of Migrant Workers Left Food Rotting in UK Fields Last Year, Data Reveals," *Guardian*, February 9, 2018; Sarah Butler, "Up to £60m in UK Crops Left to Rot Owing to Lack of Workers, Says NFU," *Guardian*, August 15, 2022.

45 Tim Stokholm, "The Mediterranean Migrant Crisis: A Critical Challenge to Global Nation-States," University of East London Centre for Social Justice and Change Working Paper No 3, January 2016.

NOTES FROM PAGES 38 TO 45

46 Marc Levinson, *The Box: How the Shipping Container Made the World Smaller and the World Economy Bigger* (Princeton, NJ: Princeton University Press, 2008); Deborah Cowen, *The Deadly Life of Logistics: Mapping Violence in Global Trade* (Minneapolis: University of Minnesota Press, 2014).

47 Catherina Zara Raymond, "Piracy and Armed Robbery in the Malacca Strait," *Naval War College Review* 62, no. 3 (Summer 2009); David Rosenberg, "The Political Economy of Piracy in the South China Sea," *Naval War College Review* 62, no. 3 (Summer 2009).

48 Matthew Mpoke Bigg, Ivan Nechepurenko and Neil Mac-Farquhar, "Russia Pulls Out of the Black Sea Grain Deal," *New York Times*, July 17, 2023.

49 Liz Alderman, "Crops 'Stored Everywhere': Ukraine's Harvest Piles Up," *New York Times*, July 28, 2022.

50 Foreign, Commonwealth and Development Office (UK), "New Intelligence Shows Russia's Targeting of a Cargo Ship," press release, September 11, 2023, gov.uk.

51 Joe Ware and Karolina Grotowska, *Cooking Up a Storm: The Climate Threat to Food Supply Chains in UK, Germany and Italy* (London: Christian Aid, September 2023).

52 Those working in the nascent field of critical logistics studies increasingly prefer this term to the misleadingly linear "supply chain." See "Supply Matrix," Field Notes Toward an Internationalist Green New Deal, internationalistgreennewdeal.org.

53 Jasbir K. Puar, *The Right to Maim: Debility, Capacity, Disability* (Durham, NC: Duke University Press, 2017).

54 Chris Vallance, "Heatwave Forced Google and Oracle to Shut Down Computers," BBC, July 20, 2022; Denis Campbell, "London NHS Trust Cancels Operations as IT System Fails in Heatwave," *Guardian*, July 21, 2022.

55 Nesrine Malik, "When State Services Fail, Citizens Pay Extra or Sink. This Is Sunak's Britain Now," *Guardian*, January 9, 2023.

56 Robert I. Rotberg, "Failed States, Collapsed States, Weak States: Causes and Indicators," in Robert I. Rotberg, ed., *State Failure and State Weakness in a Time of Terror* (Washington, DC: Brookings Institution Press, 2004).

57 David Harvey, *The Limits to Capital* (Oxford, UK: Basil Blackwell, 1982); Ruth Wilson Gilmore, *Abolition Geography: Essays Toward Liberation* (New York: Verso, 2022).

58 Ida Danewid, "The Fire This Time: Grenfell, Racial Capitalism

224

and the Urbanisation of Empire," *European Journal of International Relations* 26, no. 1 (March 2020).

59 Arline T. Geronimus, *Weathering: The Extraordinary Stress on the Body of an Ordinary Life in an Unjust Society* (London: Virago, 2023).

60 Aaron B. Frank and Elizabeth M. Bartels, eds., *Adaptive Engagement for Undergoverned Spaces: Concepts, Challenges and Prospects for New Approaches* (Santa Monica, CA: RAND Corporation, 2022).

61 David Harvey, *Rebel Cities: From the Right to the City to the Urban Revolution* (New York: Verso, 2012).

62 The Royal Society, *Geoengineering the Climate: Science, Governance and Uncertainty* (London: Royal Society, September 2009).

63 Ruth Maclean and Dionne Searcey, "Congo to Auction Land to Oil Companies: 'Our Priority Is Not to Save the Planet,'" *New York Times*, July 24, 2022; Josefine Fokuhl and Todd Gillespie, "Germany Revives Coal as Energy Security Trumps Climate Goals," Bloomberg, December 22, 2022; Severin Carrell, Peter Walker and Helena Horton, "Dismay as Rishi Sunak Vows to 'Max Out' UK Fossil Fuel Reserves," *Guardian*, July 31, 2023; Helen Davidson, "China Continues Coal Spree, Despite Climate Goals," *Guardian*, August 29, 2023; Global Energy Monitor, "India Enters an Unnecessary Coal Plant Permitting Spree in 2023," briefing, August 7, 2023, globalenergymonitor. org; Mariam Zachariah et al., *Extreme Heat in North America, Europe and China in July 2023 Made Much More Likely by Climate Change* (London: World Weather Attribution, 2023).

64 Holly Jean Buck, *After Geoengineering: Climate Tragedy, Repair, and Restoration* (New York: Verso, 2019).

65 Christoph C. Raible et al., "Tambora 1815 as a Test Case for High Impact Volcanic Eruptions: Earth System Effects," *WIREs Climate Change* 7, no. 4 (July/August 2016).

66 Elizabeth Kolbert, *Under a White Sky: The Nature of the Future* (London: Bodley Head, 2021), 179–81.

67 Some climate scientists assess that this circulation is close to shutting down already, no matter what anyone does. Peter Ditlevsen and Susanne Ditlevsen, "Warning of a Forthcoming Collapse of the Atlantic Meridional Overturning Circulation," *Nature Communications* 14, Article 4254 (July 25, 2023).

68 Clive Oppenheimer, "Climatic, Environmental and Human

Consequences of the Largest Known Historic Eruption: Tambora Volcano (Indonesia) 1815," *Progress in Physical Geography: Earth and Environment* 27, no. 2 (June 2003).

69 Brian Kahn, "No, We Shouldn't Just Block Out the Sun," *Gizmodo*, April 24, 2020, cited in Kolbert, *Under a White Sky*.

70 Buck, *After Geoengineering*, 128–33.

71 "Warming will continue beyond 2100 under all ... scenarios except [stringent mitigation]. Surface temperatures will remain approximately constant at elevated levels for many centuries after a complete cessation of net anthropogenic CO_2 emissions." Intergovernmental Panel on Climate Change, *Climate Change 2014 Synthesis Report* (Geneva: IPCC, 2014); Johan Rockström et al., "Safe and Just Earth System Boundaries," *Nature* 619 (July 6, 2023).

72 Donella H. Meadows et al., *The Limits to Growth* (New York: Universe Books, 1972).

73 Andreas Malm, *Corona, Climate, Chronic Emergency: War Communism in the Twenty-First Century* (New York: Verso, 2020). Emphasis in original.

74 Richard I. Cook, "How Complex Systems Fail," 1998.

75 Gerald K. Haines and Robert E. Leggett, eds., *CIA's Analysis of the Soviet Union, 1947–1991: A Documentary Collection* (Washington, DC: Center for the Study of Intelligence, 2001).

76 Ted Nordhaus, "Am I the Mass Murderer? Pushing Back on Climate Catastrophism Is Not a Thought Crime," Breakthrough Institute, March 29, 2022, thebreakthrough.org.

77 Cindi Katz, "Under the Falling Sky: Apocalyptic Environmentalism and the Production of Nature," in Antoni Callari, Stephen Cullenberg and Carole Biewener, eds., *Marxism in the Postmodern Age: Confronting the New World Order* (New York: Guilford Press, 1994); Sasha Lilley et al., *Catastrophism: The Apocalyptic Politics of Collapse and Rebirth* (Oakland, CA: PM Press, 2012); The Invisible Committee, *To Our Friends* (South Pasadena, CA: Semiotext(e), 2015); Leigh Phillips, *Austerity Ecology and the Collapse-Porn Addicts: A Defence of Growth, Progress, Industry and Stuff* (Washington, DC: Zero Books, 2015); Out of the Woods Collective, *Hope against Hope: Writings on Ecological Crisis* (Philadelphia: Common Notions, 2020).

2. Mutual Care

1 Kelly Hayes and Mariame Kaba, *Let This Radicalize You: Organizing and the Revolution of Reciprocal Care* (Chicago: Haymarket Books, 2023).

2 Peter Kropotkin, *Mutual Aid: A Factor of Evolution* (London: Freedom Press, 2009 [1902]).

3 Melani Cammett and Lauren M. MacLean, eds., *The Politics of Non-state Social Welfare* (Ithaca, NY: Cornell University Press, 2014).

4 Mutual Aid Disaster Relief, *Lessons Learned* (zine), June 2020, 19.

5 Dean Spade, *Mutual Aid: Building Solidarity During This Crisis (And the Next)* (New York: Verso, 2020).

6 scott crow, *Black Flags and Windmills: Hope, Anarchy, and the Common Ground Collective* (Oakland, CA: PM Press, 2014).

7 Hurricane Katrina External Review Panel, *The New Orleans Hurricane Protection System: What Went Wrong and Why: A Report* (Reston, VA: American Society of Civil Engineers, 2007); United States Department of Housing and Urban Development, Office of Policy Development and Research, *Current Housing Unit Damage Estimates: Hurricanes Katrina, Rita, and Wilma, February 12, 2006* (Darby, PA: Diane Publishing).

8 "The city's population, estimated at 485,000 in 2000, was reduced to fewer than several thousand by the end of the first week of September 2005." Kevin McCarthy et al., *The Repopulation of New Orleans after Hurricane Katrina* (Santa Monica, CA: RAND Gulf States Policy Institute, 2006).

9 Patrick Sharkey, "Survival and Death in New Orleans: An Empirical Look at the Human Impact of Katrina," *Journal of Black Studies* 37, no. 4 (March 2007); US House of Representatives, Select Bipartisan Committee to Investigate the Preparation for and Response to Hurricane Katrina, *A Failure of Initiative: Final Report of the Select Bipartisan Committee to Investigate the Preparation for and Response to Hurricane Katrina* (Washington, DC: US Government Printing Office, 2006).

10 Anderson Cooper interviewing Senator Mary Landrieu on *Anderson Cooper 360*, September 1, 2005, cnn.com; Sheri Fink, "The Deadly Choices at Memorial," *New York Times*, August 25, 2009.

11 crow, *Black Flags and Windmills*, 18; John P. Clark, *The Impossible Community: Realizing Communitarian Anarchism* (New York: Bloomsbury, 2013).

12 Rhiannon Firth, *Disaster Anarchy: Mutual Aid and Radical Action* (London, Pluto Press, 2022); crow, *Black Flags and Windmills*, 93.

13 United States Census Bureau, "Table B19013: Median Household Income in the Past 12 Months (in 2007 Inflation-Adjusted Dollars)," in *2005–2007 American Community Survey 3-Year Summary File* (December 9, 2008).

14 crow, *Black Flags and Windmills*, 103.

15 Clark, *Impossible Community*, 211.

16 The Invisible Committee, *The Coming Insurrection* (Los Angeles: semiotext(e), 2009 [2007]), 83.

17 Sam Dolnick and Corey Kilgannon, "Wind-Driven Flames Reduce Scores of Homes to Embers in Queens Enclave," *New York Times*, October 30, 2012.

18 Office of the Mayor, New York City Special Initiative for Rebuilding and Resiliency, *A Stronger, More Resilient New York* (June 11, 2013), 13.

19 "Impact of Hurricane Sandy," New York City Community Development Block Grant—Disaster Recovery, nyc.gov.

20 Michael Schwirtz, "Housing Nightmare Looms in Wake of Storm," *New York Times*, November 4, 2012.

21 *Occupy Sandy*, directed by Josh Fox (International WOW Company, 2012), at 15:13.

22 Ibid., Occupy Sandy site coordinator Justin Wedes, at 7:35.

23 These facilities included a kitchen, a medical clinic, media-outreach and legal aid tents, a clothing, bedding and hygiene supplies depot, and a 5,000-volume library housed in a tent paid for by New York music legend Patti Smith. All were destroyed by the NYPD in the course of their clearance of the park, in the predawn hours of November 15, 2011 (along with at least one of my friend Dan's WiFi routers).

24 Working Group on Principles of Consolidation, "Principles of Solidarity," New York City General Assembly, September 23, 2011, nycga.net.

25 Sharon Lerner, "How Sandy Saved Occupy," *American Prospect*, November 27, 2012.

26 Our experience was far from uncommon, nor was this kind of indifference-verging-on-hostility by any means limited to Sandy.

scott crow describes a Red Cross/FEMA site in post-Katrina Baton Rouge turning away hundreds of volunteers willing to ply the treacherous floodwaters in their own boats, "simply because they could not figure out what to do with them." crow, *Black Flags and Windmills*, 10. Clark similarly notes that the Red Cross "was conspicuous by its absence in the areas of greatest need, including the city of New Orleans." Clark, *Impossible Community*, 216.

27 Rebecca Solnit, *A Paradise Built in Hell: The Extraordinary Communities That Arise in Disaster* (London: Penguin, 2009).

28 Dean Spade, "Solidarity Not Charity: Mutual Aid for Mobilization and Survival," *Social Text* 38, no. 1 (March 1, 2020).

29 *Occupy Sandy*, at 8:31.

30 Sam Knight, "Occupy Sandy and the Future of Socialism," *Truthout*, April 5, 2014, in Peer Illner, *Disasters and Social Reproduction: Crisis Response Between the State and Community* (London: Pluto Press, 2021).

31 Nick Pinto, "Hurricane Sandy Is New York's Katrina," *Village Voice*, November 21, 2012.

32 Those suffering impacts from the storm were more than twice as likely to turn to peers for help than they were to seek assistance from any organ or echelon of government. See Kathleen A. Cagney, David Sterrett, Jennifer Benz and Trevor Tompson, "Social Resources and Community Resilience in the Wake of Superstorm Sandy," *PLOS ONE*, August 31, 2016.

33 Firth, *Disaster Anarchy*, 101.

34 Colin Ward, *Anarchy in Action* (London: Freedom Press, 1973).

35 Knight, "Occupy Sandy and the Future of Socialism."

36 Eric Ambinder and David M. Jennings, *The Resilient Social Network* (Falls Church, VA: Homeland Security Studies and Analysis Institute, September 30, 2013).

37 Spade, "Solidarity Not Charity," 133.

38 Michael Haber, "Legal Issues in Mutual Aid Operations: A Preliminary Guide," Hofstra University Legal Studies Research Paper No. 2020-06, June 5, 2020, ssrn.com.

39 "Cambio desde abajo y desde adentro: Notes on Centros de Apoyo Mutuo in post–María Puerto Rico," *Latino Studies* 16, no. 4 (December 2018); Roberto Vélez-Vélez and Jacqueline Villarrubia-Mendoza, "Mobilizing Solidarity: Hurricane María as Structural Opening for Mutual Aid," *Sociological Review* (September 2021); Brian Larkin, "The Politics and Poetics of

Infrastructure," *Annual Review of Anthropology* 42 (October 2013).

40 Sara Ahmed, *The Promise of Happiness* (Durham, NC: Duke University Press, 2010).

41 Hannah Arendt, *The Human Condition*, 2nd ed. (Chicago: University of Chicago Press, 1998 [1958]).

42 Lise Vogel, *Marxism and the Oppression of Women: Toward a Unitary Theory* (New Brunswick, NJ: Rutgers University Press, 1983).

43 Silvia Federici, *Revolution at Point Zero: Housework, Reproduction, and Feminist Struggle* (Oakland, CA: PM Press/ Common Notions, 2012).

44 Hayes and Kaba, *Let This Radicalize You*, 57–79.

45 Robyn C. Spencer, *The Revolution Has Come: Black Power, Gender and the Black Panther Party in Oakland* (Durham, NC: Duke University Press, 2016).

46 Ruth Wilson Gilmore, *Golden Gulag: Prisons, Surplus, Crisis, and Opposition in Globalizing California* (Oakland: University of California Press, 2007).

47 Martha J. Bailey and Nicolas J. Duquette, "How Johnson Fought the War on Poverty: The Economics and Politics of Funding at the Office of Economic Opportunity," *Journal of Economic History* 74, no. 2 (June 2014).

48 Sar A. Levitan, "The Community Action Program: A Strategy to Fight Poverty," *Annals of the American Academy of Political and Social Science* 385 (September 1969).

49 Section 202(a)3 of the Economic Opportunity Act of 1964, Public Law 88-452, August 20, 1964.

50 Lillian B. Rubin, "Maximum Feasible Participation: The Origins, Implications, and Present Status," *Annals of the American Academy of Political and Social Science* 385 (September 1969).

51 Memorandum from Office of Economic Opportunity Director Sargent Shriver, "Involvement of the Poor in All OEO Programs," September 9, 1966.

52 Robert Goodman, *After The Planners* (Middlesex, UK: Penguin Books, 1972).

53 Bobby Seale, *Seize the Time: The Story of the Black Panther Party and Huey P. Newton* (New York: Random House, 1970), 38.

54 Newton, able to cite state code chapter and verse since his days in the Anti-Poverty Center's law library, was famous for leading these patrols with well-thumbed law book in hand. Ibid., 131.

55 Seale statement, Sacramento, CA, May 2, 1967.

56 "Capitol Is Invaded: State Police Halt Armed Negro Band," *Sacramento Bee*, May 2, 1967.

57 Committee on Internal Security, *Gun-Barrel Politics: The Black Panther Party, 1966–1971*, H.R. Rep. No. 92–470 (Washington, DC: US Government Printing Office, 1971).

58 Huey P. Newton, *Revolutionary Suicide* (New York: Random House, 1973), 175.

59 Wallace Turner, "Witness Says Newton Shot Policeman," *New York Times*, August 8, 1968.

60 People v. Newton, 8 Cal.App.3d 359 (Cal. Ct. App. 1970), 87 Cal. Rptr. 394, May 29, 1970; Joe Street, "'Free Huey or the Sky's the Limit': The Black Panther Party and the Campaign to Free Huey P. Newton," *European Journal of American Studies* 14, no. 1 (Spring 2019). See also Emil Caldwell, "Newton Is Cleared of Charges in Slaying," *New York Times*, December 16, 1971.

61 It also led, more or less directly and immediately, to new gun-control legislation—not merely the Mulford Act, but the national Gun Control Act of 1968. Adam Winkler, *Gunfight: The Battle Over the Right to Bear Arms in America* (New York: W.W. Norton, 2011).

62 The "hate groups" encompassed included the Southern Christian Leadership Conference, headed by Rev. Martin Luther King Jr. See memorandum from FBI director J. Edgar Hoover to SAC Albany, "Counterintelligence Program: Black Nationalist Hate Groups: Racial Intelligence," March 4, 1968.

63 Ward Churchill, "To Disrupt, Discredit and Destroy: The FBI's Secret War against the Black Panther Party," in Kathleen Cleaver and George Katsiaficas, eds., *Liberation, Imagination and the Black Panther Party* (New York: Routledge, 2001).

64 Ward Churchill and Jim Vander Wall, *The COINTELPRO Papers: Documents from the FBI's Secret Wars Against Domestic Dissent* (Boston: South End Press, 1990), 139.

65 Huey P. Newton, "Black Capitalism Re-analyzed I: June 5, 1971," in *To Die for the People: The Writings of Huey P. Newton* (New York: Vintage Books, 1972).

66 Ibid.
67 Spencer, *The Revolution Has Come*, 85.
68 Joshua Bloom and Waldo E. Martin Jr., *Black Against Empire: The History and Politics of the Black Panther Party* (Oakland: University of California Press, 2013), 181.
69 See Spencer, *The Revolution Has Come*, 173, 235.
70 Earl A. Neil, "The Role of the Church and the Survival Program," *Black Panther*, May 15, 1971.
71 Spencer, *The Revolution Has Come*, 131.
72 The Panthers' Sickle-Cell Anemia Research Foundation directly screened "nearly half a million people throughout the country" in the three years from 1971: David Hilliard, ed., *The Black Panther Party: Service to the People Programs* (Albuquerque: University of New Mexico Press, 2008), 24. Black Panthers Bobby Seale and Marsha Martin discussed the program and its approach to screening for sickle-cell disease on the nationwide *Mike Douglas Show* on February 16, 1972: Alondra Nelson, *Body and Soul* (Minneapolis: University of Minnesota Press, 2011), 127.
73 "Free Food Program," in Hilliard, *Black Panther Party*, 36.
74 As reformulated in the version of March 29, 1972.
75 Mary T. Bassett, "No Justice, No Health: The Black Panther Party's Fight for Health in Boston and Beyond," *Journal of African American Studies* 23, no. 4 (December 2019).
76 Nelson, *Body and Soul*.
77 Olivia B. Waxman, "What School Didn't Teach You About the Black Panthers," *Time*, February 25, 2021.
78 Nelson, *Body and Soul*, 79.
79 Spencer, *The Revolution Has Come*, 119.
80 Hilliard, *Black Panther Party*, 5.
81 Spencer, *The Revolution Has Come*, 119.
82 Alondra Nelson, "The *Longue Durée* of Black Lives Matter," *American Journal of Public Health* 106, no. 10 (October 2016).
83 Judson L. Jeffries, *Comrades: A Local History of the Black Panther Party* (Bloomington: Indiana University Press, 2007); crow, *Black Flags and Windmills*, 33.
84 Spencer, *The Revolution Has Come*, 116.
85 Bob Avakian, "Rise and Fall of the Panthers: End of the Black Power Era," *Workers Vanguard*, no. 4, January 1972.
86 Jane Rhodes, *Framing the Black Panthers: The Spectacular Rise of a Black Power Icon* (New York: New Press, 2007), 105.

87 "How did we feed the children? We told storekeepers: 'If you don't give us a dozen eggs a day, you have a problem. You really won't have a store.' People cry, 'Oh, my God, the Panthers are ruthless! They're extortionists!' OK, but we fed our people." Elaine Brown, interviewed by George Luke, July 2, 2022.

88 "Black Panther Says He Made Bomb," *San Francisco Chronicle*, June 25, 1970, in Hugh Pearson, *The Shadow of the Panther: Huey Newton and the Price of Black Power in America* (Reading, MA: Addison-Wesley, 1994), 199.

89 Spencer, *The Revolution Has Come*, 123–4.

90 Newton, *To Die for the People*, 104.

91 Spencer, *The Revolution Has Come*, 94.

92 Elaine Brown, *A Taste of Power: A Black Woman's Story* (New York: Pantheon Books, 1992), 191.

93 Spencer, *The Revolution Has Come*.

94 Ibid.

95 Johanna Fernández, *The Young Lords: A Radical History* (Chapel Hill: University of North Carolina Press, 2020).

96 The original version of the Patients' Bill of Rights was written by Cleo Silvers. Most of the more radical provisions of the Silvers version have since been deleted. Alondra Nelson, "'Genuine Struggle and Care': An Interview with Cleo Silvers," *American Journal of Public Health* 106, no. 10 (October 2016).

97 crow, *Black Flags and Windmills*, 21.

98 Taken by Stephen Shames in Palo Alto in 1972.

99 "Greece Admits Fudging Euro Entry," BBC, November 15, 2004.

100 Kate Connolly, "Greek Debt Crisis: The View from Germany," *Guardian*, February 11, 2010.

101 Aditya Chakrabortty, "Athens Protests: Syntagma Square on Frontline of European Austerity Protests," *Guardian*, June 19, 2011; *Solidarity for All, 2014–2015: Building Hope against Fear and Devastation* (Athens: Solidarity for All, January 21, 2015), 17.

102 Ibid., 3-7.

103 Kees van Gool and Mark Pearson, "Health, Austerity and Economic Crisis: Assessing the Short-Term Impact in OECD Countries," OECD Health Working Papers No. 76, 2014; Elias Kondilis et al., "Economic Crisis, Restrictive Policies, and

the Population's Health and Health Care: The Greek Case," *American Journal of Public Health* 103, no. 6 (June 2013).

104 van Gool and Pearson, "Health, Austerity and Economic Crisis."

105 Dimitra-Dora Teloni and Sofia Adam, "Solidarity Clinics and Social Work in the Era of Crisis in Greece," *International Social Work* 61, no. 6 (November 2018); Effie Simou and Eleni Koutsogeorgou, "Effects of the Economic Crisis on Health and Healthcare in Greece in the Literature from 2009 to 2013: A Systematic Review," *Health Policy* 115, nos. 2–3 (April 2014).

106 Amalia A. Ifanti et al., "Financial Crisis and Austerity Measures in Greece: Their Impact on Health Promotion Policies and Public Health Care," *Health Policy* 113, nos. 1–2 (November 2013); Alexander Kentikelenis et al., "Health Effects of Financial Crisis: Omens of a Greek Tragedy," *Lancet* 378, no. 9801 (October 22, 2011).

107 Stefanos Bonovas and Georgios Nikolopoulos, "High-Burden Epidemics in Greece in the Era of Economic Crisis: Early Signs of a Public Health Tragedy," *Journal of Preventive Medicine and Hygiene* 53, no. 3 (September 2012); Organization for Economic Co-operation and Development, "Suicide," in *Health at a Glance: Europe 2016: State of Health in the EU Cycle* (Paris: OECD Publishing, 2016).

108 Nikolaos Vlachadis et al., "Mortality and the Economic Crisis in Greece," *Lancet* 383, no. 9918 (February 22, 2014).

109 Lower Syntagma was occupied by those espousing a variety of left, progressive and anarchist positions, and Upper Syntagma by those who tended toward nationalism. Maria Kaika and Lazaros Karaliotas, "The Spatialization of Democratic Politics: Insights from Indignant Squares," *European Urban and Regional Studies* 23, no. 4 (October 2016).

110 Helena Smith, "Greece Votes for Five-Year Austerity Plan," *Guardian*, June 29, 2011; "Greece: Warning after 'Massive' Amounts of Tear Gas Fired by Police," Amnesty International UK, June 29, 2011, amnesty.org.

111 Sissi Korizi and Antonis Vradis, "From Innocence to Realisation," *City* 16, nos. 1–2 (April 2012).

112 The Coordination Committee of Social Solidarity Clinics identifies the solidarity clinic in Rethimno, Crete, as the very first such facility operating in Greece, from 2008 onward: *Social Solidarity Clinics and Pharmacies: Making Solidarity Contagious*

(Coordination Committee of Social Solidarity Clinics and Pharmacies of Attica, 2015). Angelos Varvarousis and Giorgos Kallis, "Commoning against the Crisis," in Manuel Castells et al., eds., *Another Economy Is Possible: Culture and Economy in a Time of Crisis* (Cambridge, UK: Polity Press, 2017). Elisavet Hasa, "In the Absence of Care: Building Solidarity in Athens," *Avery Review*, no. 54 (October 2021).

113 At the movement's peak, the number of solidarity clinics operating in Greece exceeded forty: *Social Solidarity Clinics*, 2; CareNotes Collective, eds., *For Health Autonomy: Horizons of Care Beyond Austerity, Reflections from Greece* (Brooklyn: Common Notions, 2020).

114 Wolfgang Rüdig and Georgios Karyotis, "Who Protests in Greece? Mass Opposition to Austerity," *British Journal of Political Science* 44, no. 3 (July 2014).

115 John Wiltshire, "After Syntagma: Where Are the Occupiers Now?," *OpenDemocracy*, May 24, 2013.

116 Jacob Chamberlain, "'We Won't Pay' Movement Brings Guerrilla Electricity to Poverty Stricken Greece," Common Dreams, August 8, 2013, commondreams.org; Jon Henley, "Greece's Solidarity Movement: 'It's a Whole New Model—and It's Working,'" *Guardian*, January 23, 2015.

117 Elisavet Hasa, "Making-Do in Times of Crisis: Exploring the Architecture of Solidarity Clinics and Pharmacies in Athens," in Liska Chan and Elleen Stapleton, eds., *Making Do and Transformational Participatory Urbanism: Communities Claiming Space and Creating Place* (Amsterdam: Amsterdam University Press, 2024).

118 Hasa, "In the Absence of Care." A decree passed by the SYRIZA government in 2016 mandated, further, that all unused public properties of less than 100 sq m area be transferred to whatever suitable "agency of the social solidarity economy" could be found.

119 Stavros Stavrides, *Common Space: The City as Commons* (London: Zed Books, 2016).

120 Ioanna Theocharopoulou, *Builders, Housewives and the Construction of Modern Athens* (Athens: Onassis Foundation, 2022). Following the worker takeover of an owner-abandoned tile factory called Vio.Me, in Thessaloniki in 2013: Haris Malamidis, "Workers' Medical Center at Vio.Me Self-Managed Factory," in CareNotes Collective, *For Health Autonomy*.

121 Hasa, "Making-Do in Times of Crisis."

122 Ibid.

123 *Solidarity for All, 2014–2015*, 15.

124 Tonia Katerini, "Organising to Survive in Greece," *Red Pepper*, December 5, 2012.

125 Donatella Della Porta et al., *Movement Parties against Austerity* (Cambridge, UK: Polity Press, 2017); Varvarousis and Kallis, "Commoning against the Crisis," 150.

126 CareNotes Collective, "The Autonomy of Care: From Heathcare to Care Work in Greece," in *For Health Autonomy*, 39.

127 Cassie Thornton, "A Different Medicine Is Possible in Our Global Economic Crisis: Reinventing Healthcare in Greece (and the United States)," in CareNotes Collective, *For Health Autonomy*.

128 Ibid.

129 Cassie Thornton, *The Hologram: Feminist, Peer-to-Peer Health for a Post-Pandemic Future* (London: Pluto Press, 2020).

130 CareNotes Collective, "Elements of Care Work in Greece," in *For Health Autonomy*.

131 Thornton, "A Different Medicine Is Possible."

132 *Solidarity for All, 2014–2015*, 12.

133 The solidarity networks consistently upheld what we'd ordinarily think of as a left critique of society. Access to the community kitchens operated by the fascist party Golden Dawn, however, was restricted to those who could furnish proof of Greek citizenship.

134 CareNotes Collective, "The Autonomy of Care," 30.

135 Thornton, *The Hologram*, 5. Emphasis in original.

136 Hasa, "In the Absence of Care."

137 Hasa, "Making-Do in Times of Crisis."

138 *Solidarity for All, 2014–2015*, 17. Sometimes these referrals were made on a *quid pro quo* basis: Malamidis reports that the public hospital in Rethimno, Crete, offered to treat two care seekers per day gratis, in exchange for medicine from the inventory of the local solidarity clinic. Haris Malamidis, *Social Movements and Solidarity Structures in Crisis-Ridden Greece*, (Amsterdam: Amsterdam University Press, 2020), 180.

139 CareNotes Collective, "The Autonomy of Care," 30.

140 *Social Solidarity Clinics and Pharmacies*, 3.

141 *Solidarity for All, 2014–2015*, 28.

142 CareNotes Collective, "Updates on the National Solidarity Clinic Assemblies: An Interview with Ilektra Bethymouti," in *For Health Autonomy*, 140.

143 Ibid., 150.

144 Evel Economakis, "A View from Athens: Is a 'Backflip' by Syriza in the Greek Debt Crisis Negotiations Inevitable?," *New Statesman*, June 26, 2015.

145 Shao Lin et al., "What Happened to Our Environment and Mental Health as a Result of Hurricane Sandy?," *Disaster Medicine and Public Health Preparedness* 10, no. 3 (June 2016). See also Immaculata Abba, "In the Dark in Nigeria: What Poor Electricity Does to Our Minds," *Popula*, July 29, 2023.

146 Paulo Freire, *Pedagogy of the Oppressed*, trans. Myra Bergman Ramos (London: Penguin Books, 2017 [1970]).

3. Collective Power

1 Point 4 of the Charter of Constitution of Solidarity Clinics and Pharmacies, cited in Elisavet Hasa, "In the Absence of Care: Building Solidarity in Athens," *Avery Review*, no. 54 (October 2021).

2 David Graeber and David Wengrow, *The Dawn of Everything* (London: Allen Lane, 2021).

3 Janet Biehl, introduction to Janet Biehl, ed., *The Murray Bookchin Reader* (London: Cassell, 1997).

4 Curiously, he also appears to have been responsible for translating the Spanish anarchist concept of the *grupo de afinidad* into English where, as the "affinity group," it went on to inform much of the left activism of the 1960s, 1970s and 1980s.

5 Murray Bookchin, "Post-Scarcity Anarchism," in *Post-Scarcity Anarchism* (Berkeley, CA: Ramparts Press, 1971).

6 The Anarchist Library: theanarchistlibrary.org; Anarchy Archives: dwardmac.pitzer.edu.

7 Memorandum from Frank Press, Executive Office of the President, Office of Science and Technology Policy, "Release of Fossil CO_2 and the Possibility of a Catastrophic Climate Change," July 7, 1977; Bookchin, "Post-Scarcity Anarchism."

8 Murray Bookchin (writing as "Lewis Herber"), "Ecology and Revolutionary Thought," self-published in *Comment* 1, no. 1 (1964).

9 John Bellamy Foster, *Marx's Ecology: Materialism and Nature*

(New York: Monthly Review Press, 2000); Combahee River Collective, "The Combahee River Collective Statement," April 1977.

10 Murray Bookchin, "Municipalization: Community Ownership of the Economy," *Green Perspectives: Newsletter of the Green Program Project* 2 (February 1986).

11 Geneviève Reday-Mulvey and Walter R. Stahel, *The Potential for Substituting Manpower for Energy* (Geneva: Batelle Geneva Research Center, July 1977). Stahel appears to have used the term "closed-loop economy" for the first time in a 1982 paper, "The Product-Life Factor."

12 Murray Bookchin, "The Communalist Project," *Communalism: International Journal for a Rational Society* 2 (2002).

13 Murray Bookchin, "Cities: The Unfolding of Reason in History," in *The Next Revolution: Popular Assemblies and the Promise of Direct Democracy* (New York: Verso, 2015).

14 Murray Bookchin, "The Communalist Project," emphasis in original.

15 "It is a troubling fact that neither decentralization nor self-sufficiency in itself is necessarily democratic." Murray Bookchin, "The Meaning of Confederalism," in Murray Bookchin, *The Next Revolution*.

16 Not the compromised second draft: Students for a Democratic Society, *The Port Huron Statement* (New York, 1962); Dimitrios Roussopoulos, "Preface to the 2005 edition," in Dimitrios Roussopoulos and C. George Benello, eds., *Participatory Democracy: Prospects for Democratizing Democracy* (New York: Black Rose Books, 2005), x.

17 Francesca Polletta, *Freedom Is an Endless Meeting: Democracy in American Social Movements* (Chicago: University of Chicago Press, 2002), 204.

18 Gísli Pálsson, "Of Althings!," in Bruno Latour and Peter Weibel, eds., *Making Things Public: Atmospheres of Democracy* (Cambridge, MA: MIT Press, 2005); José Barreiro, *Indian Roots of American Democracy* (Ithaca, NY: Cornell University Press, 1992); Roxanne Dunbar-Ortiz, *An Indigenous Peoples' History of the United States* (Boston: Beacon Press, 2014).

19 John Chapman, Bisserka Gaydarska and Duncan Hale, "Nebelivka: Assembly Houses, Ditches, and Social Structure," in *Trypillia Mega-Sites and European Prehistory* (London: Routledge, 2016); Bisserka Gaydarska, "Fragmenting Trypillian

Megasites: A Bottom-Up Approach," in T. L. Thurston and Manuel Fernández-Götz, eds., *Power from Below in Premodern Societies: The Dynamics of Political Complexity in the Archaeological Record* (Cambridge, UK: Cambridge University Press, 2021); David Wengrow, lecture at the Architectural Association School of Architecture, London, October 14, 2022.

20 Hannah Arendt, *The Human Condition*, 2nd ed. (Chicago: University of Chicago Press, 1998 [1958]); C. L. R. James, "Every Cook Can Govern: A Study of Democracy in Ancient Greece—Its Meaning for Today," *Correspondence* 2, no. 12 (June 1956).

21 R. K. Sinclair, *Democracy and Participation in Athens* (Cambridge, UK: Cambridge University Press, 1988).

22 Peter Kropotkin, *The Great French Revolution 1789–1793* (Oakland, CA: PM Press, 2021 [1909]).

23 Graham Smith, "Popular Assemblies: From New England Town Meetings to Participatory Budgeting," in *Democratic Innovations: Designing Institutions for Citizen Participation* (Cambridge, UK: Cambridge University Press, 2009).

24 Debbie Bookchin, "The Future We Deserve," in Barcelona en Común with Debbie Bookchin and Ada Colau, *Fearless Cities: A Guide to the Global Municipalist Movement* (Oxford, UK: New Internationalist, 2019).

25 James C. Scott, *Seeing Like a State: How Certain Schemes to Improve the Human Condition Have Failed* (New Haven, CT: Yale University Press, 1998).

26 Laurence Veysey, *The Communal Experience: Anarchist and Mystical Counter-Cultures in America* (New York: Harper and Row, 1973).

27 Murray Bookchin, "The Communalist Project," emphasis in original.

28 Alberto Corsín Jiménez and Adolfo Estalella, "Assembling Neighbors: The City as Hardware, Method, and 'A Very Messy Kind of Archive,'" *Common Knowledge* 20, no. 1 (Winter 2014).

29 Elsewhere Estalella does describe a meeting of the Lavapiés assembly's working group on "migration and coexistence" with a "peak attendance [of] at least 80 people, approximately 30 of them young black Senegalese," partially conducted in Wolof. Adolfo Estalella and Alberto Corsín Jiménez, "Matters of Sense: Preoccupation in Madrid's Popular Assemblies Movement," in Anders Blok and Ignacio Farías, eds., *Urban Cosmopolitics:*

Agencements, Assemblies, Atmospheres (New York: Routledge, 2016).

30 Jo Freeman (writing as "Joreen"), "The Tyranny of Structure-lessness," self-published, 1970; Nancy Fraser, "Rethinking the Public Sphere: A Contribution to the Critique of Actually Existing Democracy," *Social Text* 25/26 (1990); Lynn M. Sanders, "Against Deliberation," *Political Theory* 25, no. 3 (June 1997).

31 In a late screed, Bookchin does address some of the issues raised by Sanders. Murray Bookchin, "Comments on the International Social Ecology Network Gathering and the 'Deep Social Ecology' of John Clark," September 20, 1995.

32 Kali Akuno, "People's Assembly Overview," in Kali Akuno and Ajamu Nangwaya with Cooperation Jackson, *Jackson Rising: The Struggle for Economic Democracy and Black Self-Determination in Jackson, Mississippi* (Montreal: Daraja Press, 2017).

33 Sherry P. Arnstein, "A Ladder of Citizen Participation," *Journal of the American Institute of Planners* 35, no. 4 (July 1969).

34 Akuno, "People's Assembly Overview," 130.

35 Iris Marion Young, *Justice and the Politics of Difference* (Princeton, NJ: Princeton University Press, 1990).

36 David Harvey, *Rebel Cities: From the Right to the City to the Urban Revolution* (New York: Verso, 2012).

37 Sarah Schulman, *Let the Record Show: A Political History of ACT UP New York, 1987–1993* (New York: Farrar, Straus and Giroux, 2021); Richard J. F. Day, *Gramsci Is Dead: Anarchist Currents in the Newest Social Movements* (Ann Arbor: Pluto Press, 2005); Hugh D'Andrade et al., "How to Make a Critical Mass: Lessons and Ideas from the San Francisco Bay Area Experience," in *Critical Mass: Bicycling's Defiant Celebration* (Oakland, CA: AK Press, 2002); Polletta, *Freedom Is an Endless Meeting*, 189.

38 Mike Gonzalez, "The Zapatistas: The Challenges of Revolution in a New Millennium," in Tom Hayden, ed., *The Zapatista Reader* (New York: Thunder's Mouth Press/Nation Books, 2002); Carne Ross, *The Leaderless Revolution: How Ordinary People Will Take Power and Change Politics in the 21st Century* (London: Penguin, 2011).

39 Marina Sitrin, "Ruptures in Imagination: Horizontalism, Autogestion and Affective Politics in Argentina," *Policy and Practice* 5 (Autumn 2007).

40 Richard Banégas, Florence Brisset-Foucault and Armando Cutolo, "Street Parliaments: Public Spaces for Speech and Citizenship in Africa," in Anne Davidian and Laurent Jean-pierre, eds., *What Makes An Assembly?* (London: Sternberg Press, 2022).

41 These are of somewhat mysterious origin, though one common folk history attributes them to longstanding practice in Quaker meetings. See Polletta, *Freedom Is an Endless Meeting*, 190.

42 For a more critical consideration of Indigenous elements in EZLN practice, see Mihalis Mentinis, *Zapatistas: The Chiapas Revolt and What It Means for Radical Politics* (Ann Arbor: Pluto Press, 2006).

43 David Graeber, "The New Anarchists," *New Left Review* 13 (January/February 2002).

44 Andrew Cornell, "Occupy Wall Street and Consensus Decision Making: Historicizing the Preoccupation with Process," in Social Text Collective, *This Is What Democracy Looks Like*, December 9, 2012.

45 Barcelona en Comú, *Fearless Cities*, 8.

46 Laura Roth and Kate Shea Baird, "Municipalism and the Feminization of Politics," *ROAR* 6 (Summer 2017).

47 Estalella and Corsín Jiménez, "Matters of Sense."

48 Marta Junqué, Caren Tepp and Mariano Fernández, "Organizing a Municipalist Platform: Structure and Confluence," in Barcelona en Comú, *Fearless Cities*.

49 Murray Bookchin, "Municipalization: Community Ownership of the Economy."

50 Ernesto Laclau and Chantal Mouffe, *Hegemony and Socialist Strategy: Towards a Radical Democratic Politics* (New York: Verso, 1985).

51 Antonio Negri, *Insurgencies: Constituent Power and the Modern State* (Minneapolis: University of Minnesota Press, 2009 [1999]); Michael Hardt and Antonio Negri, *Assembly* (New York: Oxford University Press: 2017).

52 Bruno Latour, *Aramis, or the Love of Technology*, trans. Catherine Porter (Cambridge, MA: Harvard University Press, 1996).

53 It is one of the ironies of history that, despite their hewing fairly closely to the tactics he prescribed for the acquisition of local power, virtually no one among the participants in Spanish municipalism I have spoken with spontaneously identifies Murray Bookchin as an inspiration.

54 DifRed, "Guía rápida para la dinamización de asambleas populares," #Acampadasol, May 31, 2011, madrid.tomalaplaza .net.

55 Stephen Burgen, "How to Win Back the City: The Barcelona en Comú Guide to Overthrowing the Elite," *Guardian*, June 22, 2016.

56 Ana Mendéz de Andés, personal communication, July 2023.

57 Oscar Reyes, "Rooted in the Neighbourhood: What Happened to Spain's Assemblies?," *Red Pepper*, October 18, 2012.

58 Simon Gareth Thorpe, "Let's Win Madrid: Radical Democracy and Prefigurative Constitutionality in the New Municipalism," PhD thesis, University of Warwick, 2021.

59 Movimiento de Liberación Gráfica de Madrid, *Al final, ganamos las elecciones* (Madrid, 2017).

60 Sixtine van Outryve d'Ydewalle, "Becoming Mayor to Abolish the Position of Mayor? Thinking the Line between Reform and Revolution in a Communalist Perspective," *Unbound: Harvard Journal of the Legal Left* 12 (2019).

61 Sam Jones, "Madrid's New Rightwing Council Suspends Low-Emissions Zone," *Guardian*, June 18, 2019.

62 Lavinia Steinfort and Satoko Kishimoto, "From Terrassa to Barcelona: Cities and Citizens Reclaim Public Water and Other Essential Services," Transnational Institute, April 4, 2017, tni .org.

63 Hilary Wainwright, *Reclaim the State: Experiments in Popular Democracy* (New York: Verso, 2003).

64 Staal cites an unattributed 2015 population figure for the three cantons of 4.6 million: Jonas Staal, "Theater of the Stateless," in Renée in der Maur and Jonas Staal, eds., *New World Academy Reader #5: Stateless Democracy* (2015). The lower figure is for October 2017: Fabrice Balanche, *Sectarianism in Syria's Civil War* (Washington, DC: Washington Institute for Near East Policy, 2018).

65 Bill Weinberg, "Syria's Kurdish Revolution: The Anarchist Element and the Challenge of Solidarity," *Fifth Estate* 393 (Spring 2015).

66 Michael Taussig, "The Mastery of Non-Mastery: A Report and Reflections from Kobane," *Public Seminar*, August 7, 2015.

67 Tim Weiner, "U.S. Helped Turkey Find and Capture Kurd Rebel," *New York Times*, February 20, 1999.

68 Debbie Bookchin, "How My Father's Ideas Helped the Kurds

Create a New Democracy," *New York Review of Books*, June 15, 2018.

69 Akbar Shahid Ahmed, "America's Best Allies against ISIS Are Inspired by a Bronx-Born Libertarian Socialist," *HuffPost*, December 18, 2015; Murray Bookchin, *Urbanization without Cities: The Rise and Decline of Citizenship* (New York: Black Rose Books, 1992).

70 Debbie Bookchin, "How My Father's Ideas Helped the Kurds."

71 Abdullah Öcalan, *Democratic Confederalism* (London: Transmedia Publishing, January 5, 2015).

72 Damian Gerber and Shannon Brincat, "When Öcalan Met Bookchin: The Kurdish Freedom Movement and the Political Theory of Democratic Confederalism," *Geopolitics* 26, no. 4 (2021).

73 Havin Güneşer, *The Art of Freedom: A Brief History of the Kurdish Liberation Struggle* (Oakland, CA: PM Press, 2021).

74 Michael Knapp, Anya Flach and Ercan Ayboga, *Revolution in Rojava: Democratic Autonomy and Women's Liberation in Syrian Kurdistan* (London: Pluto Press, 2016).

75 Ahmet Hamdi Akkaya and Joost Jongerden, "Reassembling the Political: The PKK and the Project of Radical Democracy," *European Journal of Turkish Studies* 14 (2012).

76 Abdullah Öcalan, "Declaration of Democratic Confederalism in Kurdistan," March 20, 2005.

77 Dilar Dirik, "Rojava: To Dare Imagining," in Dilar Dirik et al., eds., *To Dare Imagining: Rojava Revolution*, (New York: Autonomedia, 2016).

78 *Gulîstan, Land of Roses*, directed by Zaynê Akyol (Canada and Germany, 2016).

79 Knapp, Flack, and Ayboga, *Revolution in Rojava*, 86.

80 Janet Biehl, "Rojava's Communes and Councils," *New Compass*, January 31, 2015.

81 Committee of Diplomacy of Kongreya Star, *Kongreya Star: About the Work and Ideas of Kongreya Star, the Women's Movement in Rojava* (August 2016), 6.

82 Fabrice Balanche, "From Qamishli to Qamishlo: A Trip to Rojava's New Capital," Fikra Forum, May 8, 2017, washington institute.org.

83 Dilar Dirik, *The Kurdish Women's Movement: History, Theory, Practice* (London: Pluto Press, 2022); Havin Güneşer, "The Rebellion of the Oldest Colony: Jineology—the Science of

Women," in *The Art of Freedom: A Brief History of the Kurdish Liberation Struggle* (Oakland, CA: PM Press, 2021).

84 The word *jin* has since become somewhat familiar to audiences in the West in the context of *jin, jiyan, azadi,* or "woman, life, freedom," an Öcalan coinage that later became the primary slogan of the 2022 uprisings against the theocracy in Iran. Gönül Kaya, "Why Jineology? Re-Constructing the Sciences Towards a Communal and Free Life," in In der Maur and Staal, *New World Academy Reader #5;* Abdullah Öcalan, *The Sociology of Freedom: Manifesto of the Democratic Civilization,* vol. 3 (Oakland, CA: PM Press, 2020 [2003]).

85 Harriet Allsop and Wladimir van Wilgenburg, *The Kurds of Northern Syria: Governance, Diversity and Conflicts* (London: I.B. Tauris, 2019).

86 Abdullah Öcalan, *Liberating Life: Women's Revolution* (Cologne: International Initiative Edition, 2013).

87 Janet Biehl, "Revolutionary Education: Two Academies in Rojava," in In der Maur and Staal, *New World Academy Reader #5.* Despite the essentialism he displayed elsewhere, Öcalan himself was capable of acknowledging that the "female and male gender identities that we know today are constructs": Öcalan, *Liberating Life.*

88 David Graeber, interviewed by Pinar Öğünç; "No, This Is a Genuine Revolution," in Dirik et al., *To Dare Imagining.*

89 The Kurdish word for "Congress" is variously transliterated into English as both "Kongreya" and "Kongra." The organization itself has published documents under both spellings.

90 Güneşer, "Rebellion of the Oldest Colony," 37.

91 Committee of Diplomacy of Kongreya Star, *Kongreya Star,* 7.

92 Kongra Star, *Mala Jin: Empowering Women, Strengthening Society* (January 2021), 3.

93 Zîlan Diyar, "The Whole World Is Talking about Us, Kurdish Women," in In der Maur and Staal, *New World Academy Reader #5.*

94 Knapp, Flach and Ayboga, *Revolution in Rojava,* 171.

95 Katherine Finn, "Rojava Is an Unexpected Oasis of Progress in Syria," *Law Society Gazette,* November 23, 2018.

96 Knapp, Flach and Ayboga, *Revolution in Rojava,* 168.

97 Ibid., 170.

98 TATORT Kurdistan, *Democratic Autonomy in North Kurdistan: The Council Movement, Gender Liberation, and Ecology—in*

Practice, a Reconnaissance into Southeastern Turkey, trans. Janet Biehl (Porsgrunn, Norway: New Compass, 2013), 60.

99 Kongreya Star, *Mala Jin*, 10.

100 Abir Khaled, "Rojava's Prisional Systems," *Periferias* 7 (2022).

101 Graeber interviewed by Pinar Öğünç.

102 Knapp, Flach and Ayboga, *Revolution in Rojava*, 74.

103 Dirik, "Rojava: To Dare Imagining."

104 Knapp, Flach and Ayboga, *Revolution in Rojava*, 88.

105 Carol E. Lee and Courtney Kube, "Chaos in Syria, Washington after Trump Call with Erdogan Unleashed Turkish Military," NBC News, October 7, 2019.

106 Bethan McKernan, Julian Borger and Dan Sabbagh, "Turkey Unleashes Airstrikes against Kurds in North-east Syria," *Guardian*, October 9, 2019.

107 Bethan McKernan and Julian Borger, "Turkey and Russia Agree on Deal over Buffer Zone in Northern Syria," *Guardian*, October 22, 2019.

108 Rojava Information Center, "Incessant War: Turkey's Drone Campaign in North and East Syria, 2022," March 2023, rojavainformationcenter.com.

109 Knapp, Flach and Ayboga, *Revolution in Rojava*, 85.

4. Beyond Hope

1 Amy Starecheski, *Ours to Lose: When Squatters Became Home-owners in New York City* (Chicago: University of Chicago Press, 2016). You can see the actual bike for yourself at the Museum of Reclaimed Urban Space (MoRUS), at 155 Avenue C between Ninth and Tenth Streets. As MoRUS is co-located with the still very much active C-Squat, hours may, uh, vary (and access to the bike in particular may be subject to negotiation with residents).

2 Margaret Kohn, "The Power of Place: The House of the People as Counterpublic," *Polity* 33, no. 4 (Summer 2001). See also Michel Foucault, "Of Other Spaces, Heterotopias," trans. Jay Miskowiec, *Architecture, Mouvement, Continuité* 5 (1984 [1967]).

3 Thomas C. Schelling, *The Strategy of Conflict* (Cambridge, MA: Harvard University Press, 1960).

4 Samaneh Moafi, "Negative Commons," interview by Institute for Postnatural Studies, June 18, 2020, instituteforpostnatural studies.org.

5   Benjamin Foerster-Baldenius and Florian Stirnemann, *Float-ing University Berlin 2018—An Illustrated Report* (Berlin: raumlaborberlin, 2019). For more on raumlaborberlin's practice of building structures from recovered, upcycled or commodity materials on wastegrounds and urban sacrifice zones, see Markus Bader and Jan Liesegang, eds., *Building the City Together: The Osthang Project* (Berlin: raumlaborberlin, 2014).

6   The unusual degree of flexibility built into its conception allowed Floating University to set structures farther apart and deconcentrate seating areas during the COVID summers of 2021 and 2022. George Kafka, "Floating University in Berlin, Germany by Raumlabor," *Architectural Review*, September 26, 2022.

7   Charlotte Malterre-Barthes, *A Moratorium on New Construc-tion* (London: Sternberg Press, 2024).

8   Elaine Brown interviewed by George Luke, July 2, 2022.

9   Sometimes no breaking and entering is necessary, because the occupiers of a derelict site are already on the premises—as at the VIO.ME factory in Thessaloniki, Greece, occupied, operated and managed by its workers since 2013 under the wonderful slogan "Occupy, Resist, Produce." Niko Georgiades, "Occupy, Resist, Produce: Inside the Self-Managed Factory of Vio.Me," *Unicorn Riot*, April 16, 2019.

10 Mutual Aid Disaster Relief, *Workshop Facilitation Guide* (2018).

11 Michel de Certeau, *The Practice of Everyday Life*, trans. Steven Rendall (Berkeley: University of California Press, 1984), 37.

12 Paul Baran, "On Distributed Communications Networks," RAND Corporation Document P-2626, September 1962.

13 Attempts to disrupt power grids, telecommunication networks and other physical infrastructure have increased considerably in the United States over the decade from 2013. While respon-sibility for these attacks was split more or less evenly between jihadi Salafist and white-supremacist groups in the early part of this period, virtually all of the increase since 2019 can be traced to groups of the extreme right. Ilana Krill and Bennett Clifford, *Mayhem, Murder, and Misdirection: Violent Extremist Attack Plots Against Critical Infrastructure in the United States, 2016–2022* (Washington, DC: Program on Extremism at George Washington University, August 2022). See also Colin Clarke et

al., "The Targeting of Infrastructure by America's Violent Far-Right," *CTC Sentinel* 16, no. 5 (May 2023).

14 Federal Communications Commission, "Communications Status Report for Areas Impacted by Hurricane Maria," October 4, 2017, fcc.gov.

15 scott crow, *Black Flags and Windmills: Hope, Anarchy, and the Common Ground Collective* (Oakland, CA: PM Press, 2014), 100–1.

16 Joe Sacco, *Safe Area Goražde: The War in Eastern Bosnia 1992–95* (Seattle: Fantagraphics, 2000).

17 Defined as "use of hydro power on a very small scale to provide electricity for lighting, battery and mobile phone charging" in a now-lost Intermediate Technology Development Group document, "Pico Hydro Power," undated. Other, more technical definitions specify systems with a maximum output of five kilowatts or less. See Phillip Maher and Nigel Smith, *Pico Hydro for Village Power: A Practical Manual for Schemes up to 5 kW in Hilly Areas* (Department for International Development, 2001).

18 José Juan Terrasa-Soler and Daniela Lloveras-Marxuach, "Community Power as Provocation: Local Control for Resilience and Equity," *Scenario* 7 (Winter 2020); Resilient Power Puerto Rico, *Program Lookbook 2017–2022* (January 2023).

19 Arturo Massol-Deyá, "Our Energy for Our Country," *Scenario* 7 (Winter 2020).

20 "What Will Be the Impact of India's Rice-Export Ban?," *Economist*, July 26, 2023; Christina Lu and Amy Mackinnon, "Russia Declares War on Wheat, Peas, and Barley," *Foreign Policy*, July 21, 2023.

21 Michelle L. Colgrave et al., "Perspectives on Future Protein Production," *Journal of Agricultural and Food Chemistry* 69, no. 50 (December 22, 2021).

22 George Monbiot, *Regenesis: Feeding the World without Devouring the Planet* (London: Penguin, 2022).

23 Chris Smaje, *Saying NO to a Farm-Free Future: The Case for an Ecological Food System and against Manufactured Foods* (London: Chelsea Green Publishing, 2023), 53.

24 Ibid.

25 Helena K. Rene, *China's Sent-Down Generation: Public Administration and the Legacies of Mao's Rustication Program* (Washington, DC: Georgetown University Press, 2013).

26 Andrew Zumkehr and J. Elliott Campbell, "The Potential for Local Croplands to Meet US Food Demand," *Frontiers in Ecology and the Environment* 13, no. 5 (June 2015). But see Pierre Desrochers and Jayson L. Lusk, "The Inability and Undesirability of Local Croplands to Meet Food Demand," *Frontiers in Ecology and the Environment* 13, no. 8 (October 2015).

27 Zheng Zhangxin, "Tampines Blk 146 Vertical Farm Successfully Grows and Harvests Made-in-S'pore Rice," *Mothership*, February 12, 2022.

28 Alberto Corsín Jiménez, "The Right to Infrastructure: A Prototype for Open Source Urbanism," *Environment and Planning D: Society and Space* 32, no. 2 (April 2014).

29 Karl Hess, *Community Technology* (Port Townsend, WA: Breakout Productions, 1995 [1979]), 44–5.

30 "Researchers have successfully grown aloe vera, tomatoes, biogas maize, pasture grass, and lettuce in agrivoltaic experiments. Some varieties of lettuce produce greater yields in shade than under full sunlight; other varieties produce essentially the same yield under an open sky and under PV panels. Semi-transparent PV panels open additional opportunities for colocation and greenhouse production." Elnaz H. Adeh et al., "Solar PV Power Potential Is Greatest over Croplands," *Scientific Reports* 9, Article 11442 (2019).

31 International Energy Agency, *Special Report on Solar PV Global Supply Chains* (August 2022).

32 The environmental-maintenance requirements of indoor agriculture in particular introduce a new order of complexity into the growing of food, as well as all the vulnerability that attends it: as the essayist and pioneering agroecological activist Wendell Berry put it, "The control by which a tomato plant lives through January is much more problematic than the natural order by which an oak tree or a titmouse lives through January." Wendell Berry, *The Unsettling of America: Culture and Agriculture* (San Francisco: Sierra Club Books, 1977).

33 Smaje, *Saying NO to a Farm-Free Future*, 133.

34 Stephen E. Hunt, *The Revolutionary Urbanism of Street Farm* (Bristol, UK: Tangent Books, 2014).

35 Fukuoka Masanobu, *The One-Straw Revolution: An Introduction to Natural Farming*, trans. Chris Pearce, Tsune Kurosawa and Larry Korn (Emmaus, PA: Rodale Press, 1978).

36 Jason Adams, "The Constellation of Opposition," in Duane Rousselle and Süreyyya Evren, eds., *Post-Anarchism: A Reader* (London: Pluto Press, 2011).

37 Adam Greenfield, *Radical Technologies: The Design of Everyday Life* (New York: Verso, 2017), 93–6.

38 See, for example, "Open Source Hardware (OSHW) Definition 1.0," Open Source Hardware Association, oshwa.org.

39 Rachael Dal Porto et al., "Characterizing the Performance of a Do-It-Yourself (DIY) Box Fan Air Filter," *Aerosol Science and Technology* 56, no. 6 (April 2022); Jim Rosenthal, "A Variation on the 'Box Fan with MERV 13 Filter' Air Cleaner," Tex-Air Filters, August 22, 2020, texairfilters.com.

40 Liam Grace-Flood, "Open World: Habibi Works," Make:, May 9, 2018, make.co.

41 Greenfield, *Radical Technologies*, 109–10.

42 King et al. offer a list of energy systems encountered "throughout the developing world" that they found hobbled by "for want of a nail"–style critical-path dependencies: "broken windmills and micro-hydropower installations, empty biogas pits, rusting charcoal kilns, and unused solar cookers or tractors and water pumps in poor condition," many if not all of which could be restored to full operation were they but furnished with replacements for missing or broken components. Debbie L. King et al., "Mobile Open-Source Solar-Powered 3-D Printers for Distributed Manufacturing in Off-Grid Communities," *Challenges in Sustainability* 2, no. 1 (2014).

43 Eric Verploegen, Peter Rinker and Kukom Edoh Ognakossan, "Evaporative Cooling Best Practices: Producing and Using Evaporative Cooling Chambers and Clay Pot Coolers," MIT D-Lab, June 2018, d-lab.mit.edu; "Technical Sheet A23—Sand Filtration for Raw Water or Wastewater Treatment," Wikiwater, wikiwater.fr.

44 crow, *Black Flags and Windmills*, 104.

45 Ivan Illich, *Tools for Conviviality* (New York: Harper and Row, 1973). See also Andrea Vetter, "The Matrix of Convivial Technology—Assessing Technologies for Degrowth," *Journal of Cleaner Production* 197, part 2 (October 1, 2018).

46 Hess, *Community Technology*, 36.

47 "The Growing Traction of Climate Citizens Assemblies," European Climate Foundation, October 12, 2021, europeanclimate.org.

48 Quoted in Kelly Hayes and Mariame Kaba, *Let This Radicalize You: Organizing and the Revolution of Reciprocal Care* (Chicago: Haymarket Books, 2023), 61.

49 Brian Aldiss, *Billion Year Spree: The History of Science Fiction* (London: Weidenfeld & Nicolson, 1973), 293.

50 Kristin Ross, *Communal Luxury: The Political Imaginary of the Paris Commune* (New York: Verso, 2016).

51 Aaron Vansintjan, "Urbanisation as the Death of Politics: Sketches of Degrowth Municipalism," in Anitra Nelson and François Schneider, eds., *Housing for Degrowth: Principles, Models, Challenges and Opportunities* (New York: Routledge, 2019).

52 Alberto Corsín Jiménez and Adolfo Estalella, *Free Culture and the City: Hackers, Commoners, and Neighbors in Madrid, 1997–2017* (Ithaca, NY: Cornell University Press, 2023), 25.

53 "Pine Tree Gang (PTG)—White Nationalist Separatist/Cascadian Region," Terrorism Research and Analysis Consortium, trackingterrorism.org. See also Jason Luger, "Celebrations, Exaltations and Alpha Lands: Everyday Geographies of the Far-Right," *Political Geography* 96 (June 2022).

54 Ursula K. Le Guin, *The Dispossessed: An Ambiguous Utopia* (New York: HarperCollins, 1974).

55 Jem Bendell, "Deep Adaptation: A Map for Navigating Climate Tragedy," IFLAS Occasional Paper 2, July 27, 2018.

56 Prosper-Olivier Lissagaray, *History of the Paris Commune of 1871*, trans. Eleanor Marx (New York: Verso, 2012).

57 Wilton A. Gardner, "Cannon Destroy Workers' Homes," *New York Times*, February 13, 1934; "February 1934—History of Vienna," City of Vienna, wien.gv.at; Antony Beevor, *The Battle for Spain: The Spanish Civil War 1936–1939* (London: Penguin, 2006). Only the ongoing experience of the Municipios Autónomos Rebeldes Zapatistas seems to furnish a genuine exception: in Chiapas a population in excess of 350,000 has continuously self-managed by participatory assembly since December 1994.

58 Memorandum to FBI Director J. Edgar Hoover from Charles Bates, Special Agent in Charge, San Francisco Field Office, "COINTELPRO—Black Nationalist Hate Group—Racial Matters," November 30, 1970.

59 Justin Laurence, "The Chicago Freedom School Offered Food, Water and Rest to Weary Protesters Trapped Downtown—and the City Cited Them for It," *Block Club Chicago*, June 8, 2020.

60 Amanda Holpuch, "Houston Volunteers Fight Tickets for Serving Meals to Homeless People," *New York Times*, August 6, 2023.

61 State of Georgia v. Beamon, Biederman, Bilodeau et al., Fulton County Superior Court Criminal Indictment 23SC189192, August 29, 2023.

62 "New Documents Show FBI Targeting Environmental and Animal Rights Groups Activities as 'Domestic Terrorism,'" American Civil Liberties Union, December 20, 2005, aclu.org; HM Inspectorate of Constabulary, *A Review of National Police Units Which Provide Intelligence on Criminality Associated with Protest* (Birmingham, UK: HMIC, 2012); *Undercover Policing Inquiry: Tranche 1 Interim Report* (London: Undercover Policing Inquiry, June 2023); Gary T. Marx, "Thoughts on a Neglected Category of Social Movement Participant: The Agent Provocateur and the Informant," *American Journal of Sociology* 80, no. 2 (September 1974).

63 Colin Moynihan, "Activist Unmasks Himself as Federal Informant in G.O.P. Convention Case," *New York Times*, January 4, 2009.

64 Alexander Vasudevan, *The Autonomous City: A History of Urban Squatting* (New York: Verso, 2017), 225.

65 Forbidden Stories, "The Pegasus Project," July 2021, forbiddenstories.org; Ronen Bergman and Mark Mazzetti, "The Battle for the World's Most Powerful Cyberweapon," *New York Times*, January 28, 2022; Nicol Turner Lee and Caitlin Chin, "Police Surveillance and Facial Recognition: Why Data Privacy Is Imperative for Communities of Color," Brookings Institution, April 12, 2022, brookings.edu; Manal Mostafa Ali, "Real-Time Video Anomaly Detection for Smart Surveillance," *IET Image Processing*, 17, no. 5 (April 17, 2023); Eleanor Drage and Federica Frabetti, "The Performativity of AI-powered Event Detection," *Science, Technology, and Human Values*, March 27, 2023; Kaelynn Narita, "Smart Borders: Silicon Valley and Border Policing," Political Economy Research Centre, March 27, 2023, perc.org.uk.

66 Vikram Dodd and Jamie Grierson, "Greenpeace Included with Neo-Nazis on UK Counter-terror List," *Guardian*, January 17, 2020; "Terrorism Police List Extinction Rebellion as Extremist Ideology," *Guardian*, January 10, 2020.

67 "Our Focus Is Countering Terrorism, Not Lawful Protest,"

Counter Terrorism Policing, January 17, 2020, counterterrorism
.police.uk.

68 Gianluca Mezzofiore, "Golden Dawn Mob Threatens NGO for
Treating Migrants in Perama Clinic," *International Business
Times*, April 11, 2014; Yannis Palaiologos, "Greece's Neo-
Nazi Politicians Are Awaiting Trial—and as Popular as Ever,"
New Republic, September 23, 2014; "Far-Right Group Attacks
Refugee Camp on Greek Island of Chios," *Guardian*, November
18, 2016; zb, "Five Injured after Attack on Greek Anti-fascist
Center," *Freedom*, February 28, 2018, freedomnews.org.uk.

69 This is perfectly expressed in an April 2013 statement issued
by the self-proclaimed "Green Wing" of Golden Dawn. "The
leftists and the hippies tried to claim the ecologist movement as
their own, but [our] love for nature is different than theirs: The
environment is the cradle of our Race, it mirrors our culture and
civilization, making it our duty to protect it." Golden Dawn,
"The Green Wing and the Volksland Project," April 6, 2013.

70 In this regard, the same community production workshop
that pops out wind-turbine blades or supports for aquaponics
tanks in relatively peaceful times can be rapidly retooled for
the manufacture of increasingly sophisticated weaponry, like
the 3D-printed FGC-9 carbines used at scale by the insurgent
People's Defense Forces in Myanmar. (Do note that this is, of
course, wildly illegal in many jurisdictions.) Travis Pike, "The
FGC-9 in Myanmar: 3D Guns and the Future of Guerrilla
Warfare," *Sandboxx*, January 7, 2022.

Conclusion

1 David Mitchell, *The Bone Clocks* (New York: Random House,
2014).

2 You may be familiar with the Benedictine monk David Steindl-
Rast's gloss of Tarfon, which circulates widely on social media,
if generally without attribution. Entirely apropos to our considerations here, it begins by commanding that we "not be daunted
by the enormity of the world's grief."

3 Mike Davis, "Who Will Build the Ark?," *New Left Review* 61
(January/February 2010).

Index

A Paradise Built in Hell (Solnit)
    10–11
AANES *see* Rojava
abundance, politics of 119
accountability 201
action, courses of 165–6
ACT/UP 131
Adams, Jason 184–5
Adams Morgan (Washington, DC)
    183
adaptability 101
Adriana incident 35
Afrin, Silvan 160
Aganaktisménoi 98–9, 133
agrarian localism 181–2
agriculture 29–30, 182–5
agrivoltaic installations 184
Ahora Madrid 135–8, 140, 140–2,
    143–4
air freight 38
airships 212
Akif, Dorşin 155
Akuno, Kali 129, 171
Aldiss, Brian 194
Alexandras Prosfygika housing
    complex, Athens 101
Algiers Point, Louisiana 206
alienation 121
Amazon wedding-registry hack,
    Occupy Sandy 67
American Red Cross 4, 5, 63, 65,
    68–9, 72, 73
anarchism 23, 60, 72, 121
Anarchist Library 120
Anarchy Archives 120
Animal Liberation Front 203
anomaly-detection algorithms 204
aquifers, salinization of 31
Arab Spring 133, 134

Aramis, or the Love of Technology
    (Latour) 138–9
Arendt, Hannah 78, 125
Argentina 131–5
artificial intelligence 212
asambleas populares 136–7
assembly, the 124–7
    communes 152–4
    cringe factor 191
    irrelevance 192
    Lifehouses 191–4
    limitations and drawbacks
        127–31
    power 192–3
    representative legitimacy 129
    Rojava women's assemblies
        156
    rules 128
asset exposure 32
asylum seekers 205
Atelier Populaire 130
Athens, ancient 125–6
Atlantic Meridional Overturning
    Circulation 49
atmospheric warming 5
autarky 174
autonomous production 184–8
autonomy 72, 73–4, 174, 191
Avakian, Bob 91–2

Bangladesh 38
Barcelona en Comú 139–40,
    142–3, 144, 196
BDS movement 199
Beijing, PRC 31
Berkeley Free Clinic 104
Bethymouti, Ilektra 109
Big Door Brigade, Seattle 57
bioreactors 181

Black Americans
  malign neglect 80–1
  permanent emergency 95
  self-determination 82, 86
  vulnerability to premature death
    80, 85
  see also Black Panther Party for
    Self-Defense
Black Panther Party for Self-Defense
  60, 61, 209
  achievement 90–5
  ambition 91
  Breakfast for Children program
    80, 87–8, 90, 91–2, 93
  emergence 81–5
  growth 84
  leadership failings 93
  Oakland Community Learning
    Center 80, 89–90
  People's Free Food Program 87,
    88, 179
  People's Free Medical Clinics
    88–9, 90, 93–4
  property use 173
  revenue 92
  revolutionary strategies 85,
    86–7
  sexism of 92–3
  surveillance and repression of
    85–6
  survival programs 14, 80,
    80–96, 96, 115
  tactics 83–4, 92
  Ten-Point Platform and Program
    82–3, 84, 88, 89
Black Sea Grain Initiative 39–40
blockchains 212
bodily needs 76–7, 79
body, the, heat exposure impacts
  28–9
The Bone Clocks (Mitchell) 207
Bookchin, Murray 14, 118,
  118–24, 137, 139, 140–1, 143,
  144, 147, 192, 196, 209
  Communalism 120, 122–4, 124
  ideological journey 118–20
  libertarian municipalism 120,
    122–3, 124–31
  Öcalan and 148–9
  "Post-Scarcity Anarchism" 119
  social ecology 120–2, 162

"The Problem of Chemicals in
    Food" 119
  Urbanization without Cities 148
borders 34–5, 37
borderwork 35
Breakfast for Children program
  see Black Panther Party for
    Self-Defense
Brown, Elaine 92–3, 173
built environment 21
Burley, Shane 194
burnout 211
Butler, Judith 155

C40 Cities climate initiative 33
California 33, 83–4
cancer care 107
capacity-building 125
cap-and-trade schemes 8
capital flight 124
capital investment, cities 32
capitalism 53, 121
carbon credits 212
carbon capture 49–50, 210
carbon emissions 19, 30, 48
carbon offsets 8
care 77–9, 208–9, 211
care-driven organizing 79
CareNotes 108, 110
carework 78–9, 205
cargo bikes 212
Carmena, Manuela 141–2, 143–4
Carson, Rachel 120
Casa Pueblo (Puerto Rico) 179
Cascadia (region) 198
cascading disruptions 26–7
catastrophe response 22–7
catastrophic events 77
catastrophist literature 50–1
centralized institutions 175
Centros de Apoyo Mutuo (Puerto
    Rico) 77
cereal crops 180
Certeau, Michel de 174
charity 58, 60, 79, 102
Chicago Freedom School 203
chicken-keeping 183
China
  Cultural Revolution 182
  recommitment to coal-fired
    energy generation 47

source of photovoltaic panels
184
church buildings 171–2
circular economy 122–4
cities 30–3
civil disobedience 165
Civil Rights 125
Clark, John P. 11, 12
Clark, Mark 86
Cleaver, Eldridge 85, 86–7
climate crisis 5, 7, 13
climate shock 113
COINTELPRO 86, 91, 206
Colau, Ada 141, 142–3
collective action 54
    coordination of 131–5
collective decision-making 100
collective power 14, 163
    exercising 201
    as positive pressure 209
    site of 169
    theory of 117
collective resilience 158
collective self-provision 79–80
Combahee River Collective 121
Common Ground Collective (New
    Orleans) 11, 59–61, 65, 66, 77,
    96, 102, 105, 177–8, 189, 201,
    203, 209
common knowledge 189
common purpose, sense of 23
communal imagination 196
Communalism see Bookchin,
    Murray
communes 152–4, 156, 201
communication technologies 132
Community Action Programs 81
community infrastructure 166–7
community needs 61
community resilience hubs 198
community skills inventory 190–1
complex systems
    points of risk 51–2
    robustness 52–3
confederation 118, 198–9
conflict resolution 156–60
conflict risk, enhanced 40
confluences 136, 140–1
Congo, Democratic Republic of
    47–8
Coningsby, UK 17

conscientization 112
consciousness-raising 125, 131–5
consensual governance 128
conspiracy theories, COVID-19
    pandemic 24
constituent power 138
construction process, carbon release
    thereof 173
consumption 27
Contemporary Issues (journal) 119
conviviality 189–90
Cook, Richard 51–2
cooperation 58, 59
Cooperation Jackson 129, 171
"Cop City" (Atlanta) 203
Corbin, Samantha 66, 78–9
Corsín Jiménez, Alberto 128–9
Corsi-Rosenthal boxes (DIY air
    filtration device) 187
Counter Terrorism Policing (UK)
    204
COVID-19 pandemic 22–7, 40, 74,
    77, 185–6
    conspiracy theories 24
    deaths 26
    knock-on effects 24
    lifeworld contraction 23
    lockdown 23, 24, 26
    mutual aid 193–4
    official response to 23, 25
cozy catastrophe, the 194
Critical Mass (distributed
    organization) 131
crow, scott 60, 94, 105
C-Squat (New York City) 166, 176
cyanobacteria 212

Daesh 147, 150–1, 206
Davis, Mike 212
The Dawn of Everything (Graeber
    and Wengrow) 116
deaths
    COVID-19 pandemic 26
    heat 17
    refugees 35
    Superstorm Sandy 62
debility (Puar concept) 40
decarbonization 47, 49–50, 165,
    210
decency, failures of 208
decentralized organization 175

Decidim 196
decision power 117
decision-making 100, 124–31,
    191–4
deglobalization 38–9
Deleuze, Gilles 136
Delhi, India 31
deliberative assembly 118
democracy 124
Democratic Autonomy (Rojava)
    151–2
    assessment of 162–4
    communes 152–4
    public safety and conflict
        resolution 156–60
    social architecture 160–2
democratic confederalism 148–52,
    196
Democratic Confederalism (Öcalan)
    162–3
Den Pliróno ("I Do Not Pay")
    movement 100
digital fabrication 185–6, 187
dignity 88
direct action 60
direct air capture 49–50, 172
direct democracy 123
Dirik, Dilar 152, 154, 160
disaster relief 67–71, 72–5
disinvestment 21, 43–6
The Dispossessed (Le Guin) 200–1
distributed organization 174–6
doing something 5, 8, 9, 13, 15,
    144, 152, 162, 165–6, 201, 212,
    212–13
drought 30, 31

Earth First! 131
Earth Liberation Front 203
Earth system collapse 167
Ecclesia, the (Greek institution)
    125–6
ecoanarchism 204
ecological accountability 170
ecological balance 149
ecomodernists 180–1, 184
economic order, fluctuations of 112
ecosystemic collapse 50–1, 54,
    163–4
education 89–90, 94
Eemian interglacial period 163

elections, public action 6–7
electoral politics 140–1
electoral representation 6–7
electoral sentiment, shifting winds
    of 145, 163
electricity supply and generation
    176–9
empathy, failures of 208
empire, slow violence of 43
empowerment 12
energy
    access 47
    prices 47
    strategy 5–7
environmental movement 120–1
environmental stress factors 51
Erdoğan, Recep Tayyip 161, 162
European Central Bank 97
European Commission 97
Extinction Rebellion 204
extinctions 15
extractive industries
    influence of 6
    sabotage of 165

fablabs 185–6
factionalism 199–200
famine 30
farmers' markets 108
fascists 205
Fearless Cities events 195
Federal Bureau of Investigation
    (US) 86, 91
Federici, Silvia 78, 106
feedback loops 19
FEMA (Federal Emergency
    Management Agency, US) 4,
    63, 69, 72
feminism, Rojavan commitment to
    154–6
feminization of politics 155–6
financialization 133
Finn, Katherine 157–8
fishing cooperatives 108
Floating University, Berlin 172
Floyd, George 203
food and food production 39–40,
    179–85
food banks 179
food deserts 108
food insecurity 39–40

Food Not Bombs (Houston, Texas) 203
food security 180
fossil fuel dependency 5
Fox, Josh 66
Fraser, Nancy 129
Free Syrian Army 150
Freeman, Jo 129
Freire, Paulo 112
Frey, John 84–5
Fritz, Charles 11, 12
Fukuoka, Masanobu 184
fungi 180

gender equity 154–6
gender relation 149
generators (electric) 177–8
geoengineering 47, 48–9, 50, 165, 210
Germany, return to coal-fired energy generation 47
Gilmore, Ruth Wilson 43–5, 80, 112
global heating 14
    aftermath 20
    agricultural impacts 29–30
    challenge 19–20
    extent 18–19
    heat exposure impacts 28–9, 40
    and humidity 29
    impacts 27–33
    impacts on cities 30–3
    latitudes in greatest peril 28–9
    past 1.5°C 19
    and violence 36
globalization 38
Golden Dawn (Greek fascist formation) 198, 205, 206
Goodman, Robert 82
Goražde, Bosnia and Herzegovina 178
government 123
Graeber, David 116–17, 125, 137, 155, 159
Greece 11, 14, 133, 205
    10-Point Charter of Constitution of Solidarity Clinics and Pharmacies 102–3
    activist spatial practice 101
    Aganaktisménoi 98–9

ancient, 125–6
anti-austerity protest participation 100
austerity 97–9, 110
balance of trade deficit 97
deinstitutionalization of medical care 103–7
Den Plieróno ("I Do Not Pay") movement 100
economic adjustment 110
elections, 2019 110
elections, 2015 109
healthcare capacity reduced 98
Katsikas refugee camp 186
living standards 99–100
national health system 105
rationalization of state services 100–1
social kitchens 102
solidarity clinic dissolution 108–10
solidarity clinics 102–10, 116, 169, 195, 197, 201, 209
Solidarity for All network 108–10
solidarity networks 96, 96–112
sovereign debt crisis 96–9
spread of solidarity networks 100–3
Syntagma Square occupation 98–9
Thessaloniki Workers' Medical Center 104
the undocumented 105
values 102
wave of abandonment 100–1
green energy transition 47, 47–8
Green New Deal 8, 212
greenhouse effect 120–1
Greenpeace 204
grief 22
guerrilla healthcare 104

Habibi.Works (Greece) 186
habitability 31
hackspaces see makerspaces
Haiti 42
Hampton, Fred 86
Harvey, David 43–4, 46, 131
Hasa, Elisavet 197
Haudenosaunee Confederacy 125

Hayes, Kelly 57, 79
healing 211
healthcare 88–9, 93–4
  deinstitutionalization 102–10
  gating mechanism 103
  integrated 108
  mixed ecology 109
  and patient outcomes 107
  radical providers 107–8
  sites of 103
  withdrawal from public
    provision 98
  see also solidarity clinics
heat
  agricultural impacts 29–30
  effects 17
  exposure 28–9, 40
  impacts on cities 30–3
  survivability threshold 28
helplessness, sense of 5–7
Hess, Karl 183, 190
holism 90
hologram (Thornton concept) 104,
  168
homesteaders 184, 187
Hoover, J. Edgar 86
hope, trust in 8–9
horizontal turn 131, 131–5
horizontalidad 132
horizontality 58
"hostile environment" policy (UK)
  35
Houston, Texas 32
Huggins, Ericka 89–90, 92
humidity 29
hunger 30, 179
Hurricane Harvey 32
Hurricane Katrina 11, 32, 59–61,
  65, 66, 113, 177–8
Hurricane María 177, 179

ideological purity 144
Illich, Ivan 189
immigrants 35
India 37, 47, 180
Indigenous practice 133
indignados 133
indirect action 165–6
individualist responses 54
inequality, risk 58
informed consent 55

infrastructural failure 62–75
infrastructural systems 166–7
infrastructure 43
institutional state power 138
institutions, failing 8–9
insurance 32–3
insurgent counterpower 202
intercambiadero (Spanish
  institution) 197–8
interdependence, feeling of 11–12
Intergovernmental Panel on Climate
  Change 19–20
  Representative Concentration
    Pathway 31
International Monetary Fund 97
investment risk 33
invitationality 70–1
ISIS see Daesh
isolation 57, 210
Italy 23

James, C. L. R. 125
Jewish ethical tradition 211–12
jineology 154–6
Johnson, Lyndon B. 81
Johnson, Sharon 60
justice 131, 153, 158–9, 170
just-in-time logistics 39

Kaba, Mariame 57, 79
Karl-Marx-Hof, Vienna see Red
  Vienna
Khartoum, Sudan 42–3
killing degree days 30
knock-on effects, COVID-19
  pandemic 24
Kobane, Rojava 146–7
  siege of 151
Kolbert, Elizabeth 48
Kongra Star (Rojava) 155–6
Kropotkin, Peter 58, 59, 117, 194
Kuala Lumpur, Malaysia 31
Kurdish Workers' Party see PKK
Kurds 146–52, 209

labor, Marxian definition of 78
labor system 37
Laclau, Ernesto 138
lassitude 54–5
late-capitalist normalcy, resilience
  of 22

Latour, Bruno 138–9
Lavapiés (Madrid) 128
Le Guin, Ursula K. 200–1
left-libertarian tradition 117–18
liberation 73–4
libertarian municipalism 120,
    122–3, 124–31, 135, 137, 139,
    144, 196
life, parameters of 27
Lifehouses 14
    buildings 171–4
    central reservation 170
    conceptualization 167–9
    confederation 198–9
    decision-making 191–4
    establishing 170, 171–4
    food program 179–85
    greatest threat facing 198
    implications 174–6
    limitations and drawbacks
        169–71
    location 171
    maintenance and repair 187–91
    neighborhood assemblies 191–4
    network 169–70
    network organization 174–6,
        194–200
    power supply and generation
        176–9
    pragmas 199–200
    production facilities 184–8
    resource sharing 197–8
    shared technical infrastructure
        196
    state threat to 201–6
    value of 168–9
    vision 200–1
lifesystems 112
local government 140–1
local power 117–18
local state, occupation of 143
localism 23
logistical systems 22, 38–42
Long Emergency, the 14
    agricultural impacts 29–30
    as great undoing 20–1
    conceptualization 20–2
    COVID-19 pandemic example
        22–7
    deeper lesson of 112
    impacts 21, 27–33

latitudes in greatest peril 28–9
    refugees 33–7
    scale of devastation 169
    scenarios 22
    the state in 42–6
López, Marina 139–40
losses 15
Lumumba, Chokwe 130
luxury beliefs 151

Madrid, Spain 128–9
maize (grain) 30
maker community 185–6
makerspaces 185–7
Malacca Strait 39
Malik, Nesrine 42–3
Malm, Andreas 50–1
malnutrition 41, 80
market logics 116
Marx, Karl 78
Marxist economics 121
May 1968, Paris events of 130
Meatless Mondays 212
medical care see healthcare
medicines and medical devices 40,
    41
Mediterranean migration crisis 37
megacities 33
metabolic rift 121
methane 48
mêtis (Scott concept) 126
microgrids 178–9
migration, magnitude of 35–6
mindfulness 212
Mitchell, David 207
Moafi, Samaneh 172
Monobloc chairs 132, 156
Mouffe, Chantal 138
MOVE (US) 204
movement, restriction of 36
Movement for a Democratic Society
    see TEV-DEM
movement of the squares 134, 137,
    147
Mt. Sinjar massacre 151
municipalist theory 139–40
mutual aid 9–13, 57–113, 111,
    115–16
    accountability 75
    backlash against 61
    capacity for cooperation 58

mutual aid (*continued*)
  and care 77–9
  challenge to 111
  commitment 57–8, 59
  community needs 61
  conceptualization 57–8
  COVID-19 pandemic 193–4
  disaster relief 67–71, 72–5
  dormant 64
  effectiveness 76–80
  evaluation criteria 73
  feeling of interdependence
    11–12
  horizontality 58
  hybridization 66
  infrastructural systems 62–75
  instinct toward 59
  invitationality 70–1
  joy of 11
  limitations and drawbacks
    75–6, 96
  nonjudgmentality 69
  opposition to 10
  self-organization 59–61, 70–1,
    112
  sense of empowerment 12
  solidarity networks 79–80,
    80–96, 96–112
  value 75
  values 60, 66, 71, 102
Mutual Aid Disaster Relief network
  (US) 195
mutual aid groups 23
mutual care 79, 211
  site of 169
  state threat to 201–6

National Guard (US) 68
National Health Service (UK) 110
negative commons (Moafi concept)
  172
Negri, Antonio 138
neoliberalism 130
  and austerity 168
network organization 174–6
networked organizing tactics 132
networked services, dependence
  on 41–2
New Democracy (Greece) 110
new municipalism 134–5, 135–8,
  139, 149, 196, 209

"new normal," ostensible 54
New Orleans, Louisiana 11, 32,
  59–61, 65, 66, 177–8
New York City
  blackout 2, 63
  COVID-19 pandemic 74
  public-sector response 63
  revolutionary strategies 85
  Sandy deaths 62
  Special Initiative for Rebuilding
    and Recovery 73
  storm surge 1, 1–2
  Superstorm Sandy 1–4, 62–4,
    166–7, 178
  Zuccotti Park 64
  see also Occupy Sandy
Newton, Huey P. 82–3, 92, 94
  arrest and conviction 84–5
  revolutionary strategies 86–7
nonrepressive government 123
nonstate society 193, 197
North Oakland Neighborhood
  Anti-Poverty Center 82

Oakland Community Learning
  Center see Black Panther Party
  for Self-Defense
Öcalan, Abdullah 147–50, 151,
  196
  Democratic Confederalism
    148–50, 162–3
  The Sociology of Freedom
    154–5
Occupy moment 134–5
Occupy Sandy 3–5, 9, 10, 12, 14,
  62, 62–4, 62–75, 77, 96, 102,
  115–16, 147, 196, 201, 209
  achievement 72–5
  Amazon wedding-registry hack
    67
  attack on 205
  banner 65, 66
  budget 73
  carework 78–9
  commitment 72
  disaster relief 67–8, 72–5
  effectiveness 66
  intake team 67
  invitationality 70–1
  logistics 67–8
  nonjudgmentality 69

origins 62–4
outreach 69
recruitment 65–6
scale 71–2
self-organization 70–1
shared ethos 70
values 66, 71
Occupy Wall Street 62, 64, 66
ocean currents *see* Atlantic
  Meridional Overturning
  Circulation
offshoring 38
omnicrisis, permanent condition
  of 46
oppression 149
ordinary people, wisdom of 122–4
organized abandonment (Gilmore
  concept) 43–6
Ours to Lose (Starecheski) 166–7

Panama Canal 38
Paris Commune 1871 122, 124,
  196, 202
parliamentary politics 140–1
participation 117, 140–1
participatory democracy 124–7
  limitations and drawbacks
  127–31
Partido Popular (Spain) 143–4
patriarchy 121, 149
pavement burns 29
peace committees 157–8
peatlands 47–8
People's Free Food Program (BPP)
  87, 88, 179
People's Free Medical Clinics (BPP)
  88–9, 90, 93–4
permafrost thawing 19
Philippines, the 38
Phoenix, Arizona 29
pirates 39
Pirkei Avot 212
PKK (Kurdistan Workers' Party)
  147–8, 149, 154
Podemos (Spain) 138, 145
police and policing 83, 84–5, 86
policy decisions 123
political arrangements, flexibility
  117
political economy 116
political order, fluctuations of 112

political projects 138–9
politics, feminization of 155–6
Polletta, Francesca 124–5
populist parties 40
Port Huron Statement 124–5, 133
possibility 211
post-Emergency world 14
power and power structures 14,
  21, 211
  seizure of 165
power supply and generation
  176–9
powerlessness, sense of 10
pragmas 199–200
precision fermentation 181, 182,
  212
predictions 54
price instability, food and food
  production 39–40
production 27, 38, 182
protectionism 40
protein 181
protest 165, 212
psychic needs 79
Puar, Jasbir K. 40
public action, elections 6–7
public health 23
public investment, hollowing-out
  of 44
public order 46
public reason 122–4
public safety 156–60
public services, disinvestment 21
public-sector response 63
purchase signals 165
purpose, sense of 211
Putin, Vladimir Vladimirovich
  162

racism 80
Racketeer Influenced and Corrupt
  Organizations Act (Georgia)
  203
radicalization 112–13
Rahim, Malik 60
Ramadan 200
raumlaborberlin 172
Reagan, Ronald 84
recruitment 138–9, 144
Red Cross *see* American Red Cross
Red Vienna 202

refugees 8, 33–7, 105, 108, 186, 205
  from armed conflict 36
  border crossings 34–5
  deaths 35
  exploitation 37
  "hostile environment" policies
    35
  internal 34
  magnitude 35–6
  popular image 33–4
  restriction of movement 36
  terminology appertaining
    thereto 33
  working conditions 37
reinsurance firms 32
renewable energy 47, 178
representative legitimacy 129
resettlement 37
resilience 195
Resilient Power Puerto Rico 178–9
resourcefulness 192
resources, competition for 205
respect 73
responsibility 21, 115, 200–1
restorative justice 158–9, 159–60
rice (grain) 30
risk 51–2
  drivers of 20
  exposure to 58
Rojava 14, 145, 146–63, 193, 209
  achievement 162–3
  antistatism 154
  background 146–52
  commitment to feminism 154–6
  communes 152–4, 156, 201
  jineology 154–6
  justice system 157–60
  peace committees 157–8
  prison system 159–60
  public safety and conflict
    resolution 156–60
  restorative justice 158–9,
    159–60
  security formation 156–7
  social architecture 160–2
  Turkish invasion of 161
  withdrawal of US special
    operations forces from 161
  women-only governance
    structures 156
  women's assemblies 156

Ross, Kristin 196
Russia *see* Ukraine: Russian
  invasion of

Sacramento, California 83
sacrifice zones 44–5
salvage 189
Sanders, Lynn 129
savior/saved dynamic 58
scarcity 22
Schelling Point 171
Scott, James C. 126–7
seaborne cargo 38–9
Seale, Bobby 82, 88, 93, 116
Seattle, Washington
  Big Door Brigade 57
  WTO protests 1999 132
seawater rise 31
Second World War 37
self-care 211–12
self-determination 61, 161, 191
selflessness 27
self-organization 9–13, 59–61,
  70–1, 112
self-reliance 23, 174
  state threat to 201–6
self-sufficiency 174
September 11 attacks 66
sexism 92–3
sheltered environments 54
shipping 38–9
Shriver, Sargent 82
Silvers, Cleo 89
Singapore 31, 182–3
skills inventory 190–1
Smaje, Chris 181–2, 184
Sniffen, Rev. Michael 63, 65
social arrangements, flexibility 117
social breakdown 54
social ecology 162, 163, 170
social fabric, fraying of 46
social justice 149
social kitchens 102
social pathologies 121
social reproduction 205
Socialist Workers Party (US) 118
soft mitigation 8
solar power 47
solar radiation management 48–9
Solar Radiation Management
  Governance Initiative 49

solidarity 54, 60, 194
solidarity clinics (Greece) 11, 14,
    102–10, 116, 169, 195, 197,
    201, 209
    10-Point Charter of
        Constitution of Solidarity
        Clinics and Pharmacies
        102–3
    ambition 103
    archives 106
    dissolution 108–10
    egalitarian sensibility 103
    healthcare provision 103–7
    integrated healthcare 108
    shortfalls 106–7
Solidarity for All network, Greece
    108–10
solidarity networks 79–80, 80–96,
    96–112, 115
Solnit, Rebecca 10–11, 66
Somalia 42
Soviet Union 52–3, 132
Spade, Dean 73
Spain 14, 133, 139–40, 209
    Ahora Madrid 135–8, 140,
        140–2, 143–4
    asambleas populares 136–7
    Barcelona en Comú 139–40,
        142–3, 144, 196
    Ciutat Meridiana fablab 186
    confluences 135–8, 140–1
    elections of May 24, 2015 142,
        143
    intercambiadero 197–8
    local government 140–1
    Partido Popular 143–4
    Podemos 138, 145
Spanish Civil War 60, 118
spyware 204
stability 207–8
Starecheski, Amy 166–7
state, the 123, 144–5
    absence of 146–52
    failure 42–3, 96–112
    in the Long Emergency 42–6
    organized abandonment and
        43–6
    responsibility 116
    violence 202–4
State Farm (insurance company)
    33

state services, rationalization
    100–1
statism 121
Strait of Hormuz 38
stratospheric aerosol injection
    48–9, 50, 210
Street Farm 185
Students for a Democratic Society
    (US) 124–5
Sudan 42–3
Suez Canal 38
Sunak, Rishi 47
Superstorm Sandy 1–4, 62, 62–4,
    112–13
    blackout 2, 63
    damage 2
    deaths 62
    disaster relief 67–71
    electricity-generating stationary
        bicycle 166–7
    power supply and generation
        178
    public-sector response 63
    as rupture 3
    storm surge 1, 1–2
    see also Occupy Sandy
superstorms 1
supply chains 22, 38–42
    disruption 180, 184, 187
    terminology 40
survivability, heat threshold 28–9
survival programs see Black Panther
    Party for Self-Defense
syndicates of initiative 200–1
Syrian Civil War 146–7, 150,
    150–1
Syrian Democratic Forces 150
SYRIZA (Greece) 102, 108–10,
    111

Tampines Block 146, Singapore
    182–3
Tarfon (first-century CE rabbi)
    211–12
Taussig, Mick 147
technologies of permanent recourse
    188–9, 191
Tempelhof Airport (Berlin) 172
temperature
    UK record 17–18
    and violence 36

TEV-DEM (Movement for a Democratic Society, Rojava) 151, 153, 155
Thessaloniki, Greece 98–9, 104
Thornton, Cassie 11, 104, 168–9
Thunberg, Greta 212
tools, convivial 189–90
Traficantes de Sueños bookstore (Madrid) 138
translation (Latour concept) 139, 143, 144
trauma care 107
tree die-offs 19
tropical storms 32
trout farming 183
Trump, Donald, wet congeries that serve as brain of 161
Tsipras, Alex 110
Turkey 147–8
"The Tyranny of Structurelessness" (Freeman) 129

universal basic income (UBI) 212
Ukraine
  archaeological "megasites" 125
  Russian invasion of 24–5, 39–40, 180
unconscious coordination 171
undocumented, the 105
unease, sense of 7
uneven development 53
Union of the Patriotic Women of Kurdistan (YJWK) 154
United Kingdom
  Counter Terrorism Policing 204
  COVID-19 pandemic 24, 25, 40
  Eat Out to Help Out program 25
  food security 180
  green energy transition 47
  National Health Service 24, 110
  temperature record 17–18
United States of America 133
  Black experience in 44–5, 81–5
  borders 34–5
  Community Action Programs 81

Department of Homeland Security 73
  Economic Opportunity Act 81
  government expenditure 81
  healthcare provision 110
  Job Corps vocational training initiative 81
  Mulford Act 83–4
  Office of Economic Opportunity 81
  organized abandonment 44–5
  pavement burns 29
  state violence 202–4
  War on Poverty 81–2, 91
  see also Black Panther Party for Self-Defense

values 115–16
Vansintjan, Aaron 196, 198
Venezuela 42
vertical farming 182–3, 212
Veysey, Laurence 127
Vietnam 38
violence, and temperature 36
voluntarism and volunteers 3–5, 11, 76
voting 165, 212

Wallace-Wells, David 28–9
War on Poverty (US) 81–2, 91
Ward, Dana 120
Wengrow, David 116–17, 125
wet-bulb temperature 28–9, 169
wheat (grain) 30
wildfires 17
women, gender equity 154–6
women's voices 153
Workers' Medical Center, Thessaloniki 104
workshops 185
World Congress of Mayors 212
World Trade Organization 132

"year without a summer," 1815 48
Yemen 42
Young, Iris Marion 131
Young Pioneers (US) 118
YPJ (Rojava) 147

Zapatistas 60, 61, 132, 133, 147